THE COUNTRY HOUSE REMEMBERED

Telegraph,
Edensor.

Chatsworth,
Chesterfield.

Railway,
Rowsley.

29 Dec 1906

Dearest

How you would loathe this place! It crushes one by its size & is full of smart shrivelled up people. There is only <u>one</u> bathroom in the house which is kept for the King. I am going to have a good look at the library tomorrow — the best in England.

Yours

Raymond

THE COUNTRY HOUSE REMEMBERED

RECOLLECTIONS OF LIFE BETWEEN THE WARS

Edited by
Merlin Waterson

Routledge & Kegan Paul
London, Melbourne and Henley

First published in 1985
by Routledge & Kegan Paul plc
14 Leicester Square, London WC2H 7PH, England
464 St Kilda Road, Melbourne,
Victoria 3004, Australia and
Broadway House, Newtown Road,
Henley-on-Thames, Oxon RG9 1EN, England

Designed and produced
by Rock Lambert Ltd
Andoversford, Gloucestershire

Set in Monophoto Baskerville
and printed in Great Britain
by BAS Printers Limited, Over Wallop, Hampshire

British Library Cataloguing in Publication Data

Waterson, Merlin

The country house remembered : recollections of life between the wars
1. Country homes – Great Britain – History
2. Great Britain – Social life and customs – 20th century
I. Waterson, Merlin
941.083   DA566.4

ISBN 0 7102 0376 4

Frontispiece:
A *cri de cœur* from Raymond
Asquith, a guest at
Chatsworth before the First
World War. In many of the
great country houses between
the wars there was little
change. The Duchess of
Buccleuch remembers 'very
very few bathrooms . . . very
little luxury'.

CONTENTS

PREFACE

The country house toady was a familiar species between the wars. At Brideshead there was Mr Samgrass; at Rushwater House Mr Holt. 'The Arrival of a Toady' – a chapter title in Angela Thirkell's *Wild Strawberries*, published in 1932 – causes dismay at Rushwater, where everybody despises Mr Holt. Lady Emily, his tolerant hostess, remarks:

> Mr Holt is really a great deal of trouble and so terribly dull and nobody wants him, still, when somebody takes the trouble to invite themselves one feels one ought at least to be civil.

Her husband is less generous:

> He's an infernal bore, Emily. Last time he came here he invited himself for a night and stayed for three, and treated the car as if it were his own. He talks about nothing but gardens and his titled friends. I can't stand the fellow, no more can anyone else . . . I shouldn't wonder if he is keeping a diary about us all and means to publish it when he is dead, like that Weevle fellow or whatever his name was.

There have been times during the preparation of this book when I have felt Mr Holt's mantle snugly around my shoulders. It is to those still tolerant, still generous hostesses listed in the 'Who, Where and When' section, that the book owes its existence. The recollections which they have entrusted to the tape recorder will be all the more valuable as a substitute for the letters and diaries in which earlier generations often documented their lives day by day.

The selection of chatelaines and owners to be found in this book is unashamedly arbitrary, although an attempt has been made to balance the great and well-known country houses with the modest and unfamiliar, the sporting with the intellectual or artistic.

The social history of the English country house, until relatively recently, has been a neglected field, overshadowed by the study of architectural and decorative history. In trying to plot the more important trends in behaviour and fashion, there has been a tendency to overlook the exceptions, the eccentricities which have always been so characteristic of country house life. It is precisely the value of oral history such as this that it should present those contradictions, that it should record the old-fashioned as well as the pioneers and pace-setters.

Only half-hearted apology is offered for not being more objective, and for resorting so often to anecdote. There are, after all, respectable precedents for the use of parables; and anecdotes need not be true in every detail to be revealing. One of the most obvious distortions derives from limiting interviews to owners of country houses and their families, and in not including their staff or tenants. This was to keep the book to manageable proportions and to capture a certain tone of voice. Word from below stairs deserves separate treatment. Another distortion can be blamed on the medium of the tape recorder, which encourages spontaneity in some and inhibits it in others.

The conversational quality of the recollections has, I hope, survived the editing of the interviews. It is thoroughly ungracious of me to have eliminated the interviewers – particularly those chosen for their long association with the families and houses in question – and the naming of them in 'Who, Where and When' is inadequate expression of gratitude. The way in which they asked questions, and the answers they elicited, are the more interesting for sometimes being unexpected. Again, it has seemed important in the text to retain the clashes of views and evidence, and not, by editing, to force them to conform to familiar generalisations about country houses.

I am grateful to Norman and Jill Franklin for their encouragement; to my wife and family; and above all to those who have allowed their recollections to be recorded and their albums and visitors' books to be used for illustrations. Brian Shuel patiently and skilfully photographed the albums, Peyton Skipwith of the Fine Art Society produced the Sir John Lavery of the Double Cube Room at Wilton, and Laurence Whistler generously allowed his brother's paintings and drawings to be reproduced. I am grateful to the National Trust for allowing me to work on the book and for use of material from its extensive archives.

The late Duke of Beaufort *Interviewed by Mrs Richard Carew Pole*

'Master', as the 10th Duke was affectionately known, was a sobriquet acquired at the tender age of 12, when he had his first pack of hounds. His first love was ever hunting. He was, like his grandfather before him, Master of the Horse, serving 3 monarchs during his 42 years in the Royal Household. He married Lady Mary, daughter of the 1st Marquess of Cambridge in 1923, and succeeded in 1924. For 60 years he lived at Badminton and ran the 65,000-acre estates, in Gloucestershire and Wales. He died in 1984 and his widow lives on at Badminton.

Lady Bowes Lyon *Interviewed by Mrs Richard Carew Pole*

Rachael Bowes Lyon is the younger daughter of Herbert Spender-Clay, a brave soldier and an MP. Her mother was an Astor – daughter of the 1st Viscount. Rachael Spender-Clay married a banker, David Bowes Lyon, sixth son of the 12th Earl of Strathmore, in 1929. His sister Elizabeth had already married the Duke of York, later George VI. Together the Bowes Lyons recreated the garden of St Paul's Walden, Hertfordshire. Sir David died in 1961; Lady Bowes Lyon still lives in the house.

Mrs Charles Brocklebank *Interviewed by Mrs Robin Porteous*

Beatrice Brocklebank is the daughter of Falconer Madan, Bodley's Librarian and a fellow of Brasenose College, Oxford. Like Disraeli, she and her brother Geoffrey could claim to have been 'born in a library'. Unlike most of her generation, she received a formal education at a boarding school, Sherborne. Brought up in Oxford, her brother's circle included Ronald Knox, Harold Macmillan and Cyril Asquith. She married Charles Brocklebank, a member of the shipping family, in 1935, and moved to Giffords Hall in Suffolk. He died suddenly just after she and her children had gone to the United States at the start of the Second World War. Mrs Brocklebank now lives near Colchester.

Mary, Duchess of Buccleuch *Interviewed by Lady Tomkins*

Molly Buccleuch's father, Major William Lascelles, was a great-nephew of the 3rd Earl of Harewood, and her mother, Lady Sybil, a daughter of the 10th Duke of St Albans. In 1921 Mary Lascelles married Walter Dalkeith, then MP for Roxburghshire, who succeeded as 8th Duke of Buccleuch in 1935 to run estates in Scotland – Bowhill, Dalkeith, Drumlanrig, Eildon and Langholm – and in England, Boughton. Both were members of the Household: he was Lord Steward. The Duke died in 1973 and Duchess Mary now lives at Boughton.

Lady Burrell *Interviewed by the Countess of Verulam*

Judith Burrell's father, the 3rd Baron Denman, was Lord-in-Waiting to Edward VII, a Deputy Speaker in the House of Lords and a Governor-General of Australia. His equally remarkable wife, Gertrude, daughter of the 1st Viscount Cowdray, was created a Dame for her work in founding the Women's Institute. Judith Denman married Walter Burrell in 1931, and moved from Balcombe Place to a Nash castle, Knepp, also in Sussex. He succeeded to the baronetcy in 1957. A career farmer and landowner, he continues to run the Knepp estate.

WHEN

Mrs Richard Cavendish *Interviewed by Miss Vanessa de Lisle*

Pam Cavendish is the eldest daughter of Hugh Lloyd Thomas, who was briefly Secretary to Edward VIII, and a member of the Royal Household long after. Her mother was a daughter of Lord Bellew and half-sister of the former Garter King of Arms, Sir George Bellew. Her parents' home was the moated courtyard house, Compton Beauchamp, in Oxfordshire. One of three sisters, Pamela Lloyd Thomas, at the age of 19, married Richard Cavendish, only son of Lord Richard and Lady Moyra Cavendish, of Holker Hall, Cumbria. He died in 1972. Mrs Cavendish now lives in the Dower House at Holker.

Mary, Countess of Crawford & Balcarres *Interviewed by The Lady Iona Mackworth-Young*

Mary Crawford's father was the Duke of Devonshire's brother, her mother the Duke of St Albans' daughter. One of seven children, she was brought up at Holker in Cumbria. In 1925 she married David Balniel, MP for the Lonsdale division of Lancashire, a seat he held until he succeeded to the premier earldom of Scotland as 28th & 11th Earl of Crawford & Balcarres in 1940. On inheriting, the Crawfords sold Haigh Hall, near Wigan, and moved to Balcarres, in Fife. David Crawford died in 1975, having dedicated himself to art and books as a longstanding trustee of the British Museum and the Tate and National Galleries of England and Scotland, and as Chairman of the National Trust. Lady Crawford still lives at Balcarres, but retains a house on the Holker estate.

Helen, Lady Dashwood *Interviewed by Lady Tomkins*

Helen Dashwood is the daughter of a colonel in the Royal Canadian Horse Artillery. She married Sir John Dashwood in 1922, and the couple moved into the family home at West Wycombe Park. Sir John, a career diplomat, became a longstanding member of the Royal Household as Assistant Marshal of the Diplomatic Corps. He gave West Wycombe to the National Trust after the Second World War. He died in 1966, but their eldest son, Sir Fancis, is the present tenant.

Mrs John Dower *Interviewed by Miss Zillah Pettit*

Pauline Dower is the daughter of Sir Charles Trevelyan, the third baronet, whose brother was the historian G M Trevelyan. Her mother was Gertrude Bell's sister; her father MP first for the West Riding of Yorkshire and then for Newcastle-upon-Tyne. One of five children, she was brought up at Wallington in Northumberland and educated at a Quaker boarding school. In 1929 she married the author of the Dower Report, which helped to set up the National Parks – Mrs Dower has herself been Deputy Chairman of the National Parks Commission. John Dower died in 1947, and his widow now lives near Wallington, at Cambo.

Diana, Viscountess Gage *Interviewed by Mrs Tim Renton*

Diana Gage is the third daughter of Lord Richard (Dick) and Lady Moyra Cavendish. Her father was brother of the Duke of Devonshire, her mother a daughter of the Duke of St Albans. She was brought up at Holker, Cumbria, a huge amiable, Victorian house. In 1935 Diana Cavendish married Robert Boothby – a marriage which ended two years later. Her second husband, Ian Campbell Gray, was a soldier. They married in 1942 and he died four years later. In 1971 she married Rainald, Viscount Gage, of Firle Place, Sussex, as his second wife. After his death in 1976, she returned to live on the Holker estate.

The Countess of Haddington   *Interviewed by Mrs Richard Carew Pole*
Sarah Haddington is Canadian by birth, the daughter of G W Cook of Montreal. She met her husband, the 12th Earl, when he was on the staff of the Governor-General of Canada, and they married in 1923. A scientist and Fellow of the Royal Society of Edinburgh, he was for 41 years a Scottish representative peer, and has been an active trustee of Scotland's antiquities and its libary. The Haddingtons have lived at Georgian Mellerstain, Berwickshire, all their married lives.

Patricia, Viscountess Hambleden   *Interviewed by Mrs Richard Carew Pole*
Patricia Hambleden was a Herbert, a daughter of the 15th Earl of Pembroke. Her mother, Lady Beatrice, was a sister of the 6th Marquess of Anglesey. Brought up at Wilton House, Wiltshire, Lady Patricia Herbert married in 1928 William Smith, who succeeded as 3rd Viscount Hambleden the same year. He worked for the family firm, W H Smith, all his life, dying in 1949. Lady Hambleden is one of Queen Elizabeth, The Queen Mother's longest serving ladies-in-waiting. She now lives at Ewelme, in Oxfordshire, Greenlands, the Hambleden family home, having been turned into a management college.

Lady Harrod   *Interviewed by Merlin Waterson*
Billa Harrod is the daughter of a Norfolk soldier – the late Captain Cresswell – and of Dame Margaret Strickland, Sir Edward Hulton's sister. In 1938 she married the late Roy Harrod, an economics don at Christ Church, Oxford, where their friends included Gerald Berners from nearby Faringdon House, Roy Harrod worked first under Lindemann, later Lord Cherwell, in Churchill's private statistical office, and subsequently in Winston's own office. He was knighted in 1959. Lady Harrod now lives at Holt Old Rectory, the house in Norfolk where she and Roy spent their retirement.

Mrs Violet Hartcup   *Interviewed by Merlin Waterson*
Violet Hartcup's father was an admiral who ran the Malta Dockyard. To avoid the inevitable disruption of service life, the two Hammet children, Violet and Cecil were lodged by her parents with her mother's family, the Paston-Bedingfelds of Oxburgh Hall, Norfolk. When their father died on his way back from Malta, the two children remained at Oxburgh and were brought up by the present baronet's mother. Violet Hammet married Jack Hartcup, who sadly was one of the many 'living' casualties of the First World War. After his death, and that of their son in the Second World War, Mrs Hartcup returned to live at Oxburgh.

Ulla, Lady Hyde Parker   *Interviewed by Mrs Robin Porteous*
By birth and upbringing, Ulla Hyde Parker is Danish. Her father, Christian Ditlief-Nielsen, was a distinguished Old Testament scholar who made frequent visits to Oxford and Cambridge. It was on one of these that Lady Hyde Parker first met her husband-to-be, William, who succeeded to the baronetcy almost immediately after their marriage in 1931. They moved into Melford Hall, and Sir William took over the running of the estate. He died in 1951, and Lady Hyde Parker later moved back to Melford, to the wing that she had restored after a disastrous fire in the Second World War.

WHO, WHERE & WHEN

Margaret, Countess of Lichfield　　　　　　　　*Interviewed by Merlin Waterson*
Margaret Lichfield is the daughter of a Lancastrian, Henry Dawson-Greene, of Whittington
Hall. She first married Humphrey Philips of Heath House, Staffordshire. After his death at the
end of the Second World War, she married in 1949 the 4th Earl of Lichfield, a widower. They
lived at Shugborough Hall until he died in 1960 and death duties compelled the Trustees of
his heir and grandson, the present Earl, to hand the house over to the National Trust.

Loelia, Lady Lindsay of Dowhill　　　　　　*Interviewed by The Lady Mark Fitzalan Howard*
Loelia Lindsay is the daughter of the 1st Baron Sysonby, who, as Sir Frederick Ponsonby, was
a long-serving member of the Royal Household. Equerry to both Queen Victoria and Edward
VII, he was Keeper of the Privy Purse to George V. Loelia Ponsonby married, at the age of
28, as his third wife, Bendor, 2nd Duke of Westminster. They divorced in 1947 after 17 years
of marriage; Bendor died in 1953. In 1969 Loelia Westminster married Sir Martin Lindsay,
who had been a soldier, an explorer and MP for Solihull. He died in 1978.

Lady Phyllis MacRae　　　　　　　　　　　*Interviewed by Mrs Robin Porteous*
Phyllis MacRae is the daughter of the 4th Marquess of Bristol, a career sailor retiring as Rear-
Admiral. Before he succeeded he was briefly MP for Bury St Edmunds. Her mother was the
daughter of an industrialist, G E Wythes of Copped Hall, Essex. In 1921 Lady Phyllis Hervey
married a Scot – a soldier, Captain Duncan MacRae – who owned Eilean Donan Castle, now
restored. Lady Phyllis still farms quite near her parents' home, Ickworth, in Suffolk.

Lady Mander　　　　　　　　　　　　　　*Interviewed by Merlin Waterson*
Rosalie Mander is the daughter of A C Glyn Grylls, a branch of an extensive Cornish family.
Unusually for the period, she was educated at Queen's College, London and Lady Margaret
Hall, Oxford. In 1930 she married, as his second wife, Geoffrey Mander whose father Theodore,
founder of the family paint firm in Wolverhampton, had built Wightwick Manor. Geoffrey
Mander was Liberal MP for Wolverhampton. The Manders offered Wightwick to the National
Trust in 1935 and it was handed over after the war. Lady Mander is an authority on the Pre-
Raphaelites and a prolific author and biographer. Sir Geoffrey died in 1962, but Lady Mander
still has a flat in the house.

Katherine, Viscountess Mersey　　　　　　　*Interviewed by the Viscountess Mersey*
Kitty Mersey is the elder daughter of the 6th Marquess of Lansdowne, MP for West Derbyshire
until 1919. He succeeded his father, a distinguished politician and Minister, Governor-General
of Canada and Viceroy of India, in 1927, and moved with his family to Bowood, Wiltshire.
Kitty Fitzmaurice's father died in 1936; tragically, both her brothers were killed within days
of each other in 1944 and the Marquessate passed to her cousin, George Mercer-Nairne. She
herself became a peeress in her own right, succeeding her brother in the Barony of Nairne. In
1933 she married Edward Bigham, who succeeded his father, a famous shipping lawyer, in 1956.
Her husband died in 1978, and Lady Mersey still lives at Bignor, the family estate in Sussex.

The Hon Mrs John Mildmay White　　　　　　*Interviewed by Mrs Richard Carew Pole*
Helen Mildmay White is the daughter of the first Baron Mildmay of Flete, MP for Totnes for
37 years, who inherited Flete in Devon, Shoreham Place in Kent and a house in London on
his father's death in 1905. He married in 1906 Alice, daughter of the Grenfells of Taplow Court.
After his wife fell ill and entered a nursing home, Helen Mildmay became her father's hostess.

In 1945 she married Lt Commander White. Her brother, Anthony, the 2nd and last Lord Mildmay, was drowned after the 2nd World War, although the Mildmay name was preserved when Mrs White added it to her husband's. During the war, Flete was turned into a maternity hospital and later into flats by the Mutual Household Association. Commander White died in 1969 and Mrs Mildmay White now lives at Pamflete on the Flete estate.

The Duke of Richmond and Gordon   *Interviewed by The Hon Mrs David Blacker*

Freddy Richmond is the 9th Duke of Richmond and the 4th Duke of Gordon. His father was the 8th Duke and his mother an industrialist's niece, Hilda Brassey. The Duchess, Elizabeth, whom he married in 1927, is the daughter of a former vicar of Wendover, the Rev Thomas Hudson. A pioneer aviator and keen racing driver, the Duke created his own motor racing circuit at Goodwood. The Duke presided over Goodwood – house, estate and annual flat-race meeting – from 1935 until he and the Duchess moved into an elegant folly on the estate in 1969.

Anne, Countess of Rosse   *Interviewed by Miss Hermione Hobhouse*

Anne Rosse is the daughter of Colonel Leonard Messel, whose father had created the garden at Nymans. Her mother was Maude Sambourne, and it was through her that Lady Rosse, and, ultimately, the Victorian Society, inherited 18 Stafford Terrace, London. Anne Messel first married Ronald Armstrong Jones in 1925. After 9 years, they divorced and she married Michael 6th Earl of Rosse. It was a remarkable partnership: he helped to found the Georgian Group, she the Victorian Society. A famous beauty, she ran four houses – Birr, Womersley, Nymans and Stafford Terrace. Lord Rosse died in 1979 and Lady Rosse returned to live at Nymans.

Lady Marjorie Stirling   *Interviewed by Mrs Angus Stirling*

Marjorie Stirling's father, the 8th Earl of Dunmore, was a Scot and a brave soldier, fighting in the Sudan, India, and in the Boer and Great Wars, and gaining both VC and DSO. Lord-in-Waiting to George V, he commanded the Gentlemen-at-Arms. Her mother was from Skye. Brought up in Scotland, Lady Marjorie Murray married in 1926 a banker, Duncan Stirling, latterly Chairman of National Westminster. Their youngest son, Angus, is Director General of the National Trust for England.

Marcus Wickham-Boynton   *Interviewed by The Hon Mrs Nicholas Cunliffe-Lister*

Marcus Wickham-Boynton's father, Thomas, was a Wickham, his mother a Boynton, the only child of the 11th Baronet. A fine horseman and Master of the East Middleton Hunt, he inherited Burton Agnes through the Boyntons and started a stud there. Since inheriting in 1946, Marcus Wickham-Boynton has restored the Long Gallery and filled the house with modern pictures and antique furniture. To ensure continuity, he has left it to his relative, Nicholas Cunliffe-Lister, brother of the Earl of Swinton.

I VAIN CITADELS

Rex Whistler's frontispiece for *The Last of Uptake* by Simon Harcourt-Smith. 'As an institution and a way of life, the country house had seemed inviolable. The Great War put paid to that assumption.'

THE COUNTRY HOUSE REMEMBERED

One country house at least came close to perfection between the wars. Conceived in 1915, refined, embellished and enriched over the next sixty years, it is perhaps the only house created this century to which one can return again and again, and which remains completely inexhaustibly satisfying. However much devotees of their country houses may protest, Edwin Lutyens, Detmar Blow and Oliver Hill never produced that one work of indisputable genius which would have put their greatness beyond doubt. That distinction belongs to the creator of Blandings Castle. As long as Mr Beach and Mrs Twemlow were there to ensure that 'things were done properly . . . with the right solemnity', Blandings basked in eternal summer sunshine. Readers of *Something Fresh* will recall that:

> Blandings was not one of those houses – or shall we say hovels? – where the upper servants are expected not only to feed but to congregate before feeding in the Steward's Room . . . To Mr Beach and to Mrs Twemlow, the suggestion that they or their peers should gather together in the same room in which they were to dine would have been as repellent as an announcement from Lady Anne Worthington, the chatelaine, that the house party would eat in the drawing room.

And there is nothing to suggest in later accounts of life at Blandings that standards were ever allowed to slip very far while Beach presided.

If Blandings was unreal, so too in many ways was Eaton Hall, which reached an apogee of opulence during this period. 'What was extraordinary about Eaton', Loelia, Duchess of Westminster, remembers, 'was that it was already two hundred years out of date when I was there':

> I felt Eaton had stopped about the time of Versailles. The thing was on such a scale of splendour and opulence. There were simply always hundreds of people to do things – you only had to express your slightest wish. However bizarre, it was immediately accomplished. The very first visit of all I made to Eaton, I went round the wonderful greenhouses, and I idly remarked, 'You haven't got any orchids,' and the Duke said, 'No, I don't think we've ever gone in for them specially.' I never thought any more about the conversation; and when I went back to Eaton after our honeymoon, I found a whole conservatory or greenhouse full of orchids – not only that, but there was a laboratory with an orchid specialist in a white coat, mixing up pollen for new species.

Other country house owners had their own particular ideas of what was important. When Lanning Roper first stayed at Anglesey Abbey, to advise on the garden so improbably created from naked fenland in the 1930s, it was discreetly intimated that guests should not precede Lord Fairhaven to the library before dinner: he was known to dislike seeing any traces of footmarks other than his own on the passage carpet, which he insisted should be re-brushed every evening.

Despite the First World War, country house life appeared to resume its leisurely, unflustered pace. A symbol of that leisure was, for Lady Hyde Parker, the making of spills, which continued 'right up until this last war':

> Everybody had a spill box, or rather a beaker or vase, on the chimney piece in their study or morning room, filled with spills. Instead of tearing up letters, each sheet was cut lengthwise into strips of about 2–3 inches wide, and these were then folded into long 'tapers' of 14 inches wide. They were folded concertina-wise, so the ends could spread round like a fan. Like this they caught fire easily when placed near a burning log or coal. They were used instead of a match. It was such a pleasant and peaceful occupation to make unwanted letters into spills and fill the boxes. The study and library, and also the boudoir, all had spill boxes on their chimney pieces at Melford.

The attitude to house parties was similarly relaxed, provided the hostess could still rely on her well-regulated and disciplined staff. In the 1920s and 1930s, guests to Plas Newydd came and went so freely that the Marchioness of Anglesey would sometimes mistake visitors from nearby Vaynol, merely taking advantage of the swimming pool, for house guests, and ask whether they were staying long.

Swimming pools were themselves a novelty, which, as the Duke of Richmond and Gordon remembers, could be regarded as disturbing evidence of subversion:

> Everybody disapproved of it, thought it was rather fast. The Gordon Lennox family had been so tremendously orientated round Gordon Castle that to my grandfather, and to most people, salmon fishing was a sort of religion. If my father wanted to do a bit of shooting, he was seen going out salmon fishing with all his gear, and with his shotgun, for the very simple reason that on the lower reaches of the Spey there were magnificent duck; and he'd come back with half a dozen teal. But my grandfather objected: 'You either go fishing or shooting. You will not confuse things and take your gun with you.' That sort of tempo went right through the family, certainly between 1900 and I suppose 1930; so when we had built the swimming pool, and my father's brother, Esme Gordon, was staying with us, we said, 'Uncle Esme, you must come and see the swimming pool.' 'No, thank you,' he said, really quite shocked, 'as far as I'm concerned, water is a thing you get fishes out of.'

Life went on very much as before for the Duke and many of his generation:

> World War One didn't make an awful lot of difference to life, except that people started disappearing. For instance, my chauffeur, Charles Tilbury, whose home was in the Hatfield cottages, he disappeared. In a funny way, World War One did make an enormous impact at Eton, largely because one had even less food, and because the Lower Master was a very old man. He was absolutely hopeless. All the decent chaps had gone.

But there were those who sensed irrevocable change. Lady Phyllis MacRae, whose mother, the Marchioness of Bristol, had inherited an industrial fortune and was therefore more cushioned than most, had no illusions about what was happening:

> Between the two wars, everyone was trying to return to the old days before 1914. But nobody could get back; the first 'bloodless revolution' had taken place. Domestics were already difficult to get, from 1919 onwards. The estate workers, and the footmen, had gone to the War, and they did not want to come back. The butler, who had been with us from the time my parents married, was, of course, still at Ickworth, but those who had been there before the War had found out that the great big world was much more amusing than being a footman.

She was not alone in her doubts. The leisure, the aimlessness, pleasant enough for some, was thoroughly tedious for others, such as Katherine, Viscountess Mersey:

> One's life work was going to dances, and then staying as late as one possibly could; my poor mother in my first year always came too, and she got terribly tired of sitting talking to somebody's dreary father and watching us dancing ... At Bowood during the winter I had my horse and I went hunting twice a week. On the other days I had nothing to do at all. I used to do the crossword and take my dog out, and that was about all. So there wasn't enough to do, really, either in London or in the country. There was no question of doing any work. I think I did one or two things like the Young Conservatives' Association, and went to meetings, and collected half-crown subscriptions, that sort of thing. I think most of my friends would say now that they were very bored.

Taxation and the servant problem, although both were deplored, were not the cause of this gradual disillusionment. It was that attitudes to country house living were changing significantly. As Mrs John Dower records, her father, Sir Charles Trevelyan, who succeeded in 1928, hated the idea of his dining room and hall filled with servants. In 1936 Harold Nicolson was able to write in his diary for 28 June:

> Cliveden, I admit is looking lovely. The party also is lavish and enormous. How glad I am that we are not so rich I simply do not want a house like this where nothing is really yours, but belongs to servants and gardeners. There is a ghastly unreality about it all. Its beauty is purely scenic. I enjoy seeing it. But to own it, to live here, would be like living on the stage of the Scala theatre in Milan.

He had already put on record, some four years previously, in another diary entry, the life that he and Vita Sackville-West had chosen for themselves:

> It is typical of our existence that with no settled income and no certain prospects, we should live in a muddle of museum carpets, ruined castles, and penury. Yet we know very well that all this uncertainty is better for us than a dull and unadventurous security.

A feeling of insecurity pervades several of the recollections contained in this book. So too does an awareness of radical change, not just among the landed classes, but in society as a whole; and with that awareness, a willingness to adapt to an unprecedented social revolution. The doubts and self-criticisms of that generation have been articulated with peculiar frankness; and this escape from Edwardian complacency is surely one of its virtues.

Some great landowners sensed the revolution and attempted to respond positively to it. Writing to her mother in 1923, Lady Phyllis MacRae reported that Lord Leverhulme's decision to present his property on Lewis to the people of the island, was 'regarded as iniquitous, as other landlords will be expected to do likewise and naturally won't. However, whatever the poor man does will be wrong up here.'

If Leverhulme's behaviour was thought to undermine the already weakened foundations of the landed interest, Lady Phyllis' mother was herself capable of dismissing some of its most sacred principles. When, in 1925, the Marchioness' nephew, heir to the Bristol title, was dangerously ill, she insisted on regarding this as threatening personal but not dynastic tragedy: 'I suppose it is not so bad for me . . . being of the opinion that the succession should be by selection of either sex and not hereditary. Then if people marry uneugenically, I don't think it's a matter of surprise that the offspring should be

17

THE COUNTRY HOUSE REMEMBERED

non-resisters to germ invasion.' Her views on shooting were similarly unconventional:

> I managed badly and got caught for two drives shooting. I inflicted myself on Dad so that I could shut my eyes and cover my ears, which wasn't much fun for him. I saw the hare come out, hesitate whether to go back or come on – next it was rolled over and kicking instead of being all nice and alive, and one pheasant I saw too. Then I looked no more as there was no one I wanted to hate, and I knew I should if I watched because to me it seemed just mean and horrid to enjoy destroying beautiful overfed live things which are scared into coming along and people with guns just waiting and doing nothing but shoot. Primitive instinct debased! It's as well I don't go out shooting as I'd lose all my tolerance!

Such opinions were not commonly expressed in country house drawing rooms. It was the novels of the period that time and again turned to the country house as a symbol of all that was rotten in the old order. D H Lawrence's treatment of Wragby Hall and its owner, Sir Clifford Chatterley, in *Lady Chatterley's Lover* (1928), is deliberately contemptuous and cruel. Paralysed, sexually mutilated and condemned to a wheelchair by his injuries in the war that had claimed his elder brother, Sir Clifford inhabits a house 'as dreary as a disused street'; and when his wife Connie forsakes 'that great weary warren', it is for his gamekeeper and life in a farm cottage.

It was not just Wragby and the Chatterleys which suffered humiliation at Lawrence's hands. Connie was taken on a journey past a succession of great houses: 'Chadwick Hall more window than wall . . . was still kept up, but as a show piece'; Shipley was to be pulled down to make way for a housing estate; and Fritchley, 'a perfect old Georgian mansion, was even now, as Connie passed in the car, being demolished . . . it was too big, too expensive, and the country had become too uncongenial.' Connie's vision of wholesale destruction may have presented an exaggerated picture of the fate of country houses in the 1930s, but it was certainly prophetic of the post-war years.

Lawrence's view of country house life was drawn from his knowledge of the Sitwells' Renishaw and Lady Ottoline Morrell's Garsington. He hated being treated like one of the estate paupers at Garsington, and, like them, resented the gifts of huge and ugly counterpanes which Lady Ottoline had herself made out of the remnants of extravagantly coloured wool. Aldous Huxley also parodied Garsington and the Morrells in *Crome Yellow* (1921). Huxley's country houses were no longer a focal point for craftsmanship, for literary and artistic patronage. Similarly, Evelyn Waugh's Hetton

Abbey, in *A Handful of Dust* (1934), epitomised a feudal order which was as doomed as its crenellations, its shafts of polished granite, and its vast gasoliers.

There is a telling contrast between the descriptions of halycon country house life in P G Wodehouse's novels, and what he relates in his letters. In 1925, he wrote from Hunstanton Hall in Norfolk:

'The above address does not mean that I have bought a country estate. It is a joint belonging to a friend of mine, and I am putting in a week or two here. It's one of those enormous houses, about two-thirds of which are derelict. There is a whole wing which has not been lived in for half a century. You know the sort of thing – it's happening all over the country now – thousands of acres, park, gardens, moat, etc and priceless heirlooms, but precious little ready money. The income, from farms and so on, just about balances expenses.'

Twenty years later, writing to Denis Mackail in December 1945, Wodehouse was scarcely less pessimistic:

'I wish I could get the glimmering of an idea for a novel. . . . what the devil does one write about these days, if one is a specialist in country houses and butlers, both of which have ceased to exist?'

Land prices had begun to fall steadily in the 1870s, with only the shakiest of recoveries in 1921 and then a continuing decline until the late 1930s. In 1914, the *Estates Gazette* had estimated that during the preceding five years, 800,000 acres, valued at about £20 million, had changed hands. Dwindling agricultural incomes gave many landed families little choice: they could either sell out to industrial or commercial interests, or they could marry into them. The list of the great estates which came on the market, in part or in whole, just before the First World War, includes Houghton in Norfolk, Apethorpe in Northampton, Berrington in Herefordshire, Millichope in Shropshire, to name just a few. The families selling estates were among the most apparently secure: the Marquess of Ailesbury, the Earl of Carlisle, the Duke of Newcastle and the Duke of Bedford.

The resentment felt by long established but often beleaguered families of the position enjoyed by the new rich was sharpened by the vulgar and ostentatious wealth displayed by the entourage of Edward VII. Seventy years later, Lady Burrell still remembers that social tension:

It was my grandfather who made all the money, and my grandmother avoided fashionable society and felt awkward in it. I also felt out of place in grand houses and was very conscious of being *nouveau riche*, even though, in the 1930s, Knepp Castle had fourteen staff, and its own brickworks and blacksmith.

The landed society attacked by Lloyd George was already in head-long retreat. Harcourt's introduction of estate duty in 1894 had been a pointer, although at a maximum rate of eight per cent on estates worth £1 million or more, its impact was at first muted. Lloyd George's Budget of 1909 and the Rent Restriction Act of 1915 were more threatening. Then the Budget of 1919 raised death duties on a sliding scale from six per cent on estates worth over £15,000 to forty per cent on estates worth over £2 million, ensuring that the pattern of land ownership changed more radically than at any time since the Reformation. The sales recorded in the *Estates Gazette* imply that between 1918 and 1922 one quarter of the land area of England and Wales changed hands.

Many more great estates would have been broken up if a willing buyer could have been found. It was difficult enough in the 1920s and 1930s to find tenants prepared to take on estate farms, as Geoffrey Wolryche Whitmore found at Dudmaston:

> My grandfather had let things slide in the latter part of his life. Many buildings were made of our local sandstone, which crumbles away. Fences and gates were in bad order and none of the buildings were up-to-date. The consequence of this was that no tenant ever stayed at Dudmaston, which was a great drawback.
> There was no sawmill and all timber was cut up by hand by travelling pit sawyers once a year. I persuaded my father to instal a small sawmill in 1910, which helped to keep things tidy.
> In 1914, when the War started, most of the estate men left with me. At the end of the War in 1919, a whole heap of repairs needed doing. Shortly after this agriculture began to slump and things went steadily back till 1933.

Wolryche Whitmore had the energy and imagination to tackle these problems himself. He took his farms in hand, sinking wells and devising his own irrigation system. The less fertile parts of the estate he gave over to forestry, carefully integrating commercial softwoods with traditional hardwoods in a way which enhanced the landscape and established Dudmaston as a model of enlightened planting. Lady Hyde Parker's account of her husband's management of the Melford estate describes how he had to overcome similar difficulties.

Other landowners were less resourceful and resorted instead to cutting agricultural wages. Between 1920 and 1922 the weekly farm wage in Norfolk fell from 46 shillings, to 36 shillings, to 25 shillings.

In March 1923 the National Farmers' Union offered a wage of 5½d an hour for a 54-hour week; and at this the National Union of Agricultural Workers called a strike. After great bitterness and sporadic outbreaks of violence, a compromise of 25 shillings for a 50-hour week was agreed. The two sides had in effect acknowledged that both were the victims of a disastrous and apparently relentless decline in agriculture, which successive governments were either unable or unwilling to halt.

Writing in 1925, in the Epilogue to *Lyme Letters*, Lady Newton summed up the feelings of many owners of country houses:

> And what of the stately homes of England? How many of these will survive the cruel and ruthless taxation? Why are we not allowed the right to live? Why should it be a crime that we should have succeeded to places too large for present-day requirements? Why, also, should we be prevented from enjoying our homes that have come down to us from our forefathers? We only demand the right to live in them, without the amenities of former days, but this is to be denied us. What are we to do? We cannot sell, there are no buyers. We cannot afford to live in our homes, what is to become of them? . . . Well, when all is gone, and a ruthless Government has completed the ruin of the class they set out to destroy, we shall still have our self-respect and sweet memories of happy bygone days, and these, thank God, no man can take from us.

Lady Newton had come as a bride to Lyme in 1880. For many of her generation, the change was total, devastating and often made infinitely more painful by bereavement during the Great War. Death duties – frequently double death duties – compounded their loss. There was to be no dispensation: the roll of honour in innumerable parish churches lists the dead in alphabetical order, with only their rank to distinguish the sons of the country house, half-hidden by cedars across the churchyard, from the poorest agricultural labourer.

The burden was sometimes unbearable. Shugborough, for instance, had never recovered from the extravagance of the first Earl of Lichfield. With the estate weighed down with debts and mortgages, the third Earl concluded that he would not be serving his family's interests by struggling on any longer. His death in 1918 was reported as an accident: he was found to have shot himself in the woods below one of Shugborough's park monuments, the Dark Lanthorn.

Lyme and Shugborough at least survived. Others were demolished: Kirby Hall in the West Riding, Norton Priory in Cheshire, Debden Hall in Essex and Sir Robert Peel's house, Drayton Manor in Staffordshire, were among those swept away in the 1920s and the 1930s. The dissolution of great houses had happened from time to time in previous centuries, but what distinguished these earlier losses from more recent destruction was that the former were usually isolated examples, the penalty of profligacy. As an institution and a way of life, the country house had seemed inviolable. The Great War put paid to that assumption. It destroyed the myth that a country house in the right hands was, like Sir John Fisher's Dreadnoughts, indestructible. Of all the changes brought by the First World War, loss of confidence was perhaps the most significant.

In the face of depredations such as these, it was scarcely surprising that there was some closing of ranks. The cult of philistinism, which had thrived during the latter part of the nineteenth century, and which had become even more pronounced after the trial of Oscar Wilde, was no longer thought of as particularly manly or amusing. The country house owner as connoisseur, and not just as antiquarian, was less likely to be viewed askance. Excessive preoccupation with pale blue damasks and gilt fringes might raise the eyebrows of a hard-hunting country squire, but was not necessarily interpreted as a sign of moral depravity. When the second Lord Newton used to tell his Edwardian guests that the carvings in the saloon at Lyme were not really by Grinling Gibbons and that the panelling in the Long Gallery was just a sham, it was partly to annoy his wife, and partly to disassociate himself from the likes of Angela Thirkell's Mr Holt. But when the house was in imminent danger of being broken up, that was no longer a clever line. Rather than denigrate his possessions, the master of the country house might be more inclined to defend and cherish his inheritance with all the fervour of his eighteenth-century forebears.

These were not, however, the conditions for confident patronage. It is scarcely suprising that the best work of Lutyens, Detmar Blow and Goodhart-Rendel so often appears isolated and fragmentary. Even Lutyens' most fervent admirers acknowledge that the use of vernacular in his late country houses has a restraint amounting to dullness.

A fair assessment of the real stature of other country house architects of the period remains elusive. Hilles, the Cotswold manor house which Blow built for himself, worthily exemplifies the work of the Arts and Crafts movement. But Blow allowed his talents to be consumed and corrupted by the second Duke of Westminster, who spread his patronage like a debilitating disease. All too often, Blow's work qualifies for the label of 'only-little-me-ishness' which Goodhart-Rendel neatly attached to the country houses of Newton and Voysey.

Goodhart-Rendel's own buildings never seem quite to match his

abilities as a scholar – for his knowledge and appreciation of Victorian buildings was to be unrivalled for half a century – nor his perception as a critic. Like Clough Williams-Ellis, his ideas and writing are of greater interest than the executed commissions. Reviewing an RIBA competition in 1932, he concluded that 'one party yearns secretly for the vanished days when Mistress Art gloried in the richness of her wardrobe, the other prefers the nude. With the nude, as an experienced connoisseur said to me the other day, one knows the worst at once.' His alterations to Plas Newydd are, however, assured: there were not then so many planners and conservation groups to object to the change from James Wyatt's perfunctory Gothick to Goodhart-Rendel's vigorous Tudor. With his contributions, and those of Sybil Colefax and Rex Whistler, Plas Newydd is evidence that the 1920s and 1930s could produce decoration and design of real vitality, enhancing an already distinguished house. It also exemplifies an ideal of country house life, summed up in a letter of 1938 from Rex Whistler to the sixth Marquess of Anglesey, enclosing his final account for the decoration of the dining room and saying that he could not 'ever hope to repay for all those lovely days of fun & bathing & sunshine, & moonlight & enormous delicious meals'.

Rex Whistler's astonishing technique and his visual imagination stand comparison with that of any English decorative painter, of any period. The easel pictures completed towards the end of his life suggest that he was also discovering untapped subtlety and distinction in paintings which would perhaps have been taken more seriously than his earlier work. But the qualities of wit, lightness of touch and elegance which Rex Whistler shared with the Sitwells and Lord Berners should not be dismissed as mere frivolity. At the time, the choice between the classical tradition, the modern movement emanating from Paris and the Bauhaus, and the revival of a Rococo approach to decoration had wider significance. The association of monumental classicism with Fascism became inescapable in the 1930s, leading in due course to the eclipse of architects such as Lutyens and Gilbert Scott. When this political, moral dimension is taken into account, the failure to produce towering architectural and artistic achievements can better be understood, and seen perhaps in a more favourable light. The humour, humanity, the capacity for criticism provide a riposte to Auden's condemnation of a 'weakened generation', or Eliot's conclusion that these were:

Twenty years largely wasted, the years of *l'entre deux guerres*.

These qualities of wit and humanity are particularly evident in Nancy Mitford's *The Pursuit of Love*, which is all the more interesting

Opposite: 'Plas Newydd is evidence that the 1920s and 1930s could produce decoration and design of real vitality' – Rex Whistler working on the dining room mural. (*Country Life*)

because its sources can be so clearly identified. The description of Merlinford is not a generalised account of a country house, but is modelled in almost every detail on Faringdon, as recreated between the wars by Lord Berners. It is a house 'to live in, not to rush out from all day to kill enemies and animals'. Its owner, Lord Merlin, is an unashamed aesthete, whose whippets wear diamond necklaces, who fills his house with flowers and who has built 'a small but exquisite playhouse in the garden, where his astonished neighbours were sometimes invited to attend such puzzlers as Cocteau plays, the opera "Mahagonny", or the latest Dada extravagance from Paris.' However much his neighbours might despise the writing-paper with a picture of Merlinford on it, they do not refuse to attend those performances. Even Lord Alconleigh feels compelled to welcome Lord Merlin's house party to the Alconleigh ball, to save it from 'utter and unrelieved dowdiness'.

Like Rex Whistler, with whom he decorated Cecil Beaton's Circus Bedroom at Ashcombe, Lord Berners is a difficult subject for academic art historians. His talents were so varied and his jokes so important a part of his life, that his underlying seriousness can be underestimated. Behind the apparent frivolity was a profound understanding of the history of taste, in part instinctive, but in part the result of wide reading and of years spent living abroad, in Rome, Paris and Constantinople. At a time when the more stolidly conservative proponents of country house taste directed that furniture should be of dark mahogany and preferably made by Chippendale, Faringdon offered a shocking, but undeniably stylish, alternative.

Cecil Beaton's Circus Bedroom at Ashcombe, decorated by Lord Berners and Rex Whistler.

The serious study of country house design and a fuller appreciation of the decoration of different periods developed apace in the 1930s. This was more than a revival of eighteenth- and nineteenth-century antiquarianism, and certainly owed little to the crude stylistic plagiarisms of Edwardian decorators such as Amadée Joubert. A new level of understanding and scholarship is discernible in Christopher Hussey's writing for *Country Life*, in the novels of Evelyn Waugh, with their perceptive, accurate descriptions of Victorian country houses, and in John Fowler's recourse, during his early years as a decorator, to eighteenth-century painting techniques, colours and textiles. These rediscoveries are paralleled by the Sitwells' writings on Baroque and Rococo architecture, and by the fresh interest in Regency and Empire furniture, which was used to great effect by Lord Gerald Wellesley, by Ralph Dutton at Hinton Ampner, by Mario Praz, and by Lord and Lady Berwick at Attingham.

Their notoriety, their talent for self-advertisement, should not be allowed to distract attention from the lasting signficance of that generation of Oxford aesthetes who gathered around Harold Acton in the 1920s and who subsequently flung the boundaries of taste world wide. Robert Byron embarked on his lonely pilgrimage to the cities of Byzantium and the palaces of Iran. Desmond Parsons went with Harold Acton to Peking and, with his brother, Lord Rosse, organised botanical expeditions which were to enrich the gardens of Birr and Nymans.

The most precious legacy of this group of friends was a new sense of responsibility towards historic buildings, going far beyond the tenets of conservation established by William Morris and the Society for the Protection of Ancient Buildings. It is scarcely surprising that taste so little inhibited by geographical frontiers, should have been so catholic when confronted by art unfashionable in date; nor is it coincidence that in the lists of founder members of both the Georgian Group in the 1930s and the Victorian Society in the 1960s the same names crop up.

Their breadth of vision also took in garden history. At Sissinghurst, Vita Sackville-West and Harold Nicolson gave to plants an architectural framework which derived from the English seventeenth-century knot garden and the geometry of continental formal gardens. An ability to re-work, and in doing so to enhance, earlier designs, was nowhere more brilliantly demonstrated than at Blickling by Mrs Norah Lindsay, where the remodelled parterre is exactly contemporary with Sissinghurst. Taking on an over-elaborate and unmanageable jig-saw of beds designed by W E Nesfield in the 1870s, she preserved features such as the curiously shaped yews, but threw together most of the smaller borders. Four large beds were then built up into great pyramids of herbaceous plants, which in texture and colour perfectly complement the surrounding Jacobean architecture. Neither needlessly destructive, nor slavishly historical, the result has something of the subtlety of a Sickert painting, in which each layer of pigment supplements and refines the image, without completely obliterating what has gone before.

The marriage of a scholarly and a romantic view of the country house helps to explain why an institution which politically and socially seemed anachronistic, nevertheless survived. Although the catalogue of destruction during the last fifty years is a depressing one, there has not been the wholesale dissolution, comparable to that of the abbeys in the sixteenth century, which might have been expected. That fate was averted because a generation of owners of country houses was prepared, between the wars, to adapt to a way of life never envisaged by their original builders and owners. The willingness to adapt and the wish to cherish houses which were no longer

27

comfortable, or even particularly prestigious, are recurring themes of the recollections which follow. It was that same generation which assembled the case for preservation, given such eloquent expression when the Marquess of Lothian set up the National Trust's Country House Scheme in 1934. Who then would have foreseen the hundreds of thousands of visitors to country houses every year, would have dared to hope for the Historic Buildings and Monuments Commission grants, or the massive rescue operations mounted by the National Heritage Memorial Fund? It is a far cry from the years just after the First World War, when on Thursdays Lord Marshmoreton opened Belpher Castle to the public on payment of a fee of one shilling a head. As readers of *A Damsel in Distress* (1919) will recall:

> The money is collected by Keggs the butler and goes to a worthy local charity. At least, that is the idea. But the voice of calumny is never silent, and there exists a school of thought, headed by Albert, the page-boy, which holds that Keggs sticks to these shillings like glue, and adds them to his already considerable savings in the Farmers' and Merchants' Bank, on the left side of the High Street in Belpher village, next door to the Oddfellows' Hall.

Opposite:
'During the First World War, West Wycombe was more or less empty . . . Coming back after that awful war, Johnnie felt the house was too much of a burden to take on . . . Then, when Francis was born there, it somehow changed the whole picture. Johnnie felt perhaps it would be worthwhile making a tremendous effort to try and live there.'

II A GENERATION WEAKENED

West Wycombe Park – Ickworth

THE COUNTRY HOUSE REMEMBERED

Helen, Lady Dashwood

'As we rounded the drive, I gave a loud scream . . . "It's the most beautiful house I've ever seen in my life. We're not going to sell *this*."'

Opposite:
West Wycombe Park was put up for sale after the First World War, but later withdrawn from the market.

'During the First World War, West Wycombe was more or less empty, but for the last year of that war, nobody was in it, and so everything was covered with dust. It was full of lovely things but they were not properly cared for.

'Coming back after that awful war, Johnnie felt the house was too much of a burden to take on. So he sold a whole lot of things at Sotheby's. Thank goodness I didn't know about it – it was before I knew Johnnie – because he sold so many lovely things.

'I had no idea about West Wycombe. I knew vaguely that Johnnie had some property about an hour's drive from London, but I wasn't particularly interested. I gathered that there was an old barn . . . Then one day, when we were engaged, he said: "I'd like to have you down and show you where I was brought up." Oh, don't let's bother – it's up for sale, isn't it?" "Yes, it is, but I'd like to show it to you all the same." Anxious to please my nice young man, I said, "Very well." He always told the story that, as we rounded the drive, I gave a loud scream. "What's the matter, darling? Are you ill?" "No, I'm not ill, but this can't be the old barn. It's the most beautiful house I've ever seen in my life. We're not going to sell *this*."

'So, after we married in 1922, we moved in, and more or less picnicked there, because Johnnie was in the Foreign Service and we were going off to Belgium. We had an old housekeeper, a bailiff, and various people like that, and it was very dirty and not at all comfortable. Our first child – a daughter – was born there, and then we went to Brussels and I started having another baby. Johnnie didn't want me to have the baby in Brussels, because two of our chums had died having their second babies. He got in a state and said, "You've got to have it in England, whatever happens." I said, "Why take an expensive house in London? Why don't I go and picnic again at West Wycombe? Mama will come and stay with me there. It doesn't matter about heating in the summer. There are bathrooms, and I'll occupy a bedroom next to one of them. Why don't we do that?" So we did, and then, when Francis was born there, it somehow changed the whole picture. Johnnie felt perhaps it would be worthwhile making a tremendous effort to try and live there. Our first Christmas at West Wycombe was in 1922.

'I think there were 6000 acres: farmland and a lot of trees. Funnily enough, Johnnie told me that in the war, when he was in the trenches, he got a message from some government department, saying that they'd like to buy all the timber on the estate for £100,000 (a magical amount in those days). "Certainly not," he said. "What am I fighting for?" Anybody else might have said, "Well, everything's going; I don't expect to live; why not sell?"'

By direction of Sir JOHN LINDSAY DASHWOOD, Bart.

BUCKS.

Within ten minutes' walk of West Wycombe Station on the G.W. and G.C. Joint Railways, 2½ miles from High Wycombe Station and 31½ miles by road from London.

Illustrated Particulars, Plan and Conditions of Sale

OF THE

Very Valuable and Attractive

FREEHOLD COUNTY SEAT

KNOWN AS

West Wycombe Park

Dating from the Early XVIIth Century, and containing Entrance and Central Halls, Magnificent Suite of Reception Rooms, Sixteen Principal Bed Rooms, Four Bath Rooms, Ground Floor Offices and ample Servants' Accommodation.

Stabling. Garages. Two Lodges and several Cottages.

FINE UNDULATING PARK.

WOODLANDS, LAKE and HOME FARM.

The whole extending to

Over 338 Acres.

For Sale by Auction by Messrs.

GIDDY & GIDDY

At the London Auction Mart, 155, Queen Victoria Street, E.C. 4,

On WEDNESDAY, 19th JULY, 1922,

At 2.30 precisely

(unless previously Sold by Private Treaty).

LAND AGENT - Mr. W. R. BUTLER, 15, High Street, High Wycombe.

SOLICITOR - Mr. E. VERNOR MILES, 30, Theobald's Road, Bedford Row, W.C. 1; and 15, High Street, High Wycombe.

AUCTIONEERS' OFFICES :—

11a, REGENT STREET, S.W. 1; and Maidenhead and Windsor.

'I don't think Johnnie worked very hard over the estate. He worked hard at the Foreign Office, but, like everybody else of his generation, he was very worn out by that terrible war. He just wanted to live in peace and quiet.

'West Wycombe was extraordinary. The house was twice as large as it is now. The enormous servant's wing, almost as large as the main house, was totally shut up. In it, like our part of the house, were thirty or more bedrooms. We couldn't think what to do, because it was like having two enormous houses.

'I said we must get the family finances on a solid basis and find out what is going on, stop all this waste: six gardeners and nothing grown but cabbages; an enormous amount of acres and no money. We went into all the figures and found such cheating. The extraordinary thing was that the agent and the solicitor told Johnnie that the most he could take out of the estate was £1200 a year. I never knew if it was true or not; I didn't know anything about money, nor care, but when we went through the figures, we found the agent was getting £2800 and the solicitor £3200. That didn't seem to me quite right! Finally, it did become a viable estate.'

Lady Phyllis MacRae

'A good number of people did realise that life could never go back to what it was before the War, but my father, and people like him, never resigned themselves to it. He was horrified at the way of life that had to be accepted, even though it was still very lavish.

'The change came very gradually. At first it was the difference between peacetime and wartime: peacetime was so lavish compared to wartime that you did not realise you were not going back to the old life. For instance, in 1919, when I came out – I worked at the hospital here in Bury St Edmunds till 1918 – things were not right back to the way they were before the War. My father used to say, "I wouldn't have gone to a dance unless I was going to have dinner first" After the War, your hosts did not necessarily give you dinner as well; and he was horrified that there was no sit-down dinner at any of the dances. There was a buffet, and if there was anything in the way of tables, it was not an organised social affair as it was before. That never came back. A dinner party before the dance, that did begin again, but you did not have a dinner during the dance; you had a buffet, whether it was in London or in the country.

'The Season had been firmly established before 1914. People tried to revive it at once. 1919 was a wonderful Season – gay and bright, with all the men in uniform, throwing their money about any old how, they were so glad to be alive. In 1920 there were terrible strikes

Opposite:
Lady Phyllis MacRae's parents, the Marquess and Marchioness of Bristol, attending a garden party at Buckingham Palace. 'A good number of people did realise that life could never go back to what it was before the war, but my father, and people like him, never resigned themselves to it.'

– if you had a party, bricks came through your window. People were actually on the streets, walking about with a brick in their hands. It was far worse than now. There was no social security – they were starving, and when you did see a group of people having a hunger march, it was a *hunger* march. They were in rags, they were cold, they had no coats on, and they were thin and looked absolutely down-and-out. It really tore you to pieces to see them. At that time we had been lent a house in Egerton Gardens. There were children begging in the street outside. One of them, I remember, said to me when I said I had no money with me, "You've got those beads round your neck" – they were my pearls. If I could not give her anything else, could she have my beads?

'You went right back to wartime conditions. Although you might have a little party in your house – what sounds quite a big party now – and you might dance to the gramophone, you would do it upstairs in the drawing-room where no one could see you, and there was no red carpet out. It was all very small-time.

'They tried to bring back chaperones, mostly I think because the mothers had been so bored merely winding bandages and running their houses under wartime conditions that they wanted to go out to parties. I don't think they were madly keen to do the chaperoning. They tried it, but it did not really work. After all, if you had worked in a hospital during the War, you knew a good deal more about real life than the chaperones. After the War, people began to realise that women had *managed* to drive ambulances, and they had *managed* to be in the ATS (the WACS, they were called then), and they had *managed* to go over to France and work in the hospitals there. They had worked their way. They were no longer the innocents.

'I knew about suffragettes – I was thirteen just before the 1914 war. You could not read the papers then without knowing about them. After the War, you were always hearing remarks like, "Why should I not have the vote? My butler votes." There was no going back after that; when I say a bloodless revolution, that is what I mean.

'It would have been considered very caddish to get a job when there was so much unemployment. You had a home, you had money, you had everything you needed: it would have been very wrong to take anyone's job. You were expected to do a lot of voluntary work. You might be a secretary or chairman of the Women's Institute or the Red Cross; you might run the Girl Guides and Boy Scouts. You did not get paid for it. Of course if it was really necessary, people like war widows, poor things, did work. Most of them lived in poverty, and what is more, rather gracious, hidden poverty. It is really very extraordinary to think of it now, but keeping up appearances might involve having two maids, and paying them nothing.

'When I started the Boy Scouts and Girl Guides locally in 1919, I think my father regarded that as another of these bloodless revolutions. I had them up at Ickworth every week. He thought they would not come, that it was just a flash in the pan; but they came right up to the time I married.

'I suppose it was quite tough for me as a young girl to cope with the Boy Scouts; I suppose I was fairly tough. You see, if you lived in a completely true-blue, Conservative world, you either became very true-blue, or just slightly pink. I became slightly pink. The poverty and misery that there was then really hurt me; a hunger march really hurt. I was very anxious that the boys in the village should all have a chance.'

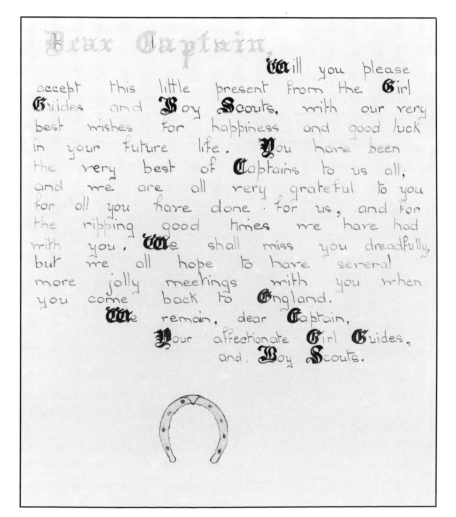

'When I started the Boy Scouts and Girl Guides locally in 1919, I think my father regarded that as . . . a flash in the pan; but they came right up to the time I married.'

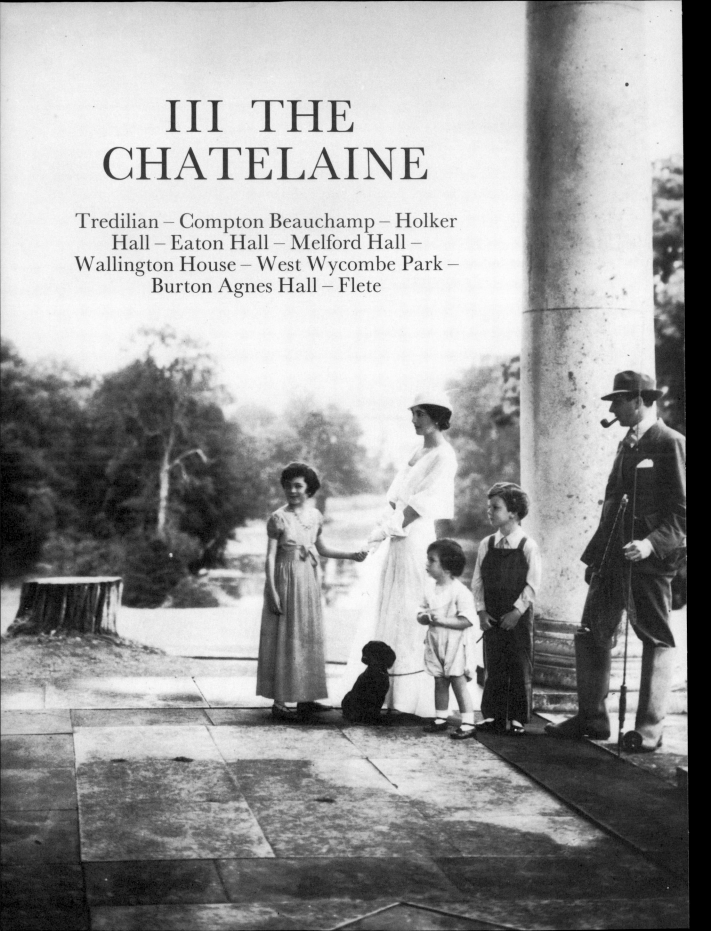

III THE CHATELAINE

Tredilian – Compton Beauchamp – Holker
Hall – Eaton Hall – Melford Hall –
Wallington House – West Wycombe Park –
Burton Agnes Hall – Flete

'Nowadays the words "Lady Bountiful" are considered dirty words. In those days they were taken literally. My grandmother was amazing: it didn't matter who wanted her – anybody in the village, anybody on the place who needed help – she was always available. She was incredibly efficient. I only saw her in the morning room, where everything was always beautifully arranged. It was where she wrote her letters, and where we were allowed to come in, any time we liked. I suspect the whole house ran from that room. I think the servants – the cook, the butler and so on – came up to her room upstairs, and everything was arranged before she appeared in the morning room, but when she was in the morning room, she was available to anyone and everyone. Every morning, at about eleven o'clock, half a bottle of champagne was brought in and placed beside her. We didn't know what it was; we just thought it was Granny's lovely medicine. She had practically none herself – the butler drank most of it! (He was called Mr Crook, and he was our hero.)

'She did the garden, she did everything. I never quite knew what my grandfather did when he was at Tredilian. He was certainly a tremendous power in India, which is where he was most of the time. There he was a multi-millionaire tea planter. When he was home from India, he used to hunt non-stop, but I never noticed any of the power in Monmouthshire. The estate had farms, a park and a wonderful grouse moor, and woods and fields.

'When my parents went to live at Compton Beauchamp, my mother automatically took on the village. There was a party for everybody at Christmas, and anybody who needed anything came to her. For instance, there was an old shepherd – an extraordinary man, who had been a schoolmaster, a shepherd and a drop-out – who used to lose his pension book practically every week. My father or my mother used to get it back for him. It was part of life – and that is just one small example.

'While I was living with my parents, I once went off, as a teenager, to stay at Welbeck, which was an incredibly grand house; the Lady Bountiful there was the Duchess of Portland. On the night of an enormous party, an old man in the village, who was dying, asked to see the Duchess. The moment all the other guests disappeared, off she went down to the village. She sat with him all night, talking to him, looking after him, until he died. Next morning, there she was at breakfast, beautifully dressed and not a word said. I happened to have my birthday at Welbeck on that same visit, and she found me the nicest present, a most beautiful watch – exactly what I wanted. I've still got it. She had time for that, yet she hadn't had a wink of sleep. Having time for everybody is the nicest thing you can say

Mrs Richard Cavendish

Opposite:
Lady Dashwood, with Sir John and the children, under the portico of West Wycombe, photographed by Cecil Beaton. (*Courtesy of Sotheby's London*)

THE COUNTRY HOUSE REMEMBERED

about anyone. That's why my mother was the prettiest, most efficient and nicest hostess I've ever known – apart from my mother-in-law. My mother only failed in one respect: she occasionally thought being a hostess was boring.

'While we were at Compton Beauchamp, Queen Mary came over from Badminton. We were much looking forward to it. My father thought: "Oh, dear me, the moat's looking rather dull. Let's put a few goldfish in for Her Majesty to see when she comes over the bridge." So an enormous crate of goldfish was tipped in just before she arrived. As they went in, the pike ate them, so not one single goldfish was left by the time she drew up. And then there she was! We had a lovely time. The honour of the day for us was that the nursery was allowed to make coffee for the Queen.

'A very shaming incident took place, though. On one of the tables in my mother's room there was a most beautiful miniature set of chess-men – Irish, black and white silver. It was a tiny travelling set. When the Queen went up to powder her nose, she went round the room and looked at everything, and admired the chess set. My mother said how delighted she was that Her Majesty liked it. The Queen went on saying how nice it was, and my mother went on saying how pleased she was that Queen Mary liked it. That was that. Then the Queen went downstairs, and the rest of the day carried on. That evening, my mother said to my father, "The Queen did love that little chess set." "Oh, did she? How do you know?" "Oh well, she admired it over and over and over again." "Well, did you not offer it to her?" "No, absolutely not – I don't want her to have it." "Oh, you must. If the Queen admires something, you've got to offer it." "Well, I don't want her to have it." Eventually my father said firmly, "You must write and offer it." So, with a fairly bad grace, she sat down and wrote to offer it. It was accepted immediately, and she had to parcel it up and send it off.

'My mother-in-law was Lady Moyra Cavendish, and I first dined at her house – before I married Richard – before Lady Astor's annual ball for the Eton and Harrow Long Leave. It was the most wonderful dinner party I've ever been to – the grandest, the biggest and the most delicious. Richard and I married in 1937, and both families strongly disapproved. At the beginning of 1938, when we were on our honeymoon at Holker (Richard's family home), my father was killed racing. We came back to London and stayed with my mother-in-law at 2 Grosvenor Crescent. She, who had been so against our marriage, was now totally forgiving, absolutely welcoming – I've never known anything like it. She decided she was going to look after me, and she did. The night we came back after my father was killed,

Opposite:
Lord Dick and Lady Moyra Cavendish at Holker with Richard and Pamela Cavendish, at Richard's coming-of-age. 'Those two really cared. They knew every single person who worked on the estate, and they knew every single tenant. It was not a question of patronage – they really cared.'

I arrived in a state of shock. She and my father-in-law were to dine at Buckingham Palace. So as to greet, welcome and look after me, they were very late at the Palace. The whole family was there; they really were fantastic. I absolutely *loved* her.

'I've always thought they were my ideal couple, because they adored each other, and they had time for anyone. There was no question of being too busy, or unable to talk, or having something else to do. If anybody came into the room when my mother-in-law was writing a letter, she'd stop. The letter would be left, exposed on the blotter, beautifully written, charming, very misspelt. She never thought of herself. She was in very bad health and had had various awful sadnesses – she lost two of her children – but her only thought was for *you* to be happy. If you wanted to play tennis, she'd play tennis. If you wanted to play golf, she'd go with you if there was nobody else. She loved games, she loved chat, she loved everything. When she lay dying, this tiny, lovely lady, desperately ill, said to me, "Oh darling, it must be so dreary for you. Why don't we get Sis over and have some fun?"

'When she prepared for a weekend at Holker, she told all her team, in the nicest possible way, exactly what she wanted, when she wanted it and how she wanted it, so that they knew what was expected of them. They adored doing it, but she never left it to them. She always checked on everything herself, always, always. But you never saw her doing it – she did it ahead, before anything happened. She'd go and see – even in the tiniest bedroom – if the light was working, if the bed was comfortable, if the flowers were fresh. And she went into every course of every meal. She was fascinated by what people liked and by what was nice and good: if she went to a little pub in Ireland and the potatoes were rather beautifully cooked, she'd find out how they were done. If she was staying in a palace, it would be exactly the same. She never bothered with pretentious things, but if something was genuinely excellent, she'd find out how it was done. Her cookery book is the funniest and sweetest thing: in among how to cook the potatoes, and do the leeks, how to clean your teeth and how to test the chimneys for smoke. She never spent anything on herself: asked once for jumble, she said, "I'm so sorry, I can't give you anything, because I actually wear my jumble." And she did, she really did!

'It was the same with my father-in-law. An MP, who looked after his land, he'd spend time with absolutely anybody who wanted to have a word. A fisherman might come up from the village when he was in the middle of a round of bridge, which he absolutely adored. "I want to see his Lordship." "And who might you be?" the butler

Rex Whistler, who painted the mural in the dining room of Plas Newydd, felt he could never 'hope to repay for all those lovely days of fun & bathing & sunshine, & moonlight & enormous delicious meals.' He did, however, find time to record the house and (detail) members of the Paget family in the Music Room. (*National Trust*)

Overleaf:
The Double Cube Room at Wilton – childhood home of the Viscountess Hambleden – painted in 1921 by Sir John Lavery, with members of her family, the Herberts. (*Royal Academy*)

The Countess of
Rosse in a
watercolour by
Charlie Baskerville
painted in 1938
when Lady Rosse
was visiting New
York. Inscribed by
the artist: 'Save it
and sell for a
fortune when I am
thoroughly dead'.

The Countess of
Rosse – chatelaine
of Birr Castle in
Ireland, Womersley
in Yorkshire and
Nymans in Sussex –
painted shortly
after her marriage
by William Acton,
brother of Harold
Acton.

would ask. "Never you mind." "There's somebody to see you, my Lord." "Oh well, show him in." Those two really cared. They knew every single person who worked on the estate, and they knew every single tenant. It was not a question of patronage – they really cared.

'When Queen Mary came to stay at Holker in 1937, the generator that made the electricity was overloaded – it always was when something special happened. All the lights went out, every single one, so candles had to be rushed to her room. But I don't think my mother-in-law saw any difference, whether it was the monarch staying or a curate coming to ask for a place. There were always the same standards – it's the best we can do, that was her thing.

'When my husband inherited, I think I really carried on in the same way my mother-in-law had done, because we have had hundreds and hundreds of people to stay since, and they've always said they couldn't see any difference. But on a tiny scale, obviously – minute. The first year that we were there we had two hundred people to stay. My husband said, "No, thank you – that's the last, you've got to cut down." So after that we changed our tune, but I think life at Holker went on in the same spirit while we were there. I hope and think it did.'

'My first impression of Eaton was this endless corridor. I arrived very late, because I had only just met the Duke, who unexpectedly asked me for the shooting party the next weekend. As I was already going to another shoot, I could only arrange to be at Eaton for one night. I took a late train on the Friday; Chester was four and a half hours away. I spent the time wondering whether I ought to have dinner on the train, or save half a crown. I was met at the station, and arrived at the side of Eaton, in the stable yard – the entrance that was always used. It was dark, and I was frightfully nervous, and suddenly, as I turned a corner, there was this enormous long corridor seeming to go absolutely out of sight. Suddenly I saw two figures advancing down it like tiny little marionettes from the other end. It was Bendor and his eldest daughter. I walked tremblingly. It was frightfully difficult to know when to start smiling. Before she took me up to my bedroom, the Duke asked me whether I'd had dinner, and I said "no". The guests were just coming out from dinner, so Bendor sent up a tray to my bedroom with a bottle of champagne on it. That was very important: I kept on nervously starting down the stairs, then coming back to my bedroom and having another glass to give myself Dutch courage.

"That was my first impression of Eaton as a guest. The first

Loelia, Lady Lindsay of Dowhill (*formerly Duchess of Westminster*)

41

weekend I had to cope as chatelaine was the National party – apart from shooting parties the Grand National was one of the two major events in the Eaton year, the other being Chester Races, which of course were on our doorstep. I had got back from my honeymoon the night before, and I had to ring for the butler to show me the way to the room where the guests were assembled, because I didn't know where it was. That weekend we had sixty-five to stay.

'When I came to live at Eaton I took a grip on things – rather foolishly, I now think. I installed the most wonderful housekeeper, who was somebody completely out of Dickens and always wore a long, black – I suppose bombazine – dress, down to the ground, with a lace apron with a black velvet bow. She was rather good looking, a stoutish character, with a bunch of keys at her waist. I used to ask her for anything I wanted, and that was passed on.

'My father had been Keeper of the Privy Purse. He looked into every kind of expense and decided where there were extravagances. He discovered, for instance, that when one slice had been carved out of a ham, the rest was a perk for the servants, so off it went and was never seen again. At Eaton, I wanted to show how frightfully efficient I was (which I wasn't), so I said I must look into everything; which put all the servants' backs up. They came to me saying that there was absolutely nothing wrong. Bendor just said, "Put all the head ones up £100", on the spot: I think it was just to try and snub me, really.

'The cook was a charming woman, but I did change quite a lot of the food – particularly the great plates of snails customarily served at the National party. Lots of guests reeking of garlic, it wasn't at all well chosen! Later on, the cook and I used to discuss the menus, usually in my bedroom. I sat up in bed, the dogs lying on top of me, and I would plan every single course for the whole weekend, in one go. I was on very good terms with her and with the butler, Percy Smith, a great character, a great gentleman, who could have been a Prime Minister. He had been with the family for years.

'At Christmas, the people on the estate used to come up to the big house for an enormous party, and all the children got given presents. I was brought up that one had to pay for any kind of privilege by trying to do what one could for other people. That was not the rule at Eaton, as was constantly drummed into my head by Bendor. If ever I did anything for a charity, which annoyed him, he always said, "Stop being the Lady Bountiful; they'll only laugh at you behind your back." That obviously didn't encourage me to play a part. Well, I didn't enjoy the part much anyway, because the terror of making a speech nearly killed me. The first one I ever

Opposite:
Eaton Hall, seat of the Duke of Westminster. 'My first impression of Eaton was this endless corridor . . . It was dark, and I was frightfully nervous, and suddenly, as I turned a corner, there was this enormous corridor seeming to go absolutely out of sight.'

Above:
The Duke and Duchess of
Westminster at the Grand
National, 'one of the two
major events in the Eaton
year'.

made, in Chester, was incredible: everyone came just to have a look at me. It was for the League of Nations, which I was then enthusiastic about, so I said I would go on the platform, and all I had to say was, "We'll now sing Hymn 299". The whole place rose to their feet and cheered at seeing me, not faintly interested in the cause!

'I wasn't really geared to be tremendously friendly, like one is nowadays with people who work for one. We never had time – we were always on the wing. The longest we used to stay at Eaton before Bendor got restless was a week to ten days.

'Where we actually lived was in a totally self-contained wing, which jutted out into the garden and had about five or six spare rooms with bathrooms. It had its own kitchen, its own pantries, its own heating system, everything, so when we weren't having a party, we never went into the big house. The big house was the second biggest house in England — the biggest was Wentworth Woodhouse, owned by the Fitzwilliams. They had two more bedrooms than we had. After the army had been let loose in the big house, it perhaps had to go – though I personally would have done everything in the world to keep it. What I felt should have been done was to keep the wing instead of building a modern house.

'One of my greatest joys, and regrets at leaving Eaton, was that the flowers were so marvellous. There was always a plethora of flowers everywhere. I can remember returning at the New Year from, I think, France, and there was a huge vase of white lilac. Oh, it was too lovely. I simply loved Eaton. Of its sort, it was so perfectly splendid. I think it's a tragedy that the whole house was razed to the ground.'

'My father-in-law died in 1931. We got officially engaged that summer, and married in November, so we didn't really even move into my husband's bachelor house, which was on the green in Long Melford. When I arrived, all his furniture had been pushed into one wing in the Hall. It all had to be sorted out, so I had a great job to do.

'In England, chatelaines employed housekeepers to look after the house because they didn't know the details. In Denmark, whether you had a big house or a small house, you, as its mistress, would know exactly how everything should be done. My mother was very worried when Willy wanted to marry me. She said, "Ulla doesn't really know cooking; she doesn't know these things yet. You must wait. I'll tell her to take a course." She was shattered when Willy said, "But that isn't necessary. We shall have a staff to do it." She

Opposite, top right:
The Duchess of Westminster with the Mayor and Corporation of Chester. "Stop being the Lady Bountiful; they'll only laugh at you behind your back."

Below:
'One of my greatest joys, and regrets at leaving Eaton, was that the flowers were so marvellous. There was always a plethora of flowers everywhere.'

Ulla, Lady Hyde Parker

said, "Who is going to instruct the staff?" "Oh, they'll know," he said, "I want to marry in three months." That was the difference.

'At the start of our marriage Willy said, "I don't want anything to do with the house; you run it." He put the money in the bank, and said, "You've got so much a year. Don't get overdrawn. You pay for everything inside the house, except light and heat." I paid the staff, the food, the subscriptions and all that. I used to keep account books right up till my son Richard married. They had fourteen columns, I remember, for wages, catering, and household furnishings (new items for the house); then they had subscriptions, my own clothing, what I spent on travelling and presents, and laundry (we ran our own laundry here).

'Right up to the Second World War, many women in England were spoilt: they had everything done for them; they never turned their hand to anything – except sitting on committees and doing social work. That I admired because it didn't exist in Denmark, which had by then already turned very socialist. I told my husband, "Really, I am staggered by the amount of staff people have over here, and how they expect everything to be done for them – clothes laid out, baths run, everything." He said, "Oh, but you should have seen what it was like before the First World War."

'Because we had death duties to pay, I didn't have as many staff at Melford as my mother-in-law had had. The house became more modernised: we put in electric light, but only in the Great Saloon, the drawing room and the dining room. Otherwise, the hall was lit by gas, and the kitchen and bedrooms by candles and gas. As we started modernising, we needed fewer people. A vacuum cleaner and modern stoves in the kitchen all meant that we cut down on staff. When I came, the kitchen had two enormous ranges and a spit, which had to be black-leaded, with the brass shining. One stood there right up to the War. Then we put in a gas stove, which wasn't too good.

'One bought what one could locally – from local shops. My mother-in-law said to me, "You must buy everything you can from the local shops." One went down to the village, but one didn't go into the shop: one sat in the car and the shopman came out in a morning coat. There was a grocer's, and a little draper's alongside it. If one went into the shop to look at anything, the shop girl would curtsy, and the village children, too.

'One was very closely involved with the life of the village. You had to know everybody in the village; and you did. I hardly knew what the Women's Institute was at the age of twenty-two, but I was made President. I had to be Vice-President of the Conservatives at Sudbury. I went down there to a meeting and hardly knew what

Pages from Lady Phyllis MacRae's account book, showing two years, 1925 and 1934.

1925 Wages

A. Kemish. Butler.	154	10	6
E. Dunn. Chauffeur.	143	1	2
E. Hof. Ladies maid	76	17	11
A. Dibley + E. Ford. nurse + nursery maid	123	3	7
M. Brown. Cook.	49	8	7
A. May. Upper Housemaid.	37	9	3
E. Evans Under Housemaid.	32	16	1
M. Parr. Kitchen maid.	25	9	6
Occasional Help	7	12	
	700	8	7

1925 House books

Milk Eggs Butter Etc.	138	19	3
Fish	50	15	7
Game + Poultry.	23	3	9
Butcher	136	19	2
Baker	30	6	5
Grocer.	310	10	4
Greengrocer.	71	8	3
	762	2	9

52 weeks at home. Average 10⅓ people in the house. About £1-8-7 per head per week.

Total 1925

Wages (including Board wages)	700	8	7
House books	761	1	9
Laundry.	55	13	7
Babies	56	4	5
Dress.	45	3	3
Doctors Dentists Nurses	108	1	10
Various (Personal)	210	3	1
Various (House hold)	192	15	4
Chemist	22	12	3
Presents + charities	3	3	
Money saved + lent			
£ Duncan, including motor	700		
	2856	13	6

1934 Wages

F. Hulme (gardener)	138	9	3
Cook.	126	13	4
Stella Hearn (Kitchen maid)	34	11	7
H. Logan	66	5	3
Upper h-maid	29	19	5
D. Balls	36	8	1
Governess	103	19	5
Nursery maid	44	13	5
Extra Help.	23	2	
	604	1	9

House Books 1934

Milk. Eggs Butter Etc.	63	18	9
Fish	15	6	8
Game + Poultry.	13	12	4
Butcher.	85	17	2
Baker.	10	14	4
Grocer	124	3	3
Greengrocer	37	16	5
Wine merchant.	3	17	9
	355	6	8

Total 1934

Wages (including Board W.)	604	1	9
House books	355	6	8
Laundry.	104	13	7
Dress	138	17	5
Children's Clothes	123	11	
Educational Extras	17	10	9
Doctors, Dentists etc	281	17	9
Chemist	17	11	4
Rent	52	10	
Rates	80	10	11
Taxes	94	8	6
Oil	25	15	1
Coal (with £5 wood)	38	12	
Coke	68	18	4
Car-hire	9	1	
Garden	14	18	10
Telephone	8	1	1
Presents + Charities	95	14	10
Car Expenses	30	18	3
Various personal	186	2	
Various Household	111	1	10
Lodging. Hotels etc.	189	17	1
Insurances.	11	17	7
John's illness Expenses	929	11	7
	3591	9	1

Sundry £ 63-19-6

I was meant to do. Colonel Burton and I were put on the platform, and I was terrified. Colonel Burton gave a splendid speech, and then he said, "I'm sure now Lady Hyde Parker would like to say a few words." It was a dreadful moment. But one gradually picked these things up.

'I was President of the mental hospital in Colchester, which didn't really involve much: I had simply to get people from all over the area to give money, and then I sent it on to the Secretary of the hospital. He wrote a quite splendid letter for the annual report, signed with my name. That was what was involved: fund-raising. I would go to a meeting, where they would say, "Now, you have to approach various people." We had a list of subscribers, and one person was put in charge of this area, and another of that area. Gradually it all came to me, and I forwarded the cheque. But you had to keep people interested.

'In those days, everything was private. I was Chairman of the District Nursing Association, and the district nurse used to come and see me. I remember her saying, "We can't let Mrs So-and-So have another baby like the last one: she was just lying there at the top of the stairs and the other children looking on." Things were primitive in those days.

'People took much harder exercise, though, they walked quite long distances. Think of Mrs Pearson of Acton Place. She must have been well over seventy and she had a lovely garden, a beautiful garden, which was her pride. She loved to come down and have lunch with me (I had many friends when I was young who were much older than myself). She would walk the couple of miles down from Acton Place to her lunch and walk back again, even though she had a couple of cars, and a chauffeur. People took a great deal of exercise – which also takes time. People don't think of that. Children would walk to and from school, which might be miles every day, and would walk to church.'

Mrs John Dower

'I can never remember a time when I wasn't familiar with Wallington. It is only a mile away from Cambo, and my grandparents loved us going down there; and as the oldest grandchild, I was at Wallington a great deal. When I was perhaps seven or eight I used to go down and spend a lot of time with my grandfather. He had been in two of Gladstone's governments as Secretary for Scotland, and my grandmother had been one of the leading Liberal hostesses in London. When I first remember them, my grandfather was a very bent old man of seventy-three, but still with a very lively mind, and

Mrs Dower's grandparents, Sir George and Lady Trevelyan. 'My grandfather used to sit in the great armchair in the library, and read to me out of Macaulay's *Homer* . . . I don't remember my grandmother in anything other than beautiful silk dresses down to the ground.'

Above, left:
The Central Hall at Wallington, as it was in Sir George Trevelyan's day.

Below:
The stables. 'My grandparents always kept carriage horses. They ran the stable on the livery system, from one in London – which all the great houses did.'

49

Pauline Dower's parents, Sir Charles and Lady Trevelyan. 'My father was Lord Lieutenant for a good many years, but he didn't use it as a social position at all . . . My mother was one of the leaders – in fact one of the founders, in 1919 – of the Women's Institute in Northumberland . . . She never failed to visit any house where there was a new baby – she was very close to all the people.'

Opposite:
Three generations at Wallington: Pauline Dower with her mother and grandmother.

my grandmother was a beautiful embroideress and also a very fine watercolour painter.

'My grandfather used to sit in the great armchair in the library, with the book-stand on a swivel in the arm, and read to me out of Macaulay's *Homer*, which was a very large book. His father, Sir Charles Edward Trevelyan, had married Macaulay's sister, so Grandfather became Macaulay's heir and also his biographer. He was a great classical scholar. He would read me the Greek and then translate it for me, and that's the way I got to know all the great Homeric stories. He enjoyed my company. I feel I was very fortunate to get to know him well and be talked to by him.

'When I went to lunch with my grandparents, I would join them in the library, and then the butler would come along, open the door, and with a little bow announce that lunch was ready. We walked along to the dining room, and the footman would stand behind my grandmother's chair, draw it out a little way, and then push it in behind her as she sat down. There was the butler carving on the sideboard, and he would place a plate, first before my grandmother, then my grandfather, and then me, and the footman would come and hand round vegetables. Then they would retire and wait outside until my grandmother rang a little bell. And I remember with the pudding course a beautiful Dundee cake was always put on the table, and you were expected to have a slice of this after the pudding. There always seemed to be room, but I don't think I could manage a piece of Dundee cake now at the end of luncheon! We never drank anything, and I was very interested, years later, to find in my grandfather's journal of April 3rd, 1903: "This day gave up wine for good." I can never remember any wine in the house.

'I don't remember my grandmother in anything other than beautiful silk dresses down to the ground – beautiful soft greys and blues, with pink piping round the edge of the bodice, and a little frilly lace. I can see my grandfather in a very well-cut knickerbocker suit with stockings.

'My grandparents always kept carriage horses. They ran the stable on the livery system, from one in London – which all the great houses did. The livery stable guaranteed to keep all its clients supplied with a pair of coach horses of the same colour and height – an exact pair. The moment a horse was ill, it was posted off to London by train from Scots Gap (because there was a railway running a mile away) and a horse of the same build and colour was returned. Until they were very old, my grandparents would drive out in their carriage of an afternoon to the nearer neighbours, to the Swinburnes of Capheaton and so on, to pay calls. But as old people, of course, they

lived much more quietly and kept very much to themselves.

'They were very close to all the people of the village and were very devoted to them. Grandfather was most interested in Cambo School – it had been built by his father – and used to visit it regularly. The tenants' party was in the afternoon each summer, so that my grandparents could see people and entertain them in the courtyard.

'My grandfather was always very generous with his servants. He left a handsome pension for both the housekeeper and the butler, and bought them each a house down south. So they left almost as soon as we moved into Wallington after his death.

'My father was Lord Lieutenant for a good many years, but he didn't use it as a social position at all. He was much more interested in the Lord Lieutenant's duties, such as the magistracy and so on. My mother was one of the leaders – in fact one of the founders, in 1919 – of the Women's Institute in Northumberland. She was very influential and was on the national executive. Before there was television and before there were cars, there was no entertainment for villagers. She started a very effective company of Girl Guides in Cambo, which lasted many years and helped the local girls tremendously. My father, years before the welfare state, started children's allowances, even including the first child, which were paid by my mother to each mother. She never failed to visit any house where there was a new baby – she was very close to all the people.'

'I never went to the bank in those days; I gave a cheque and they sent the money up. I went to the bank about once the whole time I was at West Wycombe – it must have been during the war.'

Helen, Lady Dashwood

'Housekeeping was far more complicated before the days of DDT. You couldn't just cover things and leave them for the winter, because the moths would eat the covers off them. My first winter at Knepp, the tennis balls were all eaten, and unless your clothes were beaten and put in moth-proof bags, in six months they would probably have had it.'

Lady Burrell

'A great many women, including my mother, were very good needlewomen. My mother did no less than eighteen chairs – their backs and seats – in *petit point*, to replace ones that had worn out. She did a lovely stool cover of Wilton; sadly, the colours have faded, because the wool hadn't been properly dyed. She also made several

Patricia, Vicountess Hambleden

Opposite:
Five generations at Wilton: the Viscountess Hambleden with her son Harry, her father (the Earl of Pembroke), her paternal grandmother (standing) and her great-great-aunt, the Dowager Marchioness of Lansdowne.

carpets – the original Wilton carpet factory, which was next door, had been owned by the Pembrokes. (It's nothing to do with the family now.) I can never remember her sitting idle. After dinner, if she wasn't playing bridge or bezique, she always had a piece of embroidery.'

Marcus Wickham-Boynton

'My mother wasn't in the least house-minded. She inherited the house in very good order, *qua* linen and curtains and carpets and things, because her mother, Mildred, Lady Boynton, was what one might call a good housewife and also reasonably well off. Over the years my mother really, frankly, did very little, and everything got very run down. By the end of the 1945 war, a great many of those things were virtually worn out.'

Mrs Charles Brocklebank

'Suffolk was the sort of place where you were looked on as a foreigner until you had lived there for thirty years. When I first came, people were still paying calls on each other. It was very tiresome: you hoped and prayed that people would be out, so that you might visit three houses in an afternoon. And finding your way about the Suffolk lanes was not easy – you used to waste a lot of time. You could not arrive before three o'clock and did not want to stay after four, so you had to rush about and hope that you could leave cards and not go in.

'You had to leave one – bigger – card for yourself, and two smaller ones for your husband and yourself; he didn't come, you left his card for him. There was a theory that if you turned up the corner of the card, you had actually come yourself and not sent your card by chauffeur. But you couldn't cheat very successfully; really, in the end, you had to go. In fact, you were returning their call – they called first, because they had lived there longest. Then, when you had called back, they asked you to something, you asked them back, and at that point you could both drop it if you wanted to.'

The Hon Mrs John Mildmay White

'My father became Lord Lieutenant of Devon in 1928 and went on till 1936. Whenever royalty came to the county he had to receive them, and it meant a good many meetings and ceremonies. I had to go to some of them, because after 1929 my mother was ill and was in various nursing homes, but the work was not as arduous as it is now, because people weren't expected to get about as much, or to drive such long distances. He never learnt to drive a car himself, so we always had to have a chauffeur.'

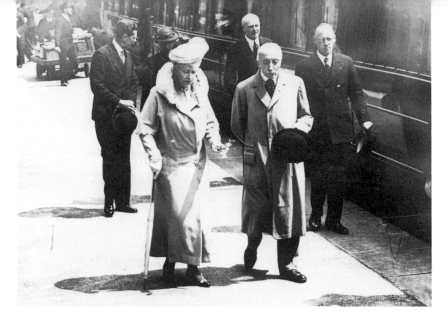

Left:
Lord Mildmay meeting
Queen Mary at Ivybridge
Station. 'My father became
Lord Lieutenant of Devon in
1928 and went on till 1936.
Whenever royalty came to the
county he had to receive
them.'

Centre and below:
Duties of a chatelaine – Helen
Mildmay launching a ship
and opening a new hut for the
local Girl Guides.

Overleaf:
The Duke of Beaufort's house
party on his waggon at the
Beaufort point-to-point.

IV THE HOUSE PARTY

Greenlands – Holker Hall – Birr Castle – Womersley –
Nymans – Eaton Hall – West Wycombe Park
– Flete – Shoreham Place – Boughton
House – Wallington House – Balcombe
Place – Goodwood House – Ickworth

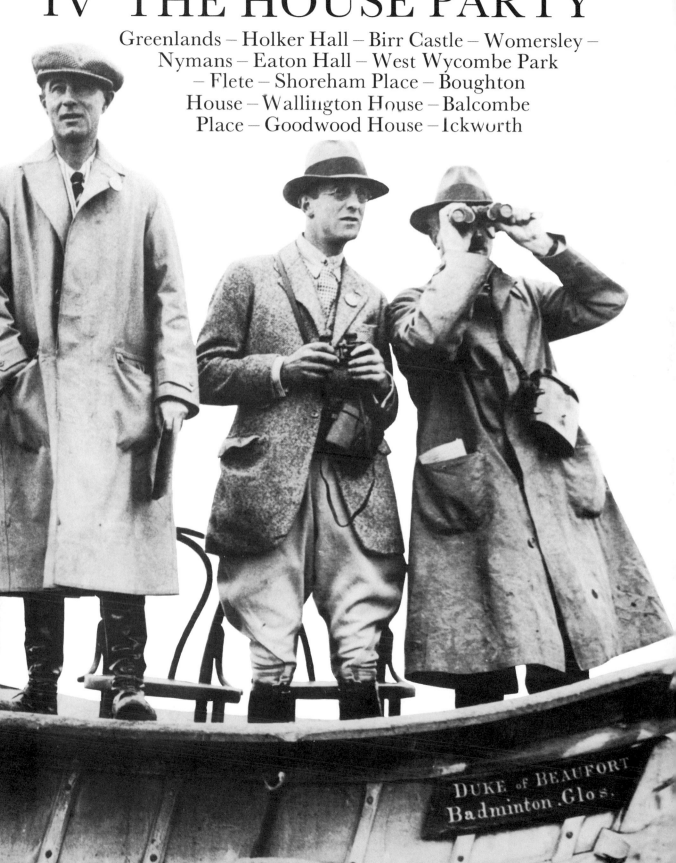

THE COUNTRY HOUSE REMEMBERED

Lady Marjorie Stirling 'When you went to stay somewhere you arrived at teatime; I always found it very alarming, driving up a long drive, not knowing what to expect. The door would be opened by the butler and you were ushered into a room full of people, nearly always strangers. It made me feel quite sick, and did for long after I married.

'It was sometimes, but not always, at a weekend; if it was a shoot it wouldn't be. I suppose people had more time in those days. If it was a grand party, you would find masses of staff to receive you and look after you. You were almost always sent with a maid, in my case my old nanny. Nanny was marvellous: she told me all sorts of interesting titbits from below stairs, and of course was very much on my side, doing anything I wanted, to the extent of going and sending me a telegram to a house where I was visiting, recalling me home!

'If it wasn't the sort of party you took your maid to, then one of the many housemaids was always detailed to look after you perfectly. Everything was laid out, what you were going to wear and all the rest of it. The housemaids were frightfully good. They always seemed to know what one should wear much better than one did oneself.

'The houses were very comfortable, but cold compared with what we would expect nowadays, although there were masses of fires everywhere, even in the corridors of some houses. And a fire in one's bedroom, which was glorious, which would be relit in the morning when one was called.

'The food was always frightfully good. It was no effort at all for the hostess – she just told the cook how many there were. At that time, English cooking, generally, was frightful, *except* country house cooking, which was very good of its kind.

'If it was a lovely house with lovely things in it, some hosts and hostesses, if they thought you were interested, took immense pleasure in showing you round them, which I liked. But it was considered bad form to remark on people's possessions: uninvited, it was very rude to say how marvellous they were. At my first dinner party, I think, to which I went with my parents, I did the most appalling thing. A simply beautiful china plate was put down in front of me, and I turned the plate up to see what it was. I got the most frightful row from my mother afterwards. Now, in my own house, I'd be delighted if anybody did that!

'One's clothes were a worry – one wasn't dressed well, not as smartly as people are now. Even for a shoot in Scotland – a seven-day shoot – you had to dress for every day of the week. And naturally that meant a different hat; and a hat box, of all things. On one visit my hat box blew off the car on the way to the station. I remember shrieking to the chauffeur, "Stop – we shall have to go back and find it!" There were very rich people who had marvellous clothes, but on the whole one just scraped through, passed muster. A small dressmaker would run up something, and every now and again one did have a nice sweater, or a nice dress. A very kind aunt gave us some special dresses; she took me to Paris to get me one. So usually one had a bit of luck.

'There was usually tennis, much swimming and golf (very grand places had a private golf course), and then in Scotland, fishing and shooting. For one big party at a house in Scotland, everybody was expected to be doing something. I was very young then, and was told to go and play squash. I'd never played squash in my life, but I found myself sent off with a very good-looking young man to the squash court. He weathered the resulting scene with great patience and kindness, and I discovered later from his wife that he was the reigning squash champion. Also on that visit was Princess Andrew of Greece, with two of her attractive and very nice daughters. Princess Andrew was charming and completely informal, and great fun. They showed me photographs of the baby they'd left at home – Prince Philip.

'The parties in Scotland – Highland gatherings – were great fun, and I think enjoyed by everybody unless they were very English and very out of it. There were parties in most large Scottish houses, and very big balls – the Northern was very large. You stayed up all night, dancing, really until daylight and breakfast. You'd wear a dress with a sash, and the men wore a kilt. You felt very very sorry for any man who wore evening dress: it's jolly difficult dancing in evening dress rather than a kilt, and it looks rather silly. You had a little card and pencil (I suppose few dances have those now), certainly at all hunt balls, and before you went to the ball you had to have your card filled in. I was actually brought out – I came out in 1921 – at the Northern Meeting in Inverness, where all my family, male and female, for generations had come out. I waited until the spring of the next year to come out in London.

'When we were young, we were sent by our parents to these house parties, and it wasn't nearly such fun. We were often very lonely. The hostess was then *in loco parentis* for her debutante guests. I was once at a big house party in Scotland, and a young man sent a note to my bedroom before breakfast, to say that he'd forgotten either a black tie, or something essential, and was driving to the village to buy it. He had a very snazzy racing car, which he knew I admired very much, and he invited me to go with him. I naturally did, and got the most fearful telling-off afterwards from my hostess. Later on, when we could choose for ourselves, we then enjoyed it very much, and after we were married, we only went away if we wanted to, and were with friends, and were asked because people wanted to see us.'

Patricia, Viscountess Hambleden

'After Billy and I were married, we lived at Greenlands, just outside Henley. We did not have a house party every weekend, but in the summer it was really rather beautiful being on the river, and one did have a lot of friends and young people. The weekend parties were fun because you got to know people in a much more relaxed way than just meeting them at parties. I'm quite pleased that some of the formality has gone out of life, but on the other hand the young did have rather a marvellous time at those weekend parties. The young and old have a lot to contribute to each other, and our parties nearly always consisted of boys and girls at the same time as couples of our age and even older. They all seemed to get on perfectly well.

'We had a lot of people to stay who were in politics, like the Halifaxes, who were great friends of ours; and we had ambassadors whom my husband had happened to meet in London, who liked to go to the country at weekends and shoot. We even had Count Bismarck – he was First Secretary at the German Embassy – and his very pretty Swedish wife, to come and shoot. I can't say I found him a very attractive gentleman. The Brazilian ambassador and his wife used to come. She had a lovely voice, she used to sing after dinner, which was a great joy. And we had other musical people: my brother-in-law, who was himself very musical, used to bring singers of all nationalities to stay, or perhaps for the day. Rex Whistler came to stay, and afterwards he wrote a beautifully illustrated letter of thanks, which is a treasure.

'We used to entertain a lot for Henley Regatta. Mr and Mrs Baldwin always used to come if they could, and the present Queen Mother and the late King – the then Duke and Duchess of York – came down here. We always had a grand lunch party on the Saturday of the Regatta and we nearly always had a party staying.

'So we had really rather a wide circle of guests. It was wide because my husband was very catholic in his tastes. They weren't all just one's friends or one's father's friends. My husband's unmarried brothers and sisters used to come to stay a tremendous amount until they got their own homes. They always came for Christmas, every year – a big family party. When I first married, I inherited all my father-in-law's relations, who used to come too – all the aunts and uncles. We had one rather eccentric relation, my mother-in-law's half-sister, Lady Winthrop Gore. She was great fun and very intelligent, but I'm bound to say a little eccentric. Regardless of weather, climate

'Rex Whistler came to stay, and afterwards he wrote a beautifully illustrated letter of thanks.'

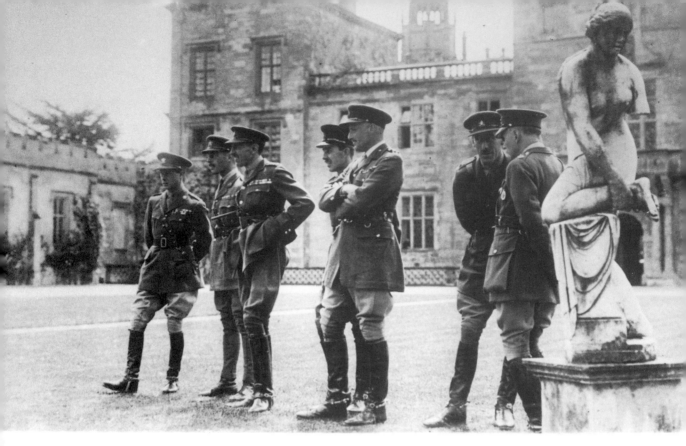

As Lady Patricia Herbert, the Viscountess Hambleden spent her childhood at Wilton, a house much visited between the wars by the royal family.

Above:
The Prince of Wales reviewing the Royal Gloucester Hussars, accompanied by Lord Apsley, the Earl of Pembroke and others.

Right:
A shooting party – overshadowed by the abdication crisis – included the Duchess of York, the Duke of Alba and members of the Herbert family.

or time of year, she would wash her hair on Friday afternoons at four o'clock. She also invariably invited herself down every three months to have her ears syringed by the local doctor. She was better than anybody at crossword puzzles and was accepted, really, as one of the family; we were all very fond of her, especially the children. And then there was a relation of my husband who lived not very far away. She ran her own farm, mended the walls and was intellectual, writing all sorts of good books. She mended her teeth with the cement she mended the walls with, which created a rather strange effect!

'I always found it quite extraordinary that one managed to fit in four meals a day at these house parties. You started off with breakfast (you came down to breakfast with the gentlemen if it was a shooting party), where you had eggs, sausages, bacon, perhaps devilled kidneys, plaice, all on a hot-plate; and then on the sideboard ham and tongue and perhaps game pie, or something like that, if you wanted it; and naturally, toast and marmalade and coffee. Lunch would always start with an egg dish or something, followed by a main course, followed by cold meats on the sideboard if anybody wanted them; pudding; cheese; and dessert. And then tea. For a big dinner party, a really posh dinner party, you would have either thick or clear soup, followed by fish, followed by the *entrée* – chicken or quails. Then you had saddle of lamb or beef; you had pudding; you had a savoury; and then you had fruit.

'Quite extraordinary – I can't think how we all ate so much. I suppose people took very small helpings of each, but they did eat rather more than we do now. I don't really think they were fatter then, though: some were fat and some were thin, same as nowadays. But nobody was as passionately interested in their figures as they are now.

'My husband would tell the butler that he'd have this, that and the other wine with dinner, depending on the menu. You had sherry offered with your soup, followed by white wine if you were having fish, followed by red wine with the *entrée* and the main course. You were waited on at all meals if there was a party – I'm not saying that we were always waited on if we were by ourselves, but we were when there was a party.

'At a shooting lunch, you obviously had to be quick, so you just had one enormous, delicious main course: for instance, pork with vegetables and so on, and then a pudding – plum or some hot pudding – and cheese. With the cheese you always had the most delicious plum cake.

'A tremendous headache for the hostess, if she had, say, sixteen

The Prince with the Countess of Pembroke.

people to stay, was to give them different neighbours at each meal for however many meals it was. There would certainly be a *placement*, but not any taking of the ladies in to dinner. That was not on at all.

'After dinner we played charades and paper games, and perhaps somebody might sing at the piano. Then there was bridge for those who liked, in another room. With youngish people, one had these round games – Clumps and things. Older generations had more sedate games, and bridge.'

Diana, Viscountess Gage

Opposite:
'We also used to go out into Morecambe Bay with the fishermen when they were cockling. You danced on the sands, up came the cockles and you flicked them into a basket.'

'There were a great many activities to choose from' at Holker, including sand yachting on Morecambe Sands.

'People didn't come as far as Cumbria just for weekends. They usually came to Holker for a week or ten days – with the whole family. Some people used to come on their way up to Scotland, and some on their way back. They always suggested themselves. My mother would say, "When would you like to come?" and then we would fit them in as best we could. They would bring lady's maids, valets and even their own sheets. Lady Wolverton and Lady Islington both brought their sheets: I suppose they thought they were better than ours. Some people considered it an insult, but my mother was delighted. It saved her own sheets.

'Linky Cecil, who was wonderful company, and Mrs Otto Sassoon and Mrs Leo Rothschild came every year, as did Lady Wolverton and her children, and, most years, the Lansdownes and their children, and Helen Mildmay. Then there was Raymond Greene, who was a hunting man, and General Pulteney. When I got a little older, young people would arrive on a sort of tour of country houses, but would have nowhere to go afterwards, and so they would stay for weeks. My mother didn't mind: they just settled down.

'Sometimes people behaved badly when they were staying away. One young man, who was being very much ragged, said, "If ever I am teased again, I shall smash up my room." He was and he did. Just cut up the sheets and smashed all the things. That's why my sister and I were never allowed to stay away without a maid, really: because my mother wanted us to be kept an eye on.

'Most of the guests got up for breakfast, but it was a very movable feast – it would probably finish about half past eleven. Then my mother used to make a list: who wanted to go riding, who was going to play lawn tennis, go fishing, play golf. There were a great many activities to choose from.

"My mother used to give something called a cotillion, which was a lovely, old-fashioned dance. You would ask about forty people and you would have a cotillion leader – David Cecil was very good at

Record of a week spent by the Herbert family at Holker. 'The house parties were continuous. When one person went, another would come.'

Aug 15ᵗʰ - 22ⁿᵈ 1925.

Mʳˢ DOUBLEDAY.   DIANA.

DIANA. LADY MOYRA. LORD RICHARD.

JOHN LYTTON DIANA.

DIANA. SIDNEY.

that. He and a woman, or a girl, would be the cotillion leaders. You'd all dance with your partner, and then people would come round with favours, like bunches of ribbon or flowers, which you could give to someone else, and then you'd dance with them. There were various figures: a girl would be given a looking-glass and a man would look over her shoulder, and if she didn't want to dance with him, she'd rub out his image in the mirror. If she did want to, she'd put the looking-glass down and get up and dance. Or the man would hold up a candle and whichever girl wanted to dance with him would blow it out. I think several people used to give cotillion parties during the 1920s. We would just wear black tie for that sort of party. In fact, we always wore a black tie, but at Belvoir, up to the last war, they always wore white tie if a woman was at dinner, or if the clergy-man came to dinner.

'A very favourite birthday treat for us was to drive in a waggonette to Windemere lakeside; you then got into a boat and rowed to an island, where you had a picnic. Then you came home, rather tired by that time. We also used to go out into Morecambe Bay with the fishermen when they were cockling. You danced on the sands, up came the cockles and you flicked them into a basket.

'The other guests might shoot, or go fishing, or they might play games; but really they just seemed to stay. The house parties were continuous. When one person went, another would come. I don't know how the servants managed, but they always seemed wonder-fully happy. Holker was a house of total sunshine and happiness. My mother loved having her friends to stay.

'My great-uncle, the eighth Duke of Devonshire, – whom my father followed at Holker – had had a large family and didn't like to entertain. He liked to have a quiet life. When my mother first came to Holker, the butler said to her, "I suppose if anybody calls, it's not at home as usual?"

Mrs Richard Cavendish

'My mother-in-law once said to me, "I don't know if I should, but I judge people by their picnics." Picnics at Holker were to dream of. You went off somewhere absolutely magical, a different place every day; if it was very hot, for instance, you went to a lovely shady wood. And then out came everything you can think of that is deli-cious. There was no question of taking servants – every single person had a packet for themselves. She thought of everything – kettles that could go onto bonfires full of water, with corks in them in case there wasn't any fresh water, and special frying pans, always pitch black. The drinks were packed separately. There were little boxes with

Virginia cigarettes, and little boxes with Turkish cigarettes, and there were always matches and cigars.

'When guests left Holker, they were given a little *papier mâché* attaché case, with the most delicious things in it. For each guest there were home-made-that-minute, feather-light scones stuffed with Morecambe Bay shrimps. All the things were wrapped individually, and labelled. And then inside the attaché case used to be put a label with stamps, so that all you had to do was to shove the empty case into the nearest Post Office and sent it back.'

'We minded passionately that guests – whether to Birr, Womersley or Nymans – were all welcomed when they arrived, and that there was never what I called a "butt" in the house party – somebody who perhaps didn't feel they fitted in. We always wanted everybody to enjoy it. Michael was always so wonderful – he was always there to greet people, and always gave that feeling of "Oh, how nice to see you". I think he really enjoyed entertaining.

'We did not entertain every weekend. For me it was always much easier to have a big party than several small ones, because you're giving out less in a kind of a way. At Birr we've had seventy-eight sitting down for luncheon – always sit-down. If people have come to see a big garden, they long to sit down.

'The vital thing is to keep people amused without making them feel too organised. I don't think they want to be *made* to play games, or *made* to do this or that. We used to play all sorts of games after dinner and then, for winter parties, always had a little card table with rather a difficult jigsaw puzzle on it, because then you were bringing people together. A lot of romances started over those jigsaws.

'Michael and I loved everything being perfect – from the bedrooms to the bathrooms to every corner of the house. It all mattered enormously. So it was a good deal of work when there were a lot of people for the weekend. It was just a matter of organisation, and punctuality. When one went to stay with other people, one noticed what they did do, or what they didn't do.

'The most important thing about being a hostess is never minding when anything goes wrong. I remember once a member of the Royal Family came to stay. The house was very full. Suddenly, at about three in the morning, there was a little tap at the door, and there were two little people with their suitcases, saying the house was on fire. Oh dear, oh dear, what had happened? In fact, the central heating had got so hot that the wallpaper had peeled off and fallen over

Anne, Countess of Rosse

69

the four-poster bed. Poor things, they thought it was the house on fire. It was just one of those things that happens in an Irish house.'

Loelia, Lady Lindsay of Dowhill *(fomerly Duchess of Westminster)*

'I never did relax completely at Eaton. I was pretty well nervous of everything. I remember my very first party of all, when I found myself – this shy, hopelessly inadequate girl – sitting between Winston Churchill and F E Smith (Lord Birkenhead), looking at the fantastic flowers spread out in front of me and the incredible food, being served snails of all things, and being pleased to be able to wear my lovely jewels. I didn't know how to cope, really.

I think the band hired from Chester was playing away, so after dinner everybody danced. It didn't amuse people like Winston and F E Smith in the slightest. They loathed it. Before you could say knife, they'd tottered round the floor once, and off. But Bendor loved it. Then, of course, he too nipped off to sit with his cronies in the smoking room, where they had the most tremendous talk about politics. I was always left having to shuffle round with some dreadful old bore of about eighty (Bendor was much too jealous to invite any younger men). The music went on, meanwhile, until guests started leaving. It seemed to me all night, but I think it must have been two in the morning.

'And then I remember the following morning the excitement of the special train from Chester to the National. As we left at about noon, most people were working, but when the train came back, the whole of Chester turned out in full force. Bendor had meanwhile taken me in a tiny mini-car back to Eaton – he couldn't bear any ostentation. That was so typical.

'Eaton had a certain way of doing things. Before I came, there was one of those huge expandable boards you shove the *placement* cards in – you can imagine how big it was for seventy-two. Bendor was fearfully bored by the difficult job of *placement*. As he never did anything that bored him, he used to put the people he wanted next to him, and perhaps two other people. Otherwise, he'd put all the cards in, and never change them for the whole of the visit. I revolutionised the *placement* system. What a nightmare it was! You always set off by putting the amusing people together, so you did quite well for a time. But you always got to the bores. Your two greatest bores met absolutely irrevocably, and you had to start to rearrange everything. I kept a list of who everybody had sat next to previously, and only once made a mistake.

'Our form of tipping was very different from other houses'. No tipping was allowed. It was made up to the servants: they got an equivalent amount according to the number of people who stayed. I know one house today where that still goes on. When I stayed there and tried to tip the housemaid who had looked after me so beautifully – this was only a few years back – she absolutely refused to take it.

'Some of the guests took full advantage of their stay. I can remember once there was a tremendous hurry to catch the train (we'd had lunch too late), and people tore out into the waiting cars. One of the elderly bachelors staying over the weekend had hoarded a mass of stationery, sealing wax, cigars, cigarettes, matches, pencils – you name it, he had it – all in a drawer, which he'd obviously meant to whip upstairs and collect. As it was, of course, he was found out. Having been given a marvellous time and told not to tip, it was pretty mean to pinch everything in sight.

'There was always a weekend tennis party around the first of August, after Wimbledon was over. Bendor was very keen on playing tennis: it was good exercise and he thoroughly enjoyed it. The bad players got the two outdoor courts. There was a marvellous *en tout cas* (it's now called a clay court) indoors, alongside the glass houses. It was very unusual in those days to have an indoor court, and it was a huge building. There was a permanent "pro" as part of the staff. In the middle of the afternoon, I'd say, "Oh, I think I'll come down and have a game at half past three", or "I'll just knock a ball about and then I think I'll practise my backhand". And then the poor man was made to play me backhands for half an hour. I became good; anybody else would have been much better, but I was good. I liked it. A couple always came to stay – Mrs Satherswaite and Jack Hilliard – who were both Wimbledon players; not the very best, but Mrs Satherswaite was fairly good.

'We did nothing except what Bendor liked, which was having dinner parties of the neighbours when there were people staying in the house. We never played charades after dinner, although there was one disastrous occasion when Michael Duff – Lord Lieutenant from Bangor – came to stay. He was rather a good mimic, and one of his great pieces of mimicry was of Queen Mary. He was incredibly funny and did it brilliantly. In the middle of acting this part one evening, in came Bendor (we were sitting in different rooms and different groups), who thought, God knows why, that Michael was imitating him. That of course was an absolute disaster. He was furious with me and extremely bad-tempered with everybody else. I tried to explain later, but he never would believe it.

'A few French people used to come over, because, after all, Bendor had a great life with Chanel, and he used to go and stay in her house in the South of France. So he had many French friends. Prince Arthur

Opposite above:
A typical house party at Eaton. 'People always say: "Oh, how did you manage those enormous parties? It must have been simply exhausting."'

Opposite below:
A shooting party at Eaton. Second from the left is Prince Arthur of Connaught, fourth from the right Princess Arthur.

Above:
'There was always a weekend tennis party around the first of August, after Wimbledon was over.' Left to right: Professor Lindemann, Joan Marjoribanks, Enid Raphael and Count Paul Munster.

Left:
A photograph of dinner at Eaton taken by the Duchess of Marlborough.

of Connaught came one year – he was a bit of a bore – and Princess Arthur, an even bigger bore. The only subject she seemed able to talk about was nursing the sick; she never came again. Although we curtsied and bowed, there wasn't a frightful flap made about their visit. I can't remember if I went and fetched them down for dinner – I hope not.

'I twice went to stay in other people's houses on my own. That was a disaster, because Bendor rang up every five minutes, asking what I was up to. I didn't do it again.

'People always say: "Oh, how did you manage those enormous parties? It must have been simply exhausting." In fact, it's far more arduous to entertain three or four than it is seventy people, because nobody knows where you are. They scattered themselves all over the house; I could sit comfortably in my own sitting room reading a good book, and they hadn't the faintest idea where I was. I sometimes did that, out of boredom. It was so hazardous having my own friends, because Bendor, after about the first year, automatically disliked them. They weren't what he called real people. He thought the curate and his wife were real people, as against the Salisburys or someone like that, who were far more rewarding to my way of thinking. Perhaps that was snobbish?'

Helen, Lady Dashwood

'We always had a garden party, at West Wycombe, to which all the neighbours and friends and all sorts of swells living in Buckinghamshire would come, in lovely cars and carriages, the ladies all looking very pretty. I don't think we ever put up a tent; the house was very big and they all flowed out onto the lawn.

'At Christmas, the house party would start the week before. On Christmas Eve the children were allowed to stay up fairly late, because the village band used to come up and play, and the village choir would sing. We had a wonderful Father Christmas costume, worn by one of the family. On one occasion I heard one of the children saying, "I wonder who'll be Father Christmas. I don't suppose it'll be Daddy again – I expect it'll be Uncle Alec." I thought, this is too bad, we must fox them; so, with a great deal of trouble, I was Father Christmas, and came in, very bent and croaky, having to be helped to my chair, and hardly able to say the names of the children. I was delighted to see looks of consternation and puzzlement on their faces: they couldn't decide who it was at all. On Christmas Day, after the stockings were opened, the whole party came back and had a lovely Christmas lunch, with turkey and plum pudding, and crackers. The butler would have decorated the tree and put it in the State

Drawing Room, but the children weren't allowed to see it until after tea on Christmas Day, when all the candles were lit, with someone standing by to snuff them out. On Christmas night we had a simple cold dinner, so that the servants could have their own party.'

'When we were at Flete by ourselves for dinner, my father wore a marvellous old blue Jaeger suit, but of course when we had people there we dressed in dinner jackets. By the time the First World War was over, putting on white ties had quite gone out. After dinner we nearly always played games of some sort, but we were were not one of the really intellectual households like Taplow Court, where you had terrifying games. We played Clumps and Coon Can and guessing games, and things like bezique and piquet and rummy, with bridge for those who liked it.

'We saw a great deal of Lady Astor, who was MP for one of the Plymouth constituencies. She was a great friend of my father and always used to come to Flete when she was at Plymouth; I went in to see her a great deal, too, at her house on Plymouth Hoe. She often had fascinating people there, like Bernard Shaw and Charlie Chaplin. Lawrence of Arabia was stationed with the Air Force at Mount Batten, near Plymouth; as Aircraftman Shaw, he used to come over on his motor bicycle.

'Guests would always tip the staff: tipping was a great thing. £1 in those days was quite a lot of money, the equivalent of at least £15 now. I think you'd normally leave £1, something like that. It was always rather a worrying and embarrassing thing if you were a girl and not married, whether you tipped the butler or not. Men would tip the butler, and everyone who had been shooting would tip the head gamekeeper at least £5.'

'We had a cricket ground quite near the house, and a village cricket team, who used to play with the local teams. At Whitsun we had a cricket match: after the racing on Whit Monday, all the jockeys used to come and play against our local team. We had a sort of party afterwards, where they all drank Pimms. The cricket wasn't very serious, but it was great fun. Summer holidays were greatly taken up with racing. There was a mass of race courses, some still here, some now gone: Torquay, Totnes, Buckfastleigh, Newton Abbot, Devon and Exeter. My brother used to ride at all of them.

'The summer holidays were always rather fun, when children and friends used to come and stay, because with the beach and everything, there was so much to do. Living at Flete, one was halfway between the moor and the sea: we used to have marvellous picnics and walks

The Hon Mrs John Mildmay White

across the moor. Of course you did it in style – the chauffeur dropped you in one place, and you'd walk ten miles across the moor and find him at the other end with tea.

'Christmas at Flete was very traditional – the usual food and things, and stockings for everyone. I always tried to think up some project for guests to do, because we had all these different ages. One year there was a tree my father wanted cut down, so we decided to do that, with all the children joining in. My father thought we were crazy. There was always shooting, and the children used to come along to that too. There was a lot of church-going, of course. The village had hand bell-ringers (which they still do), and they came along in the evening and rang. We'd all be in the hall, and they'd be given money and hot drinks.

'Life at Shoreham was mostly weekends in the summer – although we might go down there for Easter, we didn't really have people to stay then. Sometimes my father had his friends and sometimes my brother and I had our friends – we used to work out the weekends accordingly. We didn't mix them up very much. We played a lot of tennis, and went on the river in boats. The river was inhabited by rather charming little crayfish; we caught them by dangling bits of meat on long pieces of string over the edge of the boat, and hoiking the poor things out when they came to have a nibble. The garden was lovely – it ran right down to the Darenth.'

'They were never called weeekends: they were called Saturday-to-Monday; they never started until Saturday and guests always stayed until Monday. Nowadays, they start on Friday and end on Sunday evening. It was supposed to be awfully non-U to call them weekends. I remember being surprised that anyone should use the term weekend.

'Boughton was used tremendously for charity weekends and for political rallies. When Winston came, he was thrilled with the house and the history of it all; when Neville Chamberlain came, it was for a duty, to make an enormous speech to the Conservative group in the Midlands area. Winston was here the weekend before and I said to him, "We're deliberating where to the put the dais, the platform. On top of the terrace is the obvious place, but it faces due west, and if he's going to make a speech at five o'clock in the afternoon, it would really be better if we put him south to north, not looking straight into the setting sun." "By all means, put him with the wind in his teeth and the sun in his eyes," said Winston. You can imagine how impish it was. But we didn't follow his advice: we put him looking

Opposite:
At Flete, 'summer holidays were greatly taken up with racing. There was a mass of race courses, some still here, some now gone: Torquay, Totnes, Buckfastleigh, Newton Abbot, Devon and Exeter. My brother used to ride at all of them.' Helen Mildmay with friends (above left); Anthony Mildmay racing (below).

Above right:
Lord Mildmay in conversation with Leonora Cazalet (step-daughter of P G Wodehouse and wife of Anthony Mildmay's great racing friend, Peter Cazalet). 'We had a cricket ground quite near the house, and a village cricket team, who used to play with the local team.'

Mary, Duchess of Buccleuch

Above:
Winston Churchill and Lord
Harewood at Boughton.

Right:
Neville Chamberlain at
Boughton – 'An enormous
gathering it was.'

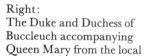

Right:
The Duke and Duchess of
Buccleuch accompanying
Queen Mary from the local
church.

Below:
Princess Elizabeth and
Princess Margaret with a
lady-in-waiting on a day bed
in the garden.

Above:
A house party at Boughton. The Duchess of Westminster is standing in the centre, the Duke of Buccleuch seated on the right.

Centre:
The Duke of Buccleuch with Sir Arthur Penn and Betty Somerset.

Below:
Tea on the terrace. Lord and Lady Balniel – later the Earl and Countess of Crawford – are in the foreground.

from south to north, under the trees of the lawn. An enormous gathering it was.'

Mrs John Dower

'My mother was a very fine pianist and used to play untiringly all sorts of dances, chiefly country dances and things like "The Lancers". She discovered fairly soon after we went to Wallington that one of our parlourmaids, Florrie, had a beautiful voice, so she encouraged her, played for her, sometimes had concerts in the drawing room for her, and allowed her to go out to concerts. I still remember with delight Florrie singing. She could read music – whether Mother taught her, I don't know.

'We did a great deal of singing with the family, and my father had a wonderful tenor voice. One of my sisters, Kitty, still has a lovely voice; my sister Marjorie plays the oboe extremely well; Geoffrey, the youngest, is a fine pianist; and my sister Patricia plays the Northumbrian pipes.

'Mother and Sybil Thorndike used to play duets (that's why there were always two pianos in the drawing room), not in the Central Hall, because the acoustics were so bad, although we used the Central Hall a great deal for dancing. During the 1930s we used to have great parties in the winter holidays. We asked people from all over the county – an enormous gathering – for a party with dancing (when it really was dancing) and a certain amount of party games.

'A good many of my father's political friends came to stay, especially for the Miners' Gala. They would occasionally bring their wives, or even their children, but guests didn't in our day bring servants. Very close family friends used also to come and stay – these were the Cassons – Sybil Thorndike and Lewis Casson.

'We used occasionally to have parties in the cellars; they were very exciting because of course there was no electric lighting. We used to write our names with candle black on the ceiling of one room, right on the far side of the cellar. We have all written our names there; it gradually wears off. It was a harmless pastime.

'We had a very amusing evening in the Central Hall at my parents' silver wedding in 1954; we re-enacted all the sort of stories which go down a family – things that my parents did when they were young. We all played different parts – a great many of us were married by then, with youngsters – so that when we re-enacted something that had happened when my mother was a child, a child of that age was chosen. As I was the oldest of the family, I played my mother. My brother George took the part of the Kaiser, who led off a dance with my mother when she was a girl of about eighteen, because her uncle,

Sir Frank Lascelles, was our ambassador in Berlin. She, being a very pretty youngster, was chosen by the Kaiser to lead off his ball. We had a tremendous actor in George, moustachioed and with a great cloak.

'We were inclined to change for evenings, not into long dresses, though I remember one of my sisters often coming down in a long dress. We would certainly change if we had been out (because we wore tweeds all day – we didn't wear trousers, at least not for a great many years). I don't think we changed until the evening, but if we'd been out and got very wet or dirty in the afternoon we would change. In the winter we would probably change at tea-time; otherwise we might come in from tennis at tea-time, and certainly would change then.

'My mother had a tailor, a man called Mr A B Little, in Newcastle, who went on making suits for me too for years, until he retired. I don't think my mother had hats made specially. Oddly enough – at least it always seemed to us odd, because my mother wasn't really interested in dress – her half-sister, Gertrude Bell, had very great taste in dress, and really liked getting her dresses and hats from Paris. She always commissioned my mother to get them – she trusted my mother to buy her clothes and send them out to Baghdad. I never knew how it worked, but Gertrude was always extremely well dressed. Nobody could say that my mother was well dressed. She was very pleasantly dressed and very characteristically dressed, but she wasn't smart.'

Gertrude Bell, Lady Trevelyan's half-sister. 'She trusted my mother to buy her clothes and send them out to Baghdad.'

Lady Burrell

'My mother, Lady Denman, was given Balcombe by my grandfather, the first Lord Cowdray, in 1907. She lived there till she died, although originally she had wanted a house in Leicestershire, in good hunting country. She spent a lot of time in London – she was creating the Women's Institute and the National Birth Control Institute – but people came to stay at weekends. If guests arrived on a summer's evening, they probably swam in the pond. On Friday evening they played billiards after dinner, or bridge, and on Saturday they played tennis or golf. They wouldn't be allowed to sit down for a moment. They always said that they returned to London exhausted on Monday morning.

'My mother did the tennis courts herself – she was the groundsman – and I should think that they were as good as any outside Wimbledon: charcoal and stone, so that the clay couldn't get into them, and not a weed on them. I think perhaps the gardener was allowed to paint the lines, but he wasn't allowed to do the draining, nor the cutting, nor the weeding. There were no weed killers or pest killers in those days, so it was all done by hand. Then she had her rock garden, and there was nothing she enjoyed more than a bonfire, in her grubbing clothes. Her grubbing clothes really were grubbing clothes; they were covered with mud and nobody else was allowed to touch them.

'A lot of people came to stay, mostly great friends who hardly counted as guests: Neville Lytton, Dennis Brown (who were both very good at tennis), Molly Sampson (who was very pretty, an Australian – I think the only friend they made while my father was Governor of Australia). Apart from the people staying, we seldom had people to lunch, because you couldn't play golf if you had neighbours to Sunday lunch. We didn't have neighbours to dinner either, because not many of them were on those terms. It was really the relations, a lot of whom lived nearby. My uncle Clive was at Balcombe House, and my mother at Balcombe Place, and my mother's sister-in-law, Alicia – they were all the greatest friends ever. And then there was Gerald Cowdray – the second Lord Cowdray – at Midhurst.'

The Duke of Richmond and Gordon

'We had quite a lot of horsey people to stay for the Goodwood week – about twenty-five altogether. Lord Lonsdale, who was a steward, used to arrive in his yellow Rolls. Everything was yellow. He was a dear old boy; everybody adored him. And then Lord and Lady Zetland, and the Duchess of Roxburgh. We used to fill the big dining room with about thirty people every night. It was really great fun.'

Lady Phyllis Macrae

'The Rotunda at Ickworth was closed during the 1914–18 war, and all entertaining was in the wing. Shooting parties continued during the winter in a small way. The whole house was opened again in 1919, but the Rotunda was closed again in 1939 and never reopened for parties.

'In the summer many members of the family came to stay, often for a whole week, and we would have several lunch and tea parties for the neighbours. We were not great dinner-partyites, however, mainly because we lived in the park, and the gates were locked overnight. There were lodge-keepers at each of the three entrances, and it was not easy to ask people to dinner, because the lodge-keeper would usually have gone to bed by the time they left, so they could not get out. We were sometimes allowed to go out and take the keys, but every door in the house had the most enormous key, which you could not possibly put in your pocket. Someone was supposed to wait up if we went out, but of course no one ever did.

As it was a house with no basement, with no one sleeping in the basement, or with a basement surround, you could not climb through a window or anything of that kind; and if you knocked on a window, you still would not be heard. If we wanted to go to a hunt ball or something, arrangments would be made, but that only happened , after all, once a year. We didn't go out much, nor did my parents go out to dinner or have dinner parties – only during the big shoots.'

Left:
Flash Kellett at Taplow Court, 'one of the really intellectual households . . . where you had terrifying games' – and also the inescapable practical joking which made house parties a nightmare for shy guests.

Below:
An inimitable record by Cecil Beaton of a house party. Those swept under the carpet include Rex Whistler, the Sacheverell Sitwells, Rosamund Lehmann and Edward Sackville-West. (*Courtesy Sotheby's London*)

Overleaf:
Hunting at Badminton. 'We would set off very early in the morning – breakfast at six o'clock, because one was out on a horse by half-past six.'

OTING & FISHING

Badminton House – Womersley – Mimizan –
Eaton Hall – World's End – Kylestrome –
Flete – Boughton House – Holker Hall – Birr
Castle – Ickworth – Wallington House

**HUNTING:
The late Duke of
Beaufort**

'Hunting was the main thing at Badminton. We started in the middle of August and went right through the first of May, six days a week in those days. We would get off very early in the morning – breakfast at six o'clock, because one was out on a horse by half-past six.

'When I was a boy, there were one hundred horses here (my father died in 1924 and we moved straight up to the big house); then there were about fifty. Every groom had to do two or three horses, but there was a head groom over them, and two or three rather senior ones who were second horsemen. We had our own blacksmith, who had a full-time job looking after the horses. The hunt had a huntsman and two whippers-in. At the end of the season, we used to have a party for everybody connected with the stables.

'I bought my own horses. I used to get practically all of them from a well-known horse-dealer: two men, the Drage brothers, who lived in the Pytchley country. Odd ones I bought from local farmers.'

**Anne, Countess of
Rosse**

'Before I married Michael I hunted with the Blackmore Vale, because my cousin was the Master; he lived in this wonderful house called Sherborne Castle, which is like a home to me. So I used to hunt a great deal with the Blackmore (those lovely banks, very exciting); and then in Sussex with the Crawley and Horsham. In fact I used to hunt three days a week.

'When I married, Michael didn't like hunting – he never had. It had always been my ambition to hunt with the Blazers. Then I thought that if he didn't hunt, and I did, I'd come home and there'd be nobody to tell what one did. It wouldn't work. We both loved gardening, and we both loved doing so much together, that I gave up the hunting.

'When I went back to Yorkshire, we had the hounds back in the house at Womersley, because that was old Badsworth country, which Michael's great-grandfather, Lord Hawke, had hunted, and his great-grandfather before him. They were the great Osbaldertons of the day. They used to keep about seventy horses in their various stables. One of the interesting pictures we've got at Womersley is of Lord Cardigan's horse, Rajah, at the Charge of the Light Brigade. He ended his days at Womersley – sent there as a great horse to finish his life.'

**Loelia, Lady Lindsay
of Dowhill** (*formerly
Duchess of Westminster*)

'Bendor got rather heavy, although still very active, so, to lose a bit of weight he became interested in boar hunting. He moved the hounds and the entire shooting match (not that that's the right

Above:
The Duke and Duchess of
Beaufort.

Left:
Judges at the Duke's hound
puppy show.

Below:
Hounds at Badminton.

expression), from Eaton down to Mimizan, where he had built himself a lovely little house on a vast lake between Biarritz and Bordeaux. He had a stable there. He sometimes bred wild boars, which were surreptitiously let out into the forest in the middle of the night. When the boars declined in number, he moved the whole *équipe* up to Rouen, to a place called Saint-Saëns, where he took a little château, which he rented right up to the last war. Then he brought the hounds and the horses back to Eaton. I hunted occasionally in a frightfully feeble way – I was much too cowardly. One of the reasons I took up embroidery was because Bendor used to spend so much time hunting that it gave me something to do while he was out all day.'

**SHOOTING:
Loelia, Lady Lindsay
of Dowhill** (*formerly
Duchess of Westminster*)

'The shoots at Eaton were on a tremendous scale, there's no doubt about that. Even looking back and having been to lots of shoots when I was a young girl, I'd never seen anything like it. The very first weekend, when I'd only just met Bendor. I was as staggered as anybody else by the performance that was put on.

'The clothes were so interesting. All the keepers were dressed in green velvet tailcoats and black bowler hats trimmed with gold braid, so that you could spot a keeper whenever you wanted to. The beaters came through the wood, just like a Breughel picture, and they wore these white smocks, which reached down sort of mid-calf (no doubt they were handed to them from their starting point), and on top of this costume, large, red felt hats with wide brims. They really did look mediaeval. But it was a good idea really, because nobody could ever make excuses for shooting a beater. They must have seen them for miles, tapping away and shouting.

'On my first shoot, I didn't know any of the people, and I thought I'd better cling to my duke while I could, because I was leaving immediately after lunch to stay somewhere else that weekend. The other guests had arrived on the Thursday night to shoot on the Friday and Saturday – they usually left on Sunday. One of the guests there was Sir James Dunn, who was Lord Beaverbrook's best friend, a very tough little Canadian nut; he never hit anything and was frightfully dangerous, because he used to swing round and pepper people.

'I don't think the shoot at Eaton was particularly good, and that's why it was moved to Wales. Bendor created a marvellous shoot near Llangollen, called World's End, at the very end of a valley, where there was a little Tudor lodge. There he put down something like 10,000 pheasants. It was scenically very Wagnerian, with great rocky cliffs soaring above one's head, and thousands of pheasants streaming over. At the first shoot the guns were too low: none of them hardly

Opposite:
The Duke of Westminster's hunting, shooting and fishing lodges – Mimizan (above), World's End (centre) and Kylestrome (below).

88

'One of the reasons I took up embroidery was because Bendor used to spend so much time hunting . . .'

The Duke shooting, assisted by his loader.

The Duchess in boar-hunting costume.

89

Above:
'Bendor created a marvellous shoot near Llangollen, called World's End, at the very end of a valley, where there was a little Tudor lodge.'

Right:
'Bendor was so keen on shooting and fishing that two or three times he did what was called the triple crown, which means that you have to shoot a stag and a brace of grouse, and catch a salmon, all in one day.'

touched a feather, though they were very good shots, and they all had to be moved higher next time. The good shots had three loaders.

'An elaborate lunch was laid on in the lodge at the head of the valley, for the guns and their wives, and nobody else. It was sent out from Eaton, and was the most super food you could possibly hope to eat. It was just over an hour and a quarter's drive from Eaton. The staff all went off at dawn with hampers and things. The ladies used to join the men at lunchtime.

'Shooting was such a part of life in those days, which thank God it isn't any more. People did lay down those enormous numbers of pheasants. Now they're mostly wild. I remember one of the keepers at World's End saying, "It's so awful the next day, when we've fed all these wretched birds, and then they come limping in."

'Bendor was so keen on shooting and fishing that two or three times he did what was called the triple crown, which means that you have to shoot a stag and a brace of grouse, and catch a salmon, all in one day. The most difficult part was the salmon. Usually people went off after the stag initially, and they'd have a long stalk perhaps, but the canny ones always caught the fish first. The brace of grouse was elusive, because the men would be tired by that time.

'Women did shoot in those days, and I went out stalking in Scotland. Strangely enough I shot a Royal – you really do have to cull in a deer forest. But certainly, I never shot any birds. I was never tempted – I'm not at all a sporting type. The stalk, which took place in the famous Scottish forest, Reay Forest, was rather thrilling, I must say. Stalking is like playing a game of hide-and-seek, because it's rather difficult to crawl over peat bogs. It was exciting, but I hate blood sports. I do feel that one of the good things that's happened nowadays is that people don't go to Africa to slaughter a lioness so that all her cubs die of starvation. That is no longer popular – and something to chalk up on the right side of the slate.'

'The first of the big shoots at Flete was in November. We would have about seven or eight guns, friends of my father, who were usually extremely good shots. Each gun had to have a loader and usually brought his own. Shoots were always mid-week, on a Tuesday, Wednesday and Thursday. The guests that my father had would never have been such good shots if they'd had to work: they went round shooting at different houses all winter.

'The estate staff were beating – and people from all around, anyone who could be useful. There would be forty or fifty of them going through the woods with the keeper in command, saying "Steady on

The Hon Mrs John Mildmay White

91

the left, forward on the right." The birds came very, very high at Flete, because it was so hilly, and you used to stand below as they were driven over. With a really good shot you would quite often see four birds dead in the air at once, always shot in the head – none of that flutter-flutter-whump. Absolutely crump – dead. It was wonderful. It's fun watching anyone doing anything really well, and it's just as much fun watching a really good shot.

'We had five keepers, and they all had boys to help with the shoot. We used to rear a tremendous lot of pheasants. All the eggs were collected up by the keepers and extra eggs bought, so that the pheasant blood was changed. Then thousands of broody hens were collected and put out in coops all around in the pheasants' big field. They sat on the eggs until they hatched out, and ran in and out of the coops, and when they got big enough they were all put out in the woods. A tremendous lot of vermin killing went on. Now the whole place is full of magpies and things like that, but in those days you hardly saw a single one.

'The women didn't normally go out to join the shoot in the morning. We usually spent the morning either going round the garden or going to look at a church. Then we used to join the men for a tremendous luncheon in one of the keeper's houses, which was quite small, and so we were rather crushed in. The food was brought down by the footmen and the butler; they came in the car, but all the food was brought in hay boxes – lovely stews and that sort of thing – by the garden horse. We drank cider and beer, and then there was cherry brandy afterwards. We all used to stay with them in the afternoon. On one of the days, when they were shooting further away, there was a specially built hut in the woods where we had our luncheon; and then the third day we had it in the house, because we shot near the house in the morning, and quite often in the afternoon as well.

'When shooting was over, we came in and had the most delicious tea, with masses of Devonshire cream, honey, jam, scones and cakes. Everybody would relax and then go to dress for dinner. My mother had put in a lot of new bathrooms in what had been old dressing rooms, so they had fireplaces, and we always had fires in the bathrooms. It really was absolutely wonderful, when you came in, quite tired after shooting, to have a leisurely bath, with towels hanging on the fireguard and all the flames bouncing up; simply lovely. The only thing was that it made you rather slow. There wasn't a bathroom for every bedroom so you couldn't stay as long as you wanted.

'We often had people to dinner after the shoots – someone like the Commander-in-Chief of Plymouth – but these wouldn't be frightfully organised occasions. With the guns, we were usually about

Left:
Lord Irwin and his children at Flete. 'We would have about seven or eight guns, friends of my father, who were usually extremely good shots.'

Below:
Amateur theatricals with a hunting theme – "The Melton Hunt Breakfast". The Marquess of Blandford, Anthony Mildmay and Colonel Green, MFH were among the actors.

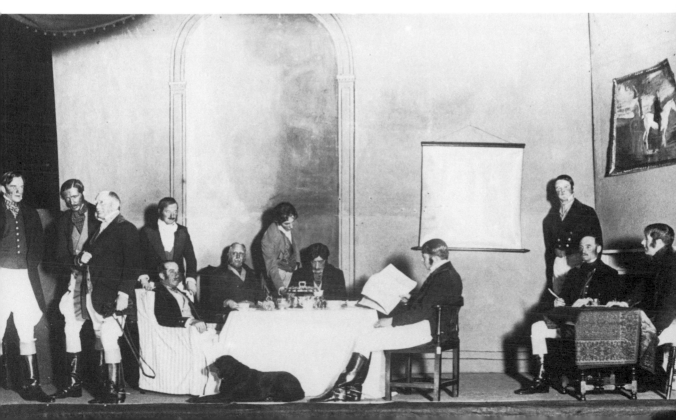

fourteen; we'd probably have dinner for about eighteen.'

Mary, Duchess of Buccleuch

'Shooting parties were usually from Monday to Friday or Saturday. I don't think they were ever at weekends. Boughton didn't have an awful lot of rooms, really, and everybody brought a maid and usually brought a valet as well, and they all had to be put up. The Queen always brought a maid, naturally, and a dresser and a lady-in-waiting and a lady-in-waiting's maid and a detective. That filled up quite a lot of the bedrooms.'

Mrs Richard Cavendish

'Holker was a lovely shoot. We didn't care for reared birds; it was wild birds. There was a lovely little grouse moor, very very good, excellent – the greatest fun and a beautiful place. Then they went after woodcock and pigeons – there was an awful lot of pigeon shooting, and flighting in duck and geese.'

Anne, Countess of Rosse

'We were regulated by certain things – the Chelsea Flower Show might take us up to London, Christmas, of course, would be spent at Birr, and after Christmas would be shooting parties. Very often we asked a large party. They were people who happened to be our friends – when they turned up, they didn't shoot at all!

'We had pheasant shooting, which I loved. And snipe, and of course woodcock, and a few grouse and a lot of wild fowl, a tremendous lot of duck of varying sorts, geese. It's very romantic, because at Birr we have the great bogs around us.'

Lady Phyllis MacRae

'At Ickworth we had two big shoots. People used to arrive on Monday, shoot on Tuesday, Wednesday and Thursday, and leave on Friday. They were other landowners, all gentlemen of leisure: they might have been in the army, or the navy, but they had all retired at the age of about forty or forty-five, so they were of course able-bodied men. Nowadays you would not get anyone to stay for five whole days and shoot for four of them.

'They used to come, not only with a wife, but also a lady's maid and very often a chauffeur and a loader, and they all expected to be put up. The loader was quite often the gentleman's gentleman – he was perhaps the first footman, who had been taught to load. A few of them did teach their chauffeurs and did not have a gentleman's gentleman, in which case they had to be valeted by the footmen.

Opposite, above:
A shoot at Drumlanrig, the Duchess of Buccleuch leading the guns. Few women shot; they would join the men at lunchtime.

Below: A shooting picnic at Drumlanrig. On the far left is the Maharajah Sodut Singh.

Two views of the same shoot
at Invermark, captured by Sir
Arthur Penn (above), and the
camera (right).

Opposite:
Beaters at the Denman shoot
at Balcombe Place.

'They reckoned on seven guns, so there would be my father and then six other guns, of which one might be someone asked in from the neighbourhood. Our parties were nearly always a matter of sitting down fourteen, which meant that there was always the fear that someone would drop out and that we would be thirteen, which happened very often. It was terribly difficult, because there was always somebody in the party who was a thirteen-not-sit-down-at-table maniac. Before the 1914–18 war our governess was always fished out of the schoolroom to make up the numbers; after the war we were both old enough, and so it was much more a matter of one of us being pushed out.'

Mrs John Dower

'Shooting was a great interest, a great delight, for my father. August 12th was always very much a sacred day for everybody. We didn't have the sort of shooting lunch at Wallington that the Edwardians had – we didn't have it laid out by a footman with a cloth and all that sort of thing. We had sandwiches, generally up at some of our high farms: Fallowlees or Redpath. In my grandparents' day, even when just the family were shooting, the coachman and footman would be in full livery with a top hat and cockade.

'We very rarely walked over dogs for grouse shooting: it was very nearly all butt shooting, with a bevy of beaters beating down on the butts. They were very long days' walking.

'George Slade, our keeper, was a splendid person. He would take us up onto the moors when we were quite young, to show us grouse nests and plovers' nests, and he also taught us to shoot and fish. We were all taught to shoot at the age of twelve, but I don't think we went up onto the moors to shoot as early as that. I cried whenever I hit anything, so he said, "Well, Miss Pauline, I'll tell your father" – so I never had to pursue this unwanted sport. One of my sisters still shoots, though. When I was very small, the dogs used to come up to the front door, where we were collected for shooting, and I was so small I could ride on a big retriever. I remember Slade objecting to my father that I was spoiling the dogs.

Even though the first thing I caught fishing was a very unattractive eel – a freshwater eel in the Wansbeck, which Slade helped me with – I became a keen fisherman; trout fishing.'

Opposite:
Fishing at Drumlanrig –
Patrick Bradshaw and Betty
Somerset.

**FISHING:
Anne, Countess of
Rosse**

'I was a tremendous salmon-fisherwoman, believe it or not, because my father salmon-fished; and I caught the largest salmon that's ever been got out of the little bit of the Dee just along by Balmoral –

a thirty-pounder, or thirty-two-pounder, I think, which was a great feat. I was very excited about that.'

Loelia, Lady Lindsay of Dowhill (*formerly Duchess of Westminster*)

'Bendor was mad also about fishing. He had the best fishing in Scotland, on the River Laxford. I don't know how many thousands of acres the estate consisted of. The house, which was on Loch More, was a typical, informal Scotch shooting lodge, with peppercorn tops. Pretty ugly, frankly, but just in such a divinely beautiful place. A huge loch, Loch Stack, flowed into the river; there was no pollution, no factories within miles. You could catch these enormous salmon, or huge sea trout or brown trout – you never knew what you were going to catch.

'He always generously gave me the top pool, which was the best pool to fish, and I really became expert at casting and loved it.'

Opposite:
Marcus Wickham-Boynton at Burton Agnes. 'Things were never the same after the First World War.'

VI PATERNAL ACRES

Burton Agnes Hall – Melford Hall – Ickworth – Eaton Hall – Badminton House – Bowhill – Langholm – Drumlanrig Castle – Dalkeith Palace – Boughton House – Flete – Wallington House – Balcombe Place – Giffords Hall – Bartlow House

Marcus Wickham Boynton

'Things were never the same after the First World War. To begin with, taxation was vastly increased: the ordinary landowner was nothing like as well off, and economies had to be made. Around 1921, agricultural depression in England was very severe and rents were either in arrears or so reduced that landowners went through a very bad period, as did their tenants. That lasted for some years, which in turn, of course, forced economies and a lower standard of upkeep on all estates. The standard of repair, I think one could say, was adequately maintained, but luxury things, such as shooting, all suffered. The home farm was run by my father, who also, during the depression, took over some other farms, which were virtually unlettable. Things were very difficult – I think he lost a lot of money during those years. Then farming gradually improved until the outbreak of the 1939 war.

'The first agent I can remember at Burton Agnes was Mr Hawes, whom we shared with our neighbouring estate, the St Quintins of Harpham. In those days the Burton Agnes estate was about 10,000 acres. He lived at Lowthorpe, and was agent at Burton Agnes, Rudston and Barmston, and at the St Quintins' estates at Harpham, Scampton and Lowthorpe. He was a high-powered and very capable gentleman. Some of the houses, which he designed or improved, form part of the Burton Agnes estate now.

'My father started the stud – his interest, of course, was in breeding hunters. He, and indeed my mother, were both devoted to foxhunting. He was Master of the East Middleton for many years and was an extremely good huntsman and very quick – you had to be if you wanted to catch the fox in open wold country. He was always interested in racing, but he was quite satisfied if his business with the stallions enabled him to pay for the hunting and the hounds.

'The stud changed over from hunters to race-horses between the wars – the switch occurred because, with the mechanisation of the army, horses were no longer required. For the 1914 war, the army had been buying hunters as remounts – a lot of my parents' horses were sold for that purpose. After the war, the blood stock industry, from the racing point of view, was expanding as the breeding of remounts was declining.

'What really started off the Burton Agnes stud was a very successful stallion, Winalot, which belonged to Joe Shepherd. Mr Shepherd had two or three mares which went to Winalot every time, and my father took an interest in the progeny. The first good horse was Spion Kop, who won the Derby. It belonged to Colonel Loder, and merely stood here under a business arrangement. By Jingo, another horse here, under the same arrangement, won the Gold Cup at Ascot. It

Marcus Wickham-Boynton's father: 'He was Master of the East Middleton for many years and was an extremely good huntsman and very quick.'

102

belonged to a Leeds timber merchant, Mr W T de Pledge, together with a number of horses trained at Lambourn by Jimmy Rhodes. Whereas Spion Kop was a successful stallion, especially as a sire for brood mares, By Jingo was a failure. Fortunately he was followed by Lola I, a horse owned by Edward Hulton, again under a business arrangement.

'My father was an extremely good judge of horses, and from 1910 to the outbreak of the 1939 war was in regular demand as a judge of hunters at the Royal, Yorkshire, Dublin and Richmond Shows. He wasn't really interested in putting a lot of capital into racing. It was only when I came along and started to take an interest in the bloodstock side that he took a financial interest in two or three foals which I had bought. My father died in 1942, shortly after my brother had died in the war, again in 1942, and I inherited Burton Agnes.'

Ulla, Lady Hyde Parker

'My husband managed the Melford estate and farmed it himself. It was considered very unusual. They spoke about it a great deal in the neighbourhood: "Have you heard? Willy farms; he's started farming." My father-in-law had broken the entail sometime in the 1920s and made the estate over to Willy, but he continued to run it himself until his death. Willy was anxious to farm, so when one of the farms fell vacant, he wanted to take it over. But he was very nervous of his father, and did not like to ask him, so he sent me! I said, "Willy wants to farm Burton's." "Certainly not. My son is a gentleman. He may shoot, and hunt, and run the estate, but not farm. Never!" I said, "If that is the case, private estates will soon not exist in England, because only the farms where families who own them have farmed for themselves have survived in Denmark." I think my father-in-law was rather taken aback to be spoken to in that way, but he thought about it and then he said, "All right, let Willy farm."

'Willy was then in his late thirties – thirty-seven. He'd always been very interested in farming. When we married, he went to Oxford and took a course during holiday time. He'd been over to Denmark and stayed with us, and I'd taken him to see several of the big estates there. In those days, farming in Denmark was very advanced, and they did it well. He got very enthusiastic about all sorts of new ideas for farming, and he grasped the important point that only the estates still in the hands of the original families had survived.

'He saw farming as a great challenge – this was in the early 1930s, when farming wasn't doing at all well. It was very hard work. You needed capital to start up. He sold one of the bigger houses on the

'My father ran Ickworth and the estate in a disciplined manner . . . He had his views and he was very mathematical: he would always measure the hayfield, measure the hay he got out of it, measure the haystack, and work out exactly how much per acre he would get.'

estate and put the money into Burton's Farm, building modern cowsheds.

'He had a farm manager as well, but he always saw to everything himself. He gave the instructions to the men, and decided what was to be done. Every morning Willy and I used to set off at eleven and ride out to look at the farm and the woodmen and everything on the estate.

'We had a big harvest supper every year for our men, celebrating when they'd finished the harvest and thanking them for the good work they'd done. It was held in the pub, The Hare, which we owned. A pig was killed and roasted outside. Up at the house we used to make dripping and all the lard for the pastry, with which the cook made enormous apple and blackberry pies.'

'My father ran Ickworth and the estate in a disciplined manner – he had been a naval officer and he would not have understood anyone who did not understand discipline. But of course you could not run your farm quite like a ship. You could fight the weather on a ship, whereas there is nothing you can do against storms on a farm. Everything had to be just so. He had his views and he was very mathematical: he would always measure the hayfield, measure the hay he got out of it, measure the haystack, and work out exactly how much per acre he would get. If it were not the same each year, he could not understand it. And of course it never was the same.

'The estate in those days was of approximately 30,000 acres in West Suffolk, 12,000 in East Suffolk, and 20,000 in Lincolnshire and 800 in Essex. We also had a house in Brighton and one in London, 6 St James's Square. So of course my father had to have an agent – you could not run all that by yourself. He certainly kept very personal accounts, not all done by someone outside the estate. He knew the names of his tenants, but he would not have known them very well personally, because he was not the sort of person who liked people very much. But he was very human, and after the First World War ended he had a peacetime party for the tenants. When his two daughters were married, the tenants were given a party too.'

Lady Phyllis MacRae

'I don't think Bendor was tremendously interested in the Eaton estate. He didn't have anything to make him particularly interested, because it all worked with such oil-like wheels.

'His agent was a gentleman called Basil Kerr; he was Bendor's most intimate friend. I should think he was very efficient. A house

Loelia, Lady Lindsay of Dowhill (*formerly Duchess of Westminster*)

Opposite, above:
The Duke and Duchess of
Beaufort in their motor being
ceremonially towed back to
Badminton after their
honeymoon by the estate
workers – a tradition that
persisted in many of the great
country houses.

Below:
The Badminton cricket team,
made up from friends of the
Duke and workers on the
estate.

and everything else was provided for him, so it was a jolly good job. There was another house at Eaton for another friend, a man called Charles Hunter, who ran all the boar hunting, which was quite a job. They were quite separate departments, but Basil Kerr was the king. At whatever moment we arrived back at Eaton, one of them would come to dinner; the wretched wife would be left alone at home.

'The Eaton estate included a lot of very good farmland, where Bendor had a most wonderful herd of cows and won the award for the best cow in the British Isles (or whatever it was) year after year. It was only because his friend the agent said, "You simply must come and see this cow, as you've won this magnificent cup," that we went off to the farmyard and out was brought the cow. I hope we made the right noises and told him how perfectly marvellously he'd done. Neither of us knew a thing about it. I said, "What beautiful eyelashes it has," or something feeble like that.

'He had rather bad luck with his stud. He really inherited the estate from his grandfather, because his father had died when he was a little boy, and Daddy Westminster, as Bendor's grandfather was always known, left his son's widow the stud, which she wasn't even faintly interested in. She hadn't any idea what to do with it, and as she was left with large death duties (most of which she didn't pay, I may say, because they really didn't get around to it), the stud was obviously one of the first things to be sold. All that wonderful line of great horses – including Ormond and Flying Fox – which goes back to the last century, was sold and dispersed, and Bendor had to start from scratch. He never really had any good horses; or only one, Twelve Pointer, which won the Lincoln. He gave me a horse, Turbine, which won a race, odd as it may seem, but as I never saw it run, I really wasn't particularly thrilled with it. We entered it in the Derby, so that I could have a runner, and it was last.'

The late Duke of Beaufort

'We did not have much land in hand in those days – we had the whole of the park, which was 1000 acres. But we didn't farm any of the other 60,000 acres at Badminton. We had sixteen gardeners and our own dairy herd – they were milked just behind the stables.

'At the top of the park, near Worcester Lodge, lived the head keeper; he had about three other keepers under him, living very near, and two others who lived further away, near two villages. Acton Turville was one; the other was near Tormarton. We didn't have very many big shoots, though. It was mainly rabbits in those days, and we were very busy keeping them down. We did rear a certain number of pheasants, but hunting was the main thing.

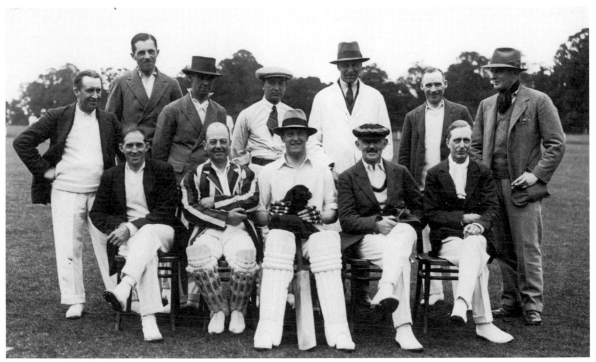

'About twelve men worked in the forestry department, with a head forester over them. We sold a lot of timber, both to firms and to individuals. People who lived all around were always asking if we had timber for sale for their own houses.

'We had our own fire engine, driven by a special fireman, which used to go all over the estate. The firemen were all our own men, who, if the fire alarms went off, quickly got into their special clothes and were driven off to the fire. We had quite a lot of fire escapes at Badminton. We used to practice escapes from the house after a special bell had been rung; the men and girls used to go down the canvas shutes with the firemen waiting at the bottom to catch us.'

Mary, Duchess of Buccleuch

'Walter never stopped dealing with the estates. We had very good factors, of course, but he saw to all the estates himself, and everything came through his hands. He knew everything that was going on, on all six estates. You see, there was Bowhill, Langholm, Drumlanrig (Eildon comes with Bowhill), Dalkeith (which was quite a big estate) and then Boughton, which for England is quite a big estate in itself – 13,000 acres. The farm at Boughton is 3000 acres, and we do it ourselves – sheep and dairy. We've got a dairy farm at Drumlanrig and a big one at Bowhill.

'All three families – the Buccleuchs, the Queensberrys, the Montagus – regarded land as a tremendous heritage and a great responsibility always. They have always been great husbanders of the land, and great foresters; they regarded it as a tremendous responsibility to be landowners. Of course, they've made the most of it, too. They've been great benefactors, providing employment and providing food and providing timber in the villages they owned. Possessions they always regarded as less important.'

The Hon Mrs John Mildmay White

'The agent ran the estate at Flete, and I think he paid the gardeners, as well as the keepers and the woodmen, the plumbers and the estate staff. The heads of staff used to have to go down once a fortnight to the estate office, on a Friday. It was quite a long way from the village – a morning's walk for them. The head gardener would go and collect the wages for the gardeners and so on and distribute them.

'An agent in those days had to be able to ride, as he had to go round all the farms – the home farm, which we farmed ourselves, and the twenty-three or twenty-four tenanted farms – to oversee the estate staff, the foresters and maintenance men. (The gardeners, keepers and grooms were totally controlled by the head gardener,

Opposite, above:
The Royal English Forestry Society visit Boughton.

Below:
The view over the estate from Flete.

head gamekeeper and stud groom.) The agent had no secretarial staff to begin with, and later on just one secretary, for there were no forms to fill in then, no PAYE, and no planning permission was needed for anything. If you wanted to build a house on your own land or add to one, you just did it, with no need to ask anyone. So the paper-work for an agent was minimal. Our agent here for many years was a friend, who inherited a beautiful castle in Wales and became Sir Seymour Boothby. He was always called in to shoot on the outskirts of the shoot.

'My father was very keen on South Devon cattle. He had some very good South Devons on the home farm, which had a manager, but, like everything else, was under the control of the agent. During the time that we were away, he had to control everything.'

Mrs John Dower

'My grandfather did not run the Wallington estate, although he would be *au fait* with what was going on. He had an agent called Nixon, who lived in Middlestead, the central house in the village. He was a very formidable, big man, rather silent. People were very much in awe of him. There were a great many estate staff, a large staff of masons, plumbers and joiners, but no electricians.

'One of the biggest things my father did was to put in electricity. You can imagine that great house with only oil and paraffin lamps on stands. When you went up to bed there were candles on the table at the bottom of the stairs; we each took one and walked up the stairs with a candle. All the downstairs oil lamps were looked after by the pantry staff, which meant taking them away, clipping the thick wicks to stop them smoking out of the glass chimneys, and then bringing them back, involving a tremendous amount of walking about the house. The upstairs lamps were looked after by the head housemaid and her staff, and taken and dealt with in the housemaids' pantry at the top of the back stairs. I think we must have been away at school when the electricity was finally installed, very effectively. A generator was put in at Close House, halfway between Wallington and Cambo, and that worked for years until the grid came.

'My father insisted on having a complete architect's examination of the house as soon as we came in 1928. It was a very good thing he did, because the architect, Cordingley from Liverpool, who was extremely careful about his work, discovered almost at once that the two wrought-iron beams – not steel beams – which, in 1853, Ruskin and Dobson had put in to hold up the cantilevered roof of the Central Hall, were cracked right through and were holding by what my architect husband called "sticktion". They were jammed together, and

110

if anybody had shaken them, the whole roof would have fallen down! So during that first, very snowy, winter of 1928, we had twenty-seven workmen in the house, the whole of the Central Hall was full of scaffolding and the roof taken off, in order to put in steel beams. Before the scaffolding was eventually taken down, we all climbed up to the very top and wrote our names in the cove of the roof.

'My father didn't want an agent who took the running of the estate entirely out of his own hands, because he was very interested in his farmers and his men. He had first a very nice Scotsman, who I think came down from working with the Forestry Commission; but, alas, his health was not good and he died within a fairly short time. I think he was followed by one of my father's farmers, who advised him about the home farm, and about the estate. By then, of course, my father had made himself familiar with the whole working of the estate, and finally he ran the farm and estate himself. He would always take advice from his men. On rent days he always had each farmer in, individually, for a separate discussion. He cared very much for his farmers, and during the very bad time in the 1930s he reduced their rent considerably, so that they could continue.

'Father inherited the whole of the estate staff: he would simply call in his own mason or joiner for any repairs. Before breakfast, he would be out to see off his estate men at 7.30 am, to discuss any particular job they were doing. He was very much *au fait* with all they were doing, discussing things with them, even though at the beginning he had an agent. He knew all his people very well indeed – he and my mother between them really were like parents to the whole estate. They visited all of the farms and were intimate with them, and really saw to it that the estate staff did all the repairs, and dealt with each farm individually. The houses on the estate had been very well built by Sir Walter Blackett in the eighteenth century, but of course they were not modernised, and there was no electricity in any of the farms until the grid came.

'My father always had a secretary to help with the paperwork, but it would be somebody local, who lived in one of the many cottages around Wallington. Judging by my father's books – they were all in his writing – he paid the wages and took the rent. He very much ran the place. My mother did the domestic side. I think it was really rather hard on her, actually: she was not brought up to an economical way of looking at things, and I still remember that it was a dreadful day when she had to bring her accounts to my father to be vetted. I don't know how often that was, whether it was once a month or once a week, but it was always dreadful.

'My father tried various leading experiments. For instance, it was still at the time when the system was to buy in Irish calves in the spring, fatten them in the summer and sell them off in the autumn. My father decided he would try crossing the best of the calves with Aberdeen Angus, keeping them over the winter – a different sort of farming, a much better use of the land and the buildings – which was a successful lead to his farmers.

'In my parents' day the tenants' party became an evening party. It took place every year after haysell and sheep-shearing, in July or August, out of doors in the courtyard. There were children's races down what was then the central path from the clock tower to the back door. Every child who ran got a prize, so it didn't much matter whether one won or not! There were between twenty and twenty-three farms. Most people would come, and all our servants too. They were treated, and they behaved, as friends (which they were). To begin with, a supper, and then dancing. Then everybody gathered round and my father told them what had been happening, both on the estate and in the world at large.'

Lady Burrell

'We farmed the home farm at Balcombe, about 180 acres, and the rest was let, on average 150 to 250 acres each. My grandfather bought bits of land and added them to the estate. He gave them to my mother; and she also bought some bits, like the wood that you can see from the house. There was a great deal of woodland – a third of the 1000 acres. We shared the agent with Grandpapa's Paddock-hurst estate, so he started with the distinct advantage that we couldn't sack him. My mother ran that side: she saw him probably about once a quarter, unless there was some severe crisis. My father was terribly ignorant about the land, but he ran the shoot. I think they had about ten or eleven days days' shooting in the year: three first-time shoots, and three second-time shoots, and then the locals. (Shooting parties that required six or seven guns had ruined all the manor houses of England, because they had all added on in order to have enough guns staying to make the shoot private and not to have to have any locals.) My father also trained his racehorses at Balcombe, which was great fun for me, because I was riding gallops at the age of twelve. He hired some stables on the downs, and swam the lame horses in the sea, but by and large he got them three-quarters fit at Balcombe.'

Mrs Charles Brocklebank

'At Giffords, where we lived from 1935 to 1940, we were very much out of village life, as the church and village are over two miles away

Sir Arthur Penn's vision of
country house entertainment.
One chatelaine recalls: 'There
was no conversation as such,
except in very special houses;
we relied on games and
practical joking during house
parties.'

Above:
A pageant in which the
Duchess of Beaufort took part
as the Duchess of
Marlborough.

Right:
The Duke of Beaufort painted
by F B Voss in 1936.

Above:
The Grosvenor Hunt by George Stubbs with the eighteenth-century huntsmen dressed in almost the same, distinctive Westminster livery described by Lady Lindsay on page 88. (*The Grosvenor Estate*)

Left:
The Duke of Beaufort's stables, painted by his friend, Lord Methuen. 'Hunting was the main thing at Badminton.'

Overleaf:
The Duke and Duchess of Buccleuch riding at Drumlanrig with their children – the present Duke, the present Duchess of Northumberland and Lady Gilmour. Painted by Edward Seago.

A tapestry of the Wallington estate, showing the Clock Tower and stables, the house, the walled garden, the bridge and the gazebo and various sporting pursuits executed by Pauline Dower.

Above:
The hall at Melford Hall.
'The hall was terracotta above
the panelling, and all the way
up the stairs. The iron railings
– the banisters – between the
gallery were black; now they
are pale grey.' (*National Trust*)

Right:
Lady Hyde Parker's bedroom
at Melford Hall. 'When I did
up the Victorian bedrooms
here, I put white curtains
under the muslin.' (*National
Trust*)

from the house. By contrast, at Bartlow, my father-in-law's house, church and house were within fifty yards of each other, and we were part of the village, most of the houses in it belonging to my father-in-law. There was hardly any mechanisation then: we had wind pumps on the farms. I remember hearing the first tractor in the 1920s. At harvest you just heard the boy warning the man on the top of the waggon that the horse was about to move forward. That was all. You could hear him calling, "Hold ye up", from far across the Cambridgeshire fields. My father-in-law ran the farm at Bartlow with a resident agent.

'At Giffords, our farm manager had seen men reaping by hand, and mowing with scythes. We had an agent, who came from Norfolk, and a farm manager on the spot. Most work on the house and estate was done by our own labour. By the time I came to deal with the estate, I had been able to pick up a lot of information about trees, fences and buildings from the people working there. They knew a great deal about the country and were extraordinarily interesting to talk to. They seemed to remember just when things had happened. "That was the year of the great flood," they would say, and they knew exactly which year it was.

'Alfred Dockerill, foreman of one of the farms at Bartlow, was always very neatly and smartly dressed, with highly polished leather gaiters, a billycock hat, and a tie pulled through a ring. His speech was almost Biblical – "he rent his coat", and he used the plural "housen". His voice, rather sing-song, sounded very like the soft creaking of machinery. He had the bluest of eyes, and a face like a ripe, slightly wrinkled red apple.

The head foreman at Giffords, John Rickett, was a tall, handsome man with a beard. In his youth, he had walked to work miles daily from his home at Abington. Besides working on several Cambridge colleges, he had cut stone on Ely Cathedral. He was very knowledgeable and well read. A wonderful craftsman, he added a porch to the church, and also a stone bridge over a stream in the park, in the manner of a bridge on the Cambridge backs.

'His habit of addressing you in the third person – not "Would you wish to look at a cottage?", but "Would Mrs Brocklebank wish . . ." – was a fairly common form of courtesy in the village. Some rare words were also in use: a "hawky" was a party or feast (corruption of "orgy"?); while, if you inquired after the health of a child, you might be told he was "fierce" – ie well and lively. The village blacksmith could be found on Sundays on his hands and knees, picking dandelions for dandelion wine. His Suffolk (or Cambridgeshire) accent was so strong that often I could not understand him.'

'The head foreman, John Rickett, was a tall, handsome man with a beard.'

A bridge built by Rickett at Giffords.

Mr and Mrs Elmer with a Suffolk ram. He was head shepherd at Giffords; she was head housemaid.

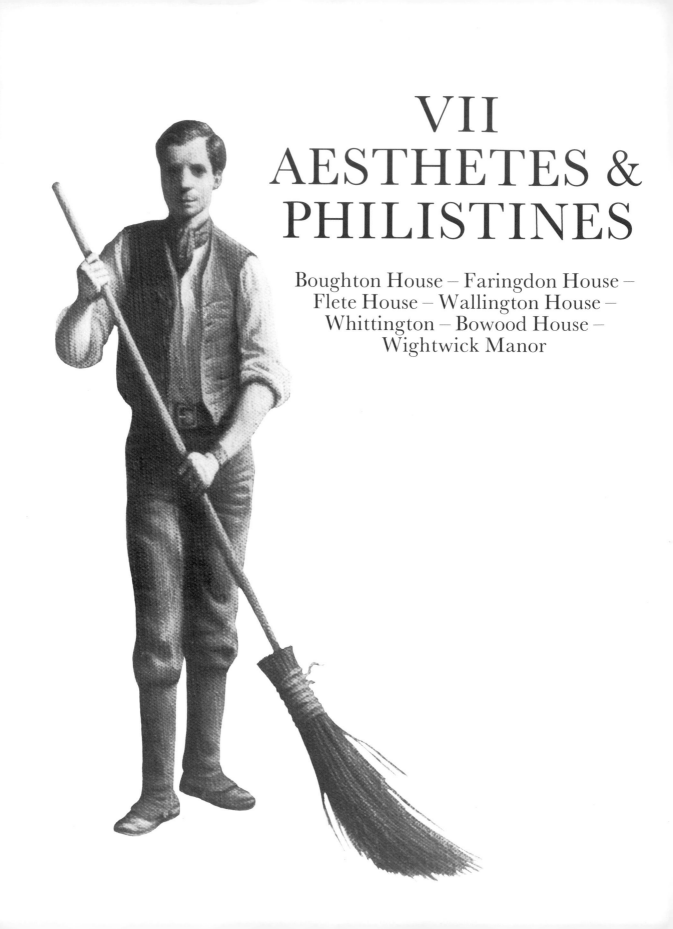

VII
AESTHETES &
PHILISTINES

Boughton House – Faringdon House –
Flete House – Wallington House –
Whittington – Bowood House –
Wightwick Manor

'I don't think people worried if their sons were bookish in those days, as long as they were hunting, shooting and fishing as well. You were allowed to be artistic, and you were allowed to have a knowledge of old things – *objets d'art*, things like architecture and anything else you chose to have – but you had to have some hunting, shooting and fishing as well. You just could not have none at all and play croquet the whole time.'

Lady Phyllis MacRae

'There was no conversation as such, except in very special houses; we relied on games and practical joking during house parties. At most country seats, time was devoted to very energetic, endless games – energetic physically, like Murder or Sardines. All over the house: it must have been awful for the host and hostess, but it was quite fun, sometimes great fun. And charades. And then tremendously intellectual paper games, of which I was absolutely terrified. My hosts and their family were always very familiar with the ones they chose, and very good at them. They were a nightmare for any shy guest, of which I was one. Even now, I remember somebody, today quite well-known, bursting into tears. Maybe young men talk more now – they're probably more intelligent. Then, at that sort of party, conversation was very rare. Some houses absolutely revelled in practical jokes: apple-pie beds and creatures in baths. One or two families were known for it. Sometimes you couldn't take it any more: you thought twice before going again.'

**Lady Marjorie
Stirling**

'At Boughton at weekends they were conversing intellectually. One foregathered before church – everybody went to church automatically – and then people would play tennis; otherwise it was conversation, really. When one had older people like the Winston Churchills and Neville Chamberlain, it was purely conversation. There were no games – a little croquet was played occasionally, but not necessarily. They didn't seem to want to play any games.'

**Mary, Duchess of
Buccleuch**

'Faringdon, Gerald Berners' house, was its own marvellous, marvellous world, in which one always felt so thrilled to be. I could never drive up to the house and not feel absolutely marvellous – never. It had to do with wit and style, and it was better if the wit and style were different from other people's. And it was better if it was funny, if there was a shock in it all. But Faringdon wouldn't have worked if it hadn't been basically so good: the carpets were exquisite; the

Lady Harrod

Opposite:
Rex Whistler portrays himself as a gardener in his mural at Plas Newydd. (*Country Life*)

115

'And then wearing a mask when you went out in the car. . .'

wallpapers wonderful; the pictures, the flowers and the curtains and things all beautiful. The food was always so marvellous too: whatever cook Gerald had was always taught to cook absolutely perfectly.

'But the jokes had to be there too. For instance, the gong for luncheon and dinner was a pretty musical box, which stood in the hall. No ringing gongs or bells – always a musical box. And then wearing a mask when you went out in the car, and putting masks on statues, and doing all sorts of funny things. Robert Heber-Percy once said that Gerald loved publicity, and loved being in the fashion. I never saw that side of him at all: I was very conscious of the desire to tease, and the desire to shock, but not the desire to be fashionable. I think it was the thing at the time. Daisy Fellowes – a friend of Gerald's – had this wonderful Gothick house, Donnington, near Newbury. She was always doing things like putting plastic flowers in her garden. I was always rather shocked, but because I felt rather snobbish about it and also liked Daisy very much, I thought that what she did was right. She was glamorous, I admired it. Daisy wasn't a tease like Gerald, though: she was a good tease, but rather malicious.

'The dining room at Faringdon had ordinary electric light, but also an oil lamp, which used to look very pretty and smell awfully nice. And it had nice portraits and a wonderful, huge round table. It was a lovely room. And even there there were jokes. I remember that there was some very nice mustard you could get, which came in little champagne bottles. That was quite funny at the time, and quite original. Then he had those lovely fishes, made of overlapping scales, and there was also a large cock. Maggie Taylor, who was the very highbrow, pretentious wife of Alan Taylor, used to go and see Gerald and yap away in her highbrow way. One day in St Giles – where Gerald had digs – he ran after her, holding this, and shouted "Maggie, Maggie, I want you to see my cock!" That was very typical of Gerald.

'He wrote very witty postcards. They were so funny. I can only remember "She *said* it was the Holy Ghost". And then there was one of the dove flying in the window, and written underneath was "Not again!" He was very blasphemous. I don't know whether he was *croyant* underneath; I should think probably not.

'He loved playing jokes on snobbish people. Poor old Sybil Colefax, who was really a very nice old lady, but snobbish, was a lion hunter. She did want to know everybody. He sent her a postcard, saying "Do come to lunch on Sunday to meet the P of W". She got terribly excited and dashed off in her best clothes, and was bitterly disappointed when she got there and Gerald said, "Oh, Lady Colefax, do you know the Provost of Worcester?"

Opposite:
'Faringdon wouldn't have worked if it hadn't been basically so good' (above left: Lord Berners with Robert Heber-Percy and his wife in the library). 'But the jokes had to be there too.'

'I don't know that Gerald planted many trees in the park. On one of the great trees round the lake he carved his name, which was a great joke, because that was always considered a dreadful thing to do – to carve your name on a tree was absolute vandalism in the 1930s. Again, it was a tease. He did build a folly, a tall tower, in the park as a present for Robert when he was twenty-one. He got his great friend, Gerry Wellesley, Gerry Wellington, to do it. He wanted it to be Gothic, but Gerry wanted it to be Classical, because that is what he liked – so the bottom is Classical, and then when Gerald came back from abroad and saw it, he made Gerry put a Gothic top to it. It's really the most useless thing in the world, although you can go up inside it. But it's rather lovely; it stands outside Faringdon in a group of trees. He also installed a lovely thing in the church at the time of Robert's birthday, a carillon of bells, which all play hymn tunes by Bishop Heber, who was Robert's ancestor. One used to lie in bed at Faringdon on Sunday mornings, *not* going to church as a sort of extra treat, and hear them. Charming.

'Gerald was a very highly cultivated man. He lived in Rome for quite a long time, and had a house there – Via Foro Romano Tre. He was a very serious composer – a very professional composer, people have said since. He did a ballet for Diaghilev, and one that Freddy Ashton, I think, did the choreography for. Music was probably the thing he was best at, and then probably next at his painting, and then possibly a third at his writing. Some of the writing is frightfully funny – you laugh aloud when you read it – and his portraits of people are very good caricatures. He was really too gifted, I think. But that's what he was like: luckily for him, he was not poor; he didn't have to earn his living; he liked all sorts of other things; he didn't have a conscience about doing something. He did the things that he loved doing, and he did them frightfully well.

'There were often very interesting people at Faringdon. I remember when Gide, who was staying in Somerville College, went out to Faringdon for a night or two. He was rather an exciting person to meet, in a black cloak, looking splendid. Amusing people from round about, like the Betjemans, would go to Sunday luncheons. The only academics who got there were ones that he liked very much anyway, like Maurice Bowra, or David Cecil, or John Sparrow, or people like us.

'Maurice Hastings rented Rousham from the Cottrell-Dormers for a bit and used to have the most wonderful parties there in the early thirties. Maurice Bowra, Roy [Harrod] and John Betjeman, all under-graduates, used to go there – all the people who were gay at that time. I don't mean that sort of gay – well, I think perhaps they

Opposite:
'Gerald was a very highly cultivated man . . . He did a ballet for Diaghilev and one that Freddy Ashton did the choreography for.' Lord Berners and Sir Frederick at Faringdon. (Note the anecdotal cock.)

were too, but that's not really the point. They were very light-hearted, and it was more fun to get drunk in beautiful surroundings. You just happened to be there and your host happened to be a frightfully jolly drunk who gave you masses to drink. I'm afraid they simply went to get drunk and have a wonderful time. They used to shoot the private parts off the statues.'

The Hon Mrs John Mildmay White

'My father was formidable in a way, I suppose but not really when you got to know him. He was, I suppose, slightly manic-depressive – either on frightfully good form or frightfully bad form. When he was on bad form he was a bit formidable. We weren't at all frightened of him, though our style of living was affected by the mood he was in. When he was on good form we would embark on tremendous parties; when he got ill we still had to carry on with the things he'd undertaken. That was a bit difficult, as there was always a slight backlog. Then he'd fly rather high, and suddenly decide he was going to have Prince George or Queen Mary to stay. Everything had to be got going and polished up – the whole house was turned upside down to make ready for her. My father never saw the necessity for anything to be done up, so when something like that was happening, one could say, "Well, if she's coming, I really do think we must have some new curtains in the drawing room," and he would say, "Yes". I would get the stuff from London and we would have them made locally.'

Mrs John Dower

'Whenever the Cassons – Sybil Thorndike and Lewis Casson – were playing in Newcastle, they used to stay at Wallington and be driven in each night to the theatre and fetched back. Sybil was marvellous. Her private talk was exactly like her acting: her voice didn't change at all, just exactly the same. One evening, when they didn't have a performance in Newcastle, they acted the great scene between Queen Catherine and Wolsey, just sitting in the library at Wallington. A great experience for us. Whether we had been into Newcastle with them or not, we all waited up, and then retired to the kitchen for a great party round the kitchen table, with the cook's beautiful brown buns and soup. Sybil would just go on talking.

'Lewis was a very quiet man, wise and rather withdrawn, with a great sense of humour. He was a very fine china mender, and whenever he stayed, we used to put up big trestle tables in the library. Any broken china would be brought in, and there Lewis would spend all his time mending. The china had come into the family in the

1790s, through the marriage of Maria Wilson of Kent to Sir John Trevelyan, as part of her dowry. I think her uncle was in the East India Company, and I suspect that is why we have so much Chinese china. The legend says that three shiploads of it sank in the Tyne, but goodness knows we've got enough.

'My uncle, G M Trevelyan, the historian, and a young friend of his, Arthur Bryant, also an historian, came up for my wedding – it was the first big function after we moved to Wallington. There was a wedding feast in the dining room – I think there were about forty of us. It was September 3rd, Cromwell's day, and my uncle was asked to propose the bride's health. It being Cromwell's day, he made a tremendous speech about Cromwell and then sat down. And because Arthur Bryant was the other guest of note, he was asked to follow. He, being a Cavalier, made a tremendous Cavalier speech, and then sat down, among growing amusement from the assembled company, because neither had mentioned the bride! I was awfully pleased, because I am a great Cromwellian myself. However, it ended happily: someone did propose my health in the end.'

Margaret, Countess of Lichfield

'I always remember a very masculine woman in a very loud check coat being brought over to Whittington by the Shuttleworths from Barbon. She sat and crossed her legs, which was unheard-of for a woman in those days. Also she smoked. Everybody was shocked: ladies never smoked. And she said, "Ha, ha, ha" and made rather coarse jokes. I can see her now – she had a face like a horse, with a huge nose, bloodshot eyes and rather rotten yellow teeth. Her hat wouldn't stay in the right place; her very ugly hair was parted in the middle and tied in an untidy knob at the back. Her clothes were really monstrous: she had a man's high collar and tie. I should imagine she was a lesbian, rather before they were known about.

'After she and the Shuttleworths had gone, my father and mother, my stepfather-to-be and all the people staying in the house all talked non-stop about this woman. Not only after she had gone, but for days afterwards. She was an authoress and supposed to be brilliantly clever. The Shuttleworths went in for these very clever, eccentric people.

'In contrast to this masculine woman, there was a very feminine man, Ernest Thesiger. He was extraordinary. He came over wearing the most beautifully cut coat in a shade of violet – almost a frock coat. It came in at the waist and had a large, purple velvet collar. He had an enormous bunch of violets – there must have been forty or fifty of them – in his left lapel. Very pretty but thought too awful.

My father gave him one look, left the room and was not seen again until he had gone. My mother realised that he wasn't being a great success (I forget who else was staying), so she said to me, "Do take Mr Thesiger and show him the wild part of the garden." That was the part farthest from the house! Off I went and showed him all the things, and told him about the trees and how they had come from Canada and how my grandfather had brought all the seeds in his pocket. Like that type of man does, Mr Thesiger went into ecstasies. He picked things and smelt them with the most Mmmmm noise: "Smell this beautiful aroma. Oh, what an aroma!" Not what a lovely smell, but what an aroma. He was lovely to imitate: I know I did him for weeks afterwards whenever I picked anything in the garden – "Oh, what an aroma!"'

Loelia, Lady Lindsay of Dowhill (*formerly Duchess of Westminster*)

'It was considered frightfully *mal vu* for people to paint their faces. I remember the very first person who started it – Lady Bingham – was very much disapproved of. She was a great friend of my mother and father; she had a hat shop in Davies Street called Rose Bentin, which was the first kind of chic. She went to Paris every Season and bought masses of models, which one then had copied to match one's dresses. She came to lunch with my parents at St James's Palace wearing a hat full of artificial cherries bobbing about, and lipstick to match. When she left I remember my mother and father saying, "How could she do anything so dreadful, and anyway, if she was going to wear lipstick, why didn't she have a discreet colour, instead of cherry red?"'

Katherine, Vicountess Mersey

'My father was an extremely good fisherman, and loved shooting and hunting. He was a Member of Parliament before the first war, and then in the Irish Guards. After the war I seem to remember him always writing. He wrote five or six books based on the Bowood papers, which had never been sorted out or gone into, and he catalogued them. My vision of him is always bent over his writing-table with a pipe in his mouth, in a cloud of smoke, writing.'

Lady Mander

'The way we lived at Wightwick in the 1930s was not typical of what is generally thought of as country house life: devoted to sport (huntin' and fishin') and Saturday-to-Monday house-parties, with cucumber sandwiches on a silver salver for tea on the lawn at five o'clock. This was because, as a Liberal Member of Parliament, my husband, Geoffrey Mander, belonged to that special class of people living in largish houses in the country but out of tune with its pursuits, and, more important, its politics.

'Historically it has been one of the strengths of England's constitution that there have always been families, with as blue blood as others, who have been what would now be called "left wing" and considered eccentric for it by the majority. It is this element which has saved the country from the extreme revolutions abroad where aristocrats have been wiped out or forced into retirement from public life. In a very minor way we were part of the tradition which has included great names in politics, such as the Howards and the Aclands – to take examples from opposite ends of the country. They tended to go in for high thinking and plain living (often teetotal), though they had as many acres and servants as the estates running with theirs. London hostesses up to about the 1920s could not invite Liberals and Conservatives to the same parties, although the divisions between them were not nearly as great as they are to-day, when personal party feelings run far less high.'

Lady Mersey's grandmother, Lady Lansdowne, in the library at Bowood – also the favourite haunt of her father. 'My vision of him is always bent over his writing table with a pipe in his mouth, in a cloud of smoke, writing.'

Overleaf:
The library at Melford Hall. 'I think, on the whole, people in country houses had not very much idea of period furniture . . . Melford had a very strong Victorian feeling. It was *dark*.'

123

VIII A FEELING FOR

Melford Hall – Eaton Hall – Faringdon House – Balcarres – Dalkeith Palace – Boughton House – Drumlanrig Castle – Bowhill House – Balcombe Place – Greenlands – St Paul's Walden – Wallington House – West Wycombe Park – Badminton House – Wightwick Manor

THE PAST

THE COUNTRY HOUSE REMEMBERED

Ulla, Lady Hyde Parker

'"You can do what you like at Melford as long as you don't spend money," Willy told me. So I got going with my book on English furniture, which interested me immensely, and I got the various periods in my mind. I rescued some lovely, painted Hepplewhite chairs from the kitchenmaid's room. Most of the library chairs I fished out from the attic. The two Regency settees in the library were in the butler's room and in the footmen's room, buried in chintz covers. When I wanted to have them done up, I got the local upholsterer, who cared for antique furniture, here. He said, "You're not going to spend money on those, are you, my lady?" The *money* was £3! To like Regency furniture wasn't done then – nobody could see the beauty in our library.

'I think, on the whole, people in country houses had not much idea of period furniture. It was Jacobean and Elizabethan oak furniture, not at all beautiful, bulbous and uncomfortable. My husband's grandfather had collected an immense amount of antique furniture – heavy oak, the pieces one sees in the porch, and so on. A great deal of that was burnt in the fire – really a blessing in disguise! The fire destroyed probably half the pictures and furniture. The house was actually in a much better state after it. And, as in lots of country houses, there had been several sales. Yet the house was, by our standards, still full and comfortable.

'I think comfort meant a great deal. I'm thinking now of the great state bedroom, the Princess's Room (because the Princess of Wales had stayed here). It had this enormous bed, rather like the Bed of Ware. There was a sofa at the foot of it, with a shawl or rug on it, so that you could get comfortable. The bed had had the most beautiful Stuart needlework – so good that Queen Mary used to come and look at it, and was rather longing to have the needlework. My father-in-law never gave it to her. Instead the hangings were cut up by the head housemaid and made into matching dust covers for two big armchairs!

'Melford had a very strong Victorian feeling. It was *dark*. Most of the colour on the walls was terracotta: the hall was terracotta above the panelling, and all the way up the stairs. The iron railings – the banisters – between the gallery, were black; now they are pale grey. And olive green was very popular then.

'I've always been interested in interior colouring. I always longed to have Melford painted in pale colours. Because in Denmark we have to spend so much time in our homes in the winter, I think on the whole we feel more conscious of them and how they are arranged. We have a lot of light colours. When I did up the Victorian bedrooms here, I put white curtains under the muslin.'

The hall at Melford Hall, before and after Lady Hyde Parker arrived in England from Denmark. 'The hall was terracotta above the panelling, and all the way up the stairs.'

The drawing room before and after. 'I always longed to have Melford painted in pale colours.' The plasterwork round the pictures was destroyed when the room was gutted by fire during the Second World War.

'I bought quite a lot of furniture for Eaton in Chester. There were no proper dressing tables, no stools in front of the dressing tables, no lights. The only lights were on cords hanging from the middle of the ceiling, which are perfectly hopeless for make-up. I remember this huge room I was shown into to change in, the first time I went there – absolutely couldn't see your face at all. I put a minimum of five lamps to a bedroom, and with the shades and all that, it really was a big job.

'I pretty well rearranged everything in the house. Bendor was wonderful about it. I don't think, looking back on it, that I made a particularly good job of it. I think I had very bad taste, really. It was the taste of the age, which was bad. Between the wars taste was bad. Perhaps "bad" is the wrong word – unimaginative would be more accurate. There was not the interest in interior decoration in the 1920s that there is now. Unlike today, when decorators are two a penny, there were very few, and no magazines like *House and Garden* and *Interiors* to give people ideas. The great breakthrough in imaginative decoration came with the late John Fowler, whose knowledge and taste were supreme.

'The most famous firm was Lenygon: most of the grand houses were done up by them. Their speciality was painting the invariable panelled drawing room a colour halfway between blue and green. If one was short of conversation, which I always was, one could ask one's neighbour if they thought the colour was blue or green. That was always good for a long discussion! The bedrooms would be peach-coloured – always.

'In the 1930s, fashion changed: to white rooms, imitating Syrie Maugham's famous drawing room in Chelsea. Then the pickling craze set in with a vengeance. Everything was pickled, regardless of suitability: you had to hang on to your beautifully polished Chippendale table, or it would be pickled in a trice. One infuriated husband had to have all his ancestral Romney and Gainsborough portrait frames regilded at vast expense, as his wife had had them stripped – it was a disaster, they were never as handsome again.'

Loelia, Lady Lindsay of Dowhill *(formerly Duchess of Westminster)*

'Gerald Berners was a highly cultivated man. I don't suppose he'd read as much about furniture and decoration as someone like Jim Lees-Milne, but I think he knew an awful lot by instinct, and by knowledge. Betjeman was very much in this *galère*, of course. He obviously did know a vast amount, but I don't think then he would have talked about it much. I think he would have gone to Rousham, for instance, for the fun, not to look at the architecture or the park

Lady Harrod

Right:
A bathroom at Eaton designed for the Duchess of Westminster. 'There was not the interest in interior decoration that there is now.'

Below:
The Duchess of Westminster at Kylestrome. The bed tester, with the arms of the Ponsonbys and the Grosvenors, was executed by her.

or the temple of worthies. At Faringdon you never saw anything being done, or talked about. It was absolutely unlike what one thinks of as "decorated" houses; it seemed absolutely natural.'

'I was brought up, by my father and my mama, very much in the artistic world. I had what I call an *oeil* to see and perceive all sorts of dates, and appreciate them. Other people might not have cottoned on so soon about the virtues of the Victorian age and the great thing about Victoriana, which was craftsmanship. We were very involved in the revival of the Royal Pavilion, which, as you know, hazarded being pulled down at one time. It was considered absolutely outrageous, even by my mother-in-law (who celebrated her 100th birthday recently). Of course now we embrace Art Nouveau and Art Deco, which even I did not particularly fancy at the time. People then thought Victorian buildings were in very bad taste. I can remember people saying, "So-and-So's bought the most ghastly Victorian house," and then they'd look at me and say, "Oh, I'm sorry." I think the whole thing comes back to people educated with an eye to symmetry. Victorian designs were not symmetrical. They were definitely going back to the mediaeval or the Renaissance. They were not easy houses to arrange, and of course a lot of Victorian houses were made inconveniently large.'

Anne, Countess of Rosse

'The care of the books at Balcarres was a family affair. For both my husband and my father-in-law, looking after the books was their recreation, and they both sat up far into the night studying, making notes, arranging and enjoying them. The rest of us helped with the oiling and airing, dusting and cleaning, and though lacking knowledge, derived pleasure in caring for them.'

Mary, Countess of Crawford and Balcarres

'When I first came to Boughton in 1936, everything was fairly primitive. And at Drumlanrig and Bowhill, the kitchens were miles and miles away; we brought them into the centre of the house, into the still rooms, and made the still rooms the kitchens.

'There was very little central heating in the houses in those days, awfully little. And one never thought of having a fire in one's bedroom, ever. At Drumlanrig there's still no central heating in the bedrooms, at all, and very very few bathrooms. There was very little luxury. We were lucky enough to have one or two bathrooms at Drumlanrig, because the house had been a hospital in the 1914–18

Mary, Duchess of Buccleuch

war, so that it had been given a certain amount of hot water. We wouldn't have had bathrooms otherwise. Electric light was just coming in when I first married, in 1921, but not many bedrooms had bedside lights; one had a light in the middle of the ceiling. Even at Holyrood there was never a bedside light: one had to climb out of bed to put the light out. You'd go miles down a passage to a communal bathroom. They had all the ambassadors in the world staying for all these great occasions in Edinburgh – they couldn't get over having to queue up for baths and finding no light beside their bed.

'The Monmouth things were scattered all over the place. A great number of them, of course, were at Dalkeith and did not even see the light of day – they were just pushed into the attics, and have only recently been resurrected. The only things that were well catalogued were the muniments. In all the houses – Boughton, Drumlanrig and Bowhill – there have been muniment rooms, and actually I think they were kept well. The great Edinburgh literary museum kept a very close watch on all our papers. We never had a whole-time archivist – there was instead a very erudite professor from Edinburgh who also worked at Boughton.

'The marvellous pictures were taken for granted. It was considered a bit vulgar then to know about one's possessions. You didn't talk about works of art. And only comparatively recently have various works of art come to light; many of the pictures weren't even identified before. A lot was inherited. Four different families merged – the Buccleuchs, the Queensberrys, the Montagus and Monmouth himself (godson of Louis XIV). We got a great deal through him. The great collector was nineteenth-century. He collected the miniatures, 800 of them; they were all in London and were moved up during the war to Drumlanrig.'

Lady Burrell

'My mother did most of the redecoration of Balcombe herself. If she did anything major, she went to young Mr Turner Lord, because she liked him, and because his firm in Mount Street had always done the repairs in Upper Grosvenor Street. She improved the house enormously, abolishing all the white lincrusta, and putting Cordoba leather round one of the rooms. She liked old furniture, which she largely collected herself. Although my grandmother had given her an enormous amount, she was always buying things.'

Patricia, Viscountess Hambleden

'My husband and I did a certain amount of decorating at Greenlands when we first went there, but nothing structural. The house already had central heating; it was rather inadequate, but we didn't do anything more to it. Strangely enough, there were a lot of bathrooms, which was very odd in those days. The only thing we did do outside was to make the conservatory into a sort of open loggia, where we used to have meals in the summer.'

'When I came, there were two bathrooms for twenty-five bedrooms, and another had been made for the Duke and Duchess of York, when they came to stay with us. The factor, always out to save money, thought what the builder was proposing to do was very extravagant, that it could be done much cheaper, so he put another bath in the same room. After a partition had been put in it, that became the ladies' bathroom! It had no ventilation, so one had to swing the door forwards and backwards to get rid of the steam. We put in four new bathrooms. We also rewired the house, which meant a certain amount of upheaval, and we made some structural changes. We changed the billiard room as well, because Lord Strathmore had taken the billiard table with him to the house that they went to in Hertfordshire.'

Lady Bowes Lyon

'Wallington had been very well furnished with Morris things by my grandmother, Lady Caroline, in about 1903. She had papered a great number of the rooms with Morris wallpapers, and astonishingly good they were; and she had put Morris curtains in the great rooms – not of course the same date as the rooms, but very handsome. And she covered the sofa and chairs in the drawing room with Morris Peacock material. My grandmother was a very skilled embroideress and extraordinarily artistic herself. When she was in London during the 1890s, she used to go to the Morris shop and choose silks and patterns of some of the May Morris designs and do them. They are the most beautiful bits of embroidery—we have still got them in the house at Wallington.

'My mother was very careful to preserve everything my grandmother had done in the house, while my father bought one thing that was absolutely right – that great Burne-Jones pastel cartoon of the lover coming into the garden. It was actually done for my mother's father's sister, who did the embroidery of the Romance of the Rose for another family house, Rounton Grange in Yorkshire – this was the cartoon for it. I think my father may even have bought it from Burne-Jones himself. It was his first present to my mother when they got married.'

Mrs John Dower

**Helen, Lady
Dashwood**

'We modernised the plumbing and that sort of thing. We didn't have enough money to do very much. Sir Robert, Johnnie's father, had been very modern about the heating, luckily. He had put in a number of colossal but rather attractive Victorian radiators, which really weren't bad at all. He also put a billiard table in what is now the Palmyra Room. It had a marble floor, which Johnnie removed when he turned the room into a servants' hall and a telephone room; and he put a perfectly hideous light for the billiards above the table. (Francis restored all that, after the last war.)

'Johnnie made the old kitchen into a squash court, in about 1926. It was exactly the right size, so you can see how huge it must have been. He made a great mistake, though, because he made the King's Room – my favourite room in the house – into the kitchen instead. It took me years before I could turn it back again.

'There were a great many rooms in the old servants' wing (which Francis pulled down after the Second World War). On one occasion, it seemed to me that some of the busts in the colonnade were missing, and the man I was talking to about it said, "Oh, I expect they will be in the Bust Room, my lady." "The Bust Room? Where's that?" He looked rather surprised and said, "Don't you know?" "No, I don't. Take me and show me." It was in the old wing – I'd lived in the house for fifteen years and I'd never known there was such a thing – in a bedroom, with a staircase leading out of it onto the second or third floor, and it was absolutely full of busts. Some of them were quite good.'

**The late Duke of
Beaufort**

'My wife and I married in 1923 and we went to live in a house in the village called The Cottage. My father died a year later: my mother moved down to The Cottage and we moved straight up to the big house. It was in very good order. There were plenty of servants, both male and female, and except for the occasional repairs, things which occur in any big house – painting and patching up some of the ceilings – there was really very little we had to do. My father had put in all the bathrooms that there are now. We did put in a certain amount of central heating, especially in some of the rooms which were not used a lot. We put in the electricity in 1934 – it was quite a job.'

Lady Mander

'When I married and first came to Wightwick in the 1930s, I regarded the place as old-fashioned and uncomfortable – which it was, and is – but as I was much more interested in our small house in Westmins-

Above:
At West Wycombe, 'Johnnie made a great mistake, because he made the King's Room – my favourite room in the house – into the kitchen.'

Left:
'It took me years before I could turn it back again' – Lady Dashwood and the children helping to restore the ceiling of the King's Room.

ter I made no attempt to "do Wightwick over". This was lucky, as it meant that when the National Trust accepted it later very little that was original had been changed.

'The house was built in 1887 and 1901, a monument to Victorian standards of conspicuous inconvenience, which meant that it was prestigious to make no concessions to easy running. If coal had to come from an outside coal house, there was male staff to bring it in and maids to put lumps on the fire when the bell was rung for them. Bathrooms or running water in bedrooms were unnecessary when there were housemaids to carry up brass cans of hot water, and so long as the smell of cooking was kept from the delicate nostrils of guests it did not matter how far food had to be carried from the kitchens. In a genuine mediaeval house the buttery would have been across the way from the hall, as it is in colleges, not a knight's move along a passage, as in our mock-Tudor design. Even now, with my small kitchen converted from the pantry devoted to washing the silver, there are still two steps down to the morning room, which makes it impossible to employ a labour-saving trolley.

'All the windows had casement curtains, which made them darker than they are now. In the 1930s, all those were torn down. Now they all have to go back. There wasn't all this thing then about conservation; the Trust has gone too far really. People's watercolours just hung on the walls then; frankly, it was luck if they didn't fade. We wanted more light, so we got rid of the curtains.

'When my husband first considered trying to sell the property in the 1920s, it was described in the *Country Life* advertisement of November 27th, 1920, as "one of the most unique (*sic*) half-timbered houses in England combining medieval atmosphere and modern convenience in keeping with the finest traditions of Jacobean (*sic*) domestic architecture" – which shows that estate agents' special language doesn't change. My husband was still anxious to find a solution to it in the 1930s when it was even more difficult and expensive to run and we were both away so much in London. Happily it was on a walking tour of the Roman Wall that we stayed at Wallington, where Sir Charles Trevelyan (another "eccentric" family!) suggested we offer it to the National Trust. Although we thought nothing so comparatively modern and unfashionable could be accepted, we applied. The Trust in 1937, after some deliberation, took the forward-looking view that the wheel of fashion would come full circle and the despised Victorian era be appreciated again, as indeed has proved to be the case. The property was the first to be given absolutely in the lifetime of the donor and it was a step we never regretted. The house at once took on new life with its sense of security and we set

Opposite:
Sir Geoffrey and Lady Mander showing one of the William Morris tapestries to the Clement Attlees. Wightwick 'was predominantly connected with the work of William Morris and the firm he established.'

136

about acquiring things to add to original treasures. We were lucky in those years to get to know several descendants of the Pre-Raphaelites. We received many generous gifts, besides pictures on permanent loan, from those who were glad to find them appreciated and displayed for enjoyment. If only we had bought more then!

'As the house was predominantly connected with the work of William Morris and the firm he established, we were very pleased to welcome his daughter, May. Thrilled to hear of somewhere devoted to her father, she hired a car from Kelmscott with her companion, the famous Miss Lobb. At that time, before we had conducted tours, we put up explanatory notices on the walls. Beside the original Trellis wall-paper with its flowers and birds hung a label saying that the birds were by Philip Webb. She was most indignant: "My father could draw a bird as well as Philip Webb if he wanted to."

'Another Morris connection was Morris's secretary and recent director of the Fitzwilliam, Sir Sydney Cockerell. In his retirement he loved attending debates at the House, and would ring up early (too early after an all-night sitting) to ask for a ticket. My husband could always get him a place in the Distinguished Strangers' Gallery, where he would sit all day, bringing his lunch of penny buns in a paper bag. His bread-and-butter letter, as it were, of thanks would include strips of Morris' original designs for the Kelmscott Press.

'The friendship I cherish most is that with the Rossetti family. The contents of the house in St Johns' Wood, where Mrs Angeli and her sister (daughters of William Michael Rossetti) were living in the war, had a time bomb on the day they were about to leave for the country. Their precious pictures and other possessions were rescued by civil defence workers and stacked on the pavement outside. Mrs Angeli, who had nursed John Rothenstein on her knee as a baby, appealed to him as the then Director of the Tate Gallery, and he was able to send an ambulance for the things. They remained in the basement of the Gallery until after the War, when we asked Mrs Angeli if she would consider putting them on loan to Wightwick. The Tate parted with them without demur – not quite what would have happened in 1984 when the big Pre-Raphaelite Exhibition was held there.'

Opposite:
'I made no attempt to "do Wightwick over". This was lucky, as it meant that when the National Trust accepted it later very little that was original had to be changed.' In the drawing room, 'All the windows had casement curtains, which made them darker than they are now. In the 1930s, all those were torn down.'

Overleaf:
The formal parterre at Bowood. The wing and the house facing the camera have now been demolished.

IX THE GARDEN

Compton Beauchamp – Holker Hall – St Paul's Walden – Wallington House – Flete – Shoreham Place – Wilton House – West Wycombe Park – Oxburgh Hall – Melford Hall – Bartlow House – Faringdon House – Eaton Hall – Wightwick Manor – Goodwood House – Badminton House

**Mrs Richard
Cavendish**

'My father loved the garden at Compton Beauchamp so much that every time he arrived home, he never went into the house; he used to get out of the car and rush straight through the courtyard to see what had been happening. He knew all the great gardeners of the time – people like Fred Sterne – and I've got quite a lot of his gardening notes now.

'When I first got to Holker, there were five or six enormous greenhouses going full blast, and *malmaison* houses, and gardenia houses. But they all fell down during the Second World War. The head gardener was Mr Fenner, and my mother-in-law and he were tremendous friends. My children thought he was Mr McGregor, out of Beatrix Potter – he was a very frightening-looking man, but a brilliant gardener.

'My mother-in-law had been an excellent gardener, and so had her predecessor, Aunt Evie Devonshire. She got lovely plants from Bodnant, from Muncaster, and from Leonardslee – you name it. The gardeners there used to send her things, just saying, "I think this ought to be at Holker." She enjoyed all this tremendously, but crowded the plants slightly. We have such a legacy from those days; there are still a few of those incredibly good plants left at Holker.'

Lady Bowes Lyon

'When we had friends to stay for weekends at St Paul's Walden, unless they were rather elderly, we'd get them all working in the garden on some project. The weekend really focused around the garden.

'David and I planned it together. One of his great things was recreating the *allées*. The bones of the eighteenth-century garden were still there, but they had got so fantastically overgrown that we could hardly see the shape. We replanted the beech hedges where they had originally been. We bought £2-worth of beech trees – about 10,000 trees, I think – and grew them in the kitchen garden for four years. Now, when the hedges of the *allées* are cut, we reckon it must be twelve miles, cutting the four sides.

'We had a head gardener, Tebbetts, and I suppose about four kitchen garden staff. They grew all the vegetables, but their pride and joy was the double herbaceous border in the kitchen garden. They weren't pleasure gardeners, they were kitchen gardeners. An old fashioned gardener like Tebbetts would eye very carefully what his neighbours were doing at the Harvest Festival, to make sure that he had the biggest marrow. We always had to decorate the church, and the garden was opened for charity: I think we have opened the garden for the National Gardens Scheme for something like fifty years.'

Opposite, above:
'The bones of the eighteenth-century garden were still there, but they had got so fantastically overgrown that we could hardly see the shape. We replanted the beech hedges where they had originally been.'

Below, left:
A staircase cascading down a bank at St Paul's Walden.

Below, right:
Sir David Bowes-Lyon with his head gardener, Tebbetts (left).

'There was a very well-known head gardener, Edward Keith, at Wallington in my grandparents' day, and on into our day. He was a great sweet-pea grower and used to win major cups for them in the London shows. During the sweet-pea season, we always had the most wonderful array in the house, and when there were guests, Keith used to bring up little buttonholes of two sweet-peas and lay them out before breakfast, so that all adults went about with a buttonhole.

'Judging from old photographs, there were certainly four or five gardeners under Keith. He was also in charge of the great conservatory built by my grandfather, which he had developed from the much lower greenhouses and furnished with beautiful Italian things – a fountain, a marble seat, a marble font, and great earthenware tubs, which now hold fuschias.

'All we needed in the way of vegetables and fruit was produced in the kitchen garden, and the gardeners generally brought the vegetables and fruit the half mile up to the house. But there were so many strawberries and raspberries that we were allowed to go down to the garden whenever we wanted, to eat them and bring them by the basketful up to the house. My mother didn't have direct dealings with the gardeners. The cook would be told by them what vegetables there were, and she would then say, "Well, Keith says so-and-so . . ."

'My father was very interested in the garden; Wallington was already a great eighteenth-century garden when we took over. I used to go down to the garden a good deal – it was across a road. I remember one delicious, bucolic scene: we had a very nice friend, Edward North, staying. I remember seeing him sauntering up the main path of the garden; he was wearing a green tweed jacket and under one arm he had an enormous cabbage. He was walking very, very slowly, just looking at the flowers.'

Mrs John Dower

Opposite, above:
At Wallington, herbaceous borders were gradually replaced by grass.

Below:
'The great conservatory built by my grandfather, which he had developed from the much lower greenhouses and furnished with beautiful Italian things – a fountain, a marble font, and great earthenware tubs.'

The Hon Mrs John Mildmay White

'We only had twelve gardeners at Flete – some people had anything up to thirty – under a head gardener, who didn't really do very much except wander round seeing that others were doing what they should, though he used to do the skilled greenhouse work. If there was real trouble, something the head gardener couldn't cope with, he would go to the butler, and the butler would go to my father. It had to go through the right channels, but my father was the ultimate arbiter, even though he didn't know anything about gardening.

'Gardeners started at fourteen. If the head gardener was very keen to get them, he would sneak them away from school before that, and they would just be sent back to school on the days that the inspector was coming. So they came at about thirteen and a half. Even if their homes were in the village, they still had their midday meal cooked for them here, and they lived in the bothy – kept clean by a local woman – which adjoined the head gardener's house. I suppose this was in order that they should be to hand, because they used to start very early in the morning (5.45 in the summer), to open up the greenhouses; otherwise the sun ruined everything. They were allocated different jobs: two would do the greenhouses, others did the bedding-out or the vegetables. The head gardener would show them how to pot up and then, after they had done a certain amount, they would be promoted to a different job; but while they were at that job, they stuck to it.

'They grew all the vegetables for the house, and lovely peaches, grapes and nectarines. The owner of the house was never allowed to do any picking of peaches or grapes. I can remember getting the most fearful telling-off from the head gardener, because I had picked my own peach.*

'All our food was bought locally, and when we were in London all sorts of things used to come up from Flete. Twice a week the garden cart and garden horse used to go the four miles to Ivybridge station with large hampers of vegetables and things from the farm – chicken and eggs and cream and butter – and they would all come up by train to London.

'The gardeners had a weekend off every three weeks, but they didn't get bank holidays unless they asked for it. When I asked one of the gardeners why not everybody asked for it, he said, "Oh well, nobody thought about asking for it." On Saturdays, they had to work all day.

'Originally, all the flowers in the house were done by the gardeners. I used to go through all the seed lists for the flowers with the head gardener. He used to order the vegetable seeds, because he knew the sort of things we wanted, but I used to do all the planning of the borders with him. About 1930, people began to take an interest in how flowers were done, so I became rather keen on doing the flowers myself; I took it out of the hands of the two gardeners, although

Opposite, above:
Flete gardens open to the public. 'We only had twelve gardeners at Flete – some people had anything up to thirty.'

Below:
'Originally, all the flowers in the house were done by the gardeners . . . About 1930, people began to take an interest in how flowers were done, so I became rather keen on doing the flowers myself. I took it out of the hands of the two gardeners.'

---

* At Blandings Castle, Lord Emsworth experienced similar difficulties:

'As a general rule, the procedure for getting flowers out of Angus McAllister [his head gardener] was as follows. You waited till he was in one of his rare moods of complaisance, then you led the conversation gently round to the subject of interior decoration, and then, choosing your moment, you asked if he could possibly spare a few to be put in vases. The last thing you thought of doing was to charge in and start helping yourself.' (*Lord Emsworth and the Girl Friend*)

they still had to pick the flowers for me. I discovered recently that it wasn't a frightfully popular move, because they loved coming into the house to do them.

'At least it got them out of family prayers. Before, if the gardeners happened to be in the house doing the flowers, they had to attend. What they used to do when they heard the prayer bell go was to sneak out of the side door and disappear for a smoke under the terrace. Then, after a quarter of an hour, they would come back and finish off the flowers. They weren't too keen on attending prayers. The hymn used to be chosen by everyone in succession, until one of the hall boys chose a hymn called "I was a wandering sheep". Everyone was in fits of laughter; after that, it was vetted a bit more carefully.

'At Shoreham the garden was at its absolute peak in June and July. We had a beautiful rose garden – it was a wonderful place for growing roses – and lovely herbaceous borders, which I used to organise. At Flete the garden didn't really have to be at its peak till August. There we had an August and September and October sort of garden, an autumn garden. In the spring, of course, there were bulbs everywhere – one didn't have to *make* it especially spring-like; it just *was*.'

Patricia, Viscountess Hambleden

'When my grandfather was alive, there were fifty gardeners at Wilton. The head gardener was called Mr Chalice. He used to walk about eight miles round the entire garden every day, in a top hat and tails, but I don't think his hands ever got dirty. Each side of the bridge on the way to the two gardens, two trees were planted, and they were called Mr and Mrs Chalice. They are now, I'm sorry to say, quite enormous.'

Helen, Lady Dashwood

'Mr Jolivet, whose grandfather had worked at Versailles, designed the garden originally in the eighteenth century. Then Capability Brown, who was working nearby at Stowe, lent one of his men, Thomas Brown, to Sir Francis Dashwood, and he worked at West Wycombe for twenty years. It was a landscape garden: there was no pleasure garden and no herbaceous border. But my father-in-law and mother-in-law planted all sorts of silly middle-class flowers all round the house, which was perfectly crazy. Pictures taken about 1921 show rose standards around the colonnade, and when I arrived there were these little standards all around. They looked too silly for words, and didn't suit the Capability Brown design at all, so I

Above:
At West Wycombe, 'Mr Jolivet, whose grandfather had worked at Versailles, designed the garden originally in the eighteenth century.'
(*Country Life*)

Left:
A temple above a waterfall. 'It was a landscape garden: there was no pleasure garden and no herbaceous borders.'
(*Country Life*)

had them removed. I didn't reorganise the garden otherwise, even though what the gardeners grew was really horrid. I didn't know about gardens, so I let it go on as it was.'

Diana, Viscountess Gage

'Somebody asked Winnie, Duchess of Portland, how many gardeners they had. She couldn't remember. She sent for the head gardener. He had to send for somebody else.'

Mrs Violet Hartcup

'Nobody except myself cared about the the garden at Oxburgh. My uncle only cared about his trees; and my aunt never went into the garden. She wasn't a garden person at all, although she used to do the flowers. The garden started to run downhill during the first war; nobody was left except old men. And of course when a place goes down, it becomes impossible to get it up again. The wilderness had box hedging and gravel paths. It was kept up a bit, but the Second World War finished everything.

'The poor old head gardener, Coe, who had been at Oxburgh for years, was a very bad-tempered man. He came one day to my uncle and said, "Sir Henry, I can't grow flowers if you don't give me a greenhouse." (The previous one was falling down.) "Well, what's it going to cost?" my uncle asked. "£25." "Good gracious, what an awful lot of money!" But Coe got his greenhouse. Then the war came, and the first bombs fell quite close here, and one splintered the greenhouse to bits. My uncle was very amusing about it. "There! Nag, nag, nag, nag to build a greenhouse, and the whole thing is blown up by the blasted Germans."

'In those days people really did work – there were five in the garden and they didn't put down their tools if there was just a yard or two more to do. When Fred Greef, our new head gardener after Coe, who stayed with us thirty years, had a box of plants to bed out, he would never think of stopping just because it was four o'clock. They were brought up on the place and loved it. Things have changed. I don't blame anybody – it's just that life has changed.

'Fred Greef brought in the flowers for the house and for the chapel, and left them outside the pantry. Granny or I did them – there were always heaps of flowers. There was always a huge vegetable garden, too, with a marvellous strain of raspberries.

'When they were children, my mother and the others loved the kitchen garden. She was very trim and very agile: there was one particular apple tree in the garden, a russet, that her sisters and brothers used to make her climb to get the apples. If Grandpapa came along,

THE GARDEN

At Oxburgh, 'M'ladies' wood was perfectly charming. It had a stream, and a drawbridge which would pull up. There was a little waterfall down into the stream, then another waterfall – all beautifully kept, with trees, gravel paths and more box hedging.'

one of those on guard would say "Cooee!" Then all the rest – the cowards – would run off. She thought Grandfather would never notice her. But he came under the apple and said, "Come down if you can," and walked on. She felt so stupid. I remember the tree well; it was ploughed up during the Second World War.

'M'ladies' wood was perfectly charming. It had a stream, and a drawbridge which would pull up. There was a little waterfall down into the stream, then another waterfall – all beautifully kept, with trees, gravel paths and more box hedging. You could walk all the way round, over another little bridge. For an old lady like my grand-mother, the walk was enough. I did my lessons there, and my brother and I used to fish there for trout. I was always the lucky one; so we would change places, and then I'd catch one where he'd been all afternoon. It was just a matter of luck, or perhaps patience.'

Ulla, Lady Hyde Parker

'The head gardener at Melford, Pomfret, was in charge of four gardeners and the "boy". And under him they certainly were! We called him just Pomfret, but he was addressed and referred to as Mr Pomfret by the gardeners. In spite of his unimposing appearance, Pomfret had quite an air about him. How this was achieved, I often wondered. He was neither tall nor strongly built; he was pale, with pale hair and pale blue, rather red-rimmed eyes; and as the ovals of his eyes were set not horizontally but vertically, this gave him rather a mournful look. His long, pale, thin moustache drooped over his mouth and down either side to his chin. I don't think I ever saw a smile on his face or his eyes light up.

'It was Pomfret's dress which gave one the feeling that he was of importance, for he always wore a black bowler hat, a green baize apron covering the front of his black trousers and jacket, and a white shirt. From the large pocket in the front of his green apron hung pieces of raffia, and inside the pocket were his secateurs.

'In spite of working out of doors, he was pale-complexioned, but then he spent a great deal of time in his potting shed, making a mix-ture of sand loam and leaf mould, with a large heap on the table in front of him for potting up seedlings and plants, and in the green-houses and vineries regulating the ventilation, and debudding carnations.

'In the vineries there were two vines: one for the dark grapes and one for the white Muscatels. Pomfret would move about at ground level, or on ladders when the grapes were in bloom, with a stick in his hand, at the end of which was tied a rabbit tail. He would gently touch the tiny grape blooms with the tip of the tail and then touch another flower on a different bunch, pollinating the blooms so that they would bear fruit.

'He sowed seeds into boxes; then, when little plants appeared, he pricked them out into larger boxes and placed them in frames, which were kept open, or partly open, with shorter or longer pieces of wood placed between the frame and its glazed top, according to the weather and the season.

'He produced really beautiful carnations, orchids and exotic house plants out of his greenhouses. The pot plants were transferred, when they had reached their full beauty, to a large octagonal oak table, which stood just inside the front hall, on the right as you entered. It was covered with zinc trays made to fit, and these were filled with small pebbles, so that plants could be watered without causing damage to the table. The lovely bank of plants Pomfret filled the trays with created a screen, so that the hall was not open to view as soon as anybody stepped inside.

'Greenhouse flowers were all cut and brought into the various rooms daily at 10 am and arranged by Pomfret. The dining room table had priority: eight little crystal vases were filled with the finest carnations, orchids, or whatever the choice blooms were at that moment, and placed between the silver candlesticks. The butler had no say in this, nor in Pomfret's arrangement of peaches, pears, grapes, plums and apples, which were piled up in beautiful pyramids on the dessert dishes on the sideboard. Pomfret reigned supreme: no one dared interfere.

'If I took a peach from a wall while passing through the garden on a summer's day, Pomfret knew at once, and in spite of informing me most politely that one was missing, he managed to convey that he knew perfectly well who the culprit was and that he disapproved strongly. But how much better a newly-picked peach tastes still hot from the sun and eaten from hand, with its juice seeping through one's fingers, than served on a dessert plate, eaten with a fruit knife and fork!

'Early each summer, the wide border, which ran the whole length of the tall brick wall dividing the kitchen garden from the moat and the road, was planted out with annual flowers of various heights and colours. The number of flowers raised from seed each year was quite amazing. There were larkspur, zinnias, helichrysum, petunias, love-in-a-mist, scabias, lobelias, alyssum, foxgloves (at the back), mignonettes, African marigolds, antirrhinum and so on. They were planted out in great clumps like a herbaceous border. How wonderful it looked when they all came into flower.

'Pomfret was always rather late in getting these flowers planted

'The pot plants were transferred when they had reached their full beauty to a large octagonal table which stood just inside the front hall on the right as you entered.'

Overleaf, left:
'In the spring there were thousands of bulbs, thousands of them, mostly daffodils. It was beautiful.'

Right:
Lady Hyde Parker's mother and son by the garden pavilion wall at Melford Hall. 'Early each summer, the wide border, which ran the whole length of the tall brick wall . . . was planted out with annual flowers of various heights and colours.'

153

out. The sun would shine more strongly each day and the ground would become drier and drier. My mother, who loved gardening, would say to me, "Really, dearest, you must tell Pomfret to get his plants out; they will never survive in this weather. Their roots are growing out of the bottom of their boxes." I would then say to Pomfret, "The annuals ought to go out, Pomfret." His answer was always, "All in good time, your ladyship, all in good time." And I would reply, "But you will never be able to water that long bed, and the plants will need no end of water to survive." "Ah, my lady, it will work out, it will all work out." And, sure enough, it always did. Pomfret at last would give orders to have plants put out. The soil would look like a desert, the sun would shine and the plants would droop, but, sure enough, that night it would pour and pour with rain, and after that the whole border would glow in gorgeous colours. This happened year after year. It was a great mystery how Pomfret knew it was going to rain when there was not one cloud to be seen in the clear blue sky.

'Pomfret and I only crossed swords once, and this was over moving a lovely, old-world, rose. I love and have always loved roses. I could see in my mind's eye just how beautiful that rose bush, with its great cream blooms just flushed with the palest pink, would look in the centre of a bed of roses, then on the west lawn. So I asked Pomfret to dig it up and plant it in the bed. In those days when ones' employees' replies only took three forms – "Yes, my lady", "No, my lady", or "Very good, my lady" – it gave me quite a shock when Pomfret replied, "But my lady, it cannot be done at this time of year – the rose is in bloom." I said, "You must dig a deep hole, fill it with water, then lift the rose with a great deal of earth round its roots and place it in the bed. Water it round the top as well, after more soil has been put round it and stamped down." Pomfret almost refused. I went into Willy's study, which was used as an office. His secretary was there, but I blurted out my order to Pomfret and his reply. Saying nothing, Willy got up from his chair by the desk, walked out of the room and onto the library steps, calling to Pomfret, who came and stood in front of him on the path. I had followed Willy and now stood beside him. Willy looked at Pomfret and said firmly, "Pomfret, when her ladyship gives you an order, you carry it out at once. If she asks you to plant the roses with their roots in the air, you do it. Is that understood?" "Very good, Sir William," was Pomfret's short answer, and the rose was moved at once.

'I did not know what to think of Willy's order. A strange feeling came over me: so, I had complete authority, this was clear; but was my knowledge really adequate? From that day onward, I ordered and received a weekly paper called *The Amateur Gardener*. I read it dutifully and also began reading books on gardening. But I never achieved Pomfret's knowledge. That was based not on books, but on years and years of experience; watching the wind, the sky and even the birds and the movement of tiny animals and insects. Still, I'm glad to say, the rose lived and bloomed year after year.

'On Sundays, Pomfret sang in the choir in Melford church, and processed in his white surplice at the end of the procession with the other senior men. He was always there without fail. Mrs Pomfret was never seen in church, and lived her life between the gardener's cottage and the apple house opposite, at the back of which she had her wash house and large copper in part of the same building. She brewed beer in this copper; from my boudoir window I could see her trotting backwards and forwards between these two buildings with a quick, wobbling gait, for she was bow-legged. She was a short, stout, dark-haired woman with a loud voice and a sharp tongue. My father-in-law before me had watched her with amusement, when, after a stroke, he had had to lie on a day bed in the boudoir, facing the window.

'In those days, the water mill was going strong, and carts drove up in front of the bridge with sacks of corn to be ground. The gardeners had to control the water in the stream with the sluice gate just inside our square pond, as this our ancient water level. Two great wooden bungs, at the end of long poles, were fitted tightly into two large openings in a great piece of wood fixed to the side of the pond, so that water could be let at will into or out of the river.

'June was the time we cut the reeds on the fish ponds; they were cut just under the water. That's how the ponds were kept clean, and it was beautiful, clear water. The gardeners did this tremendous work, going out in a boat, with waders. It took them ages. In the spring there were thousands of bulbs, thousands of them, mostly daffodils. It was beautiful. We only scythed when we saw about four inches of grass and were sure that the leaves of the daffodils had died down. If you cut the grass sooner, of course, it kills the bulbs. That's the great worry with modern machinery: it's much more difficult for shrubs and trees to reseed themselves these days, because the whole place is inevitably much tidier, in a different, mechanistic, sort of way.'

'After we took over Bartlow House in 1926, when my father-in-law died, we had only one gardener, Willy Albon, who, single-handed, kept everything in order: the lawns, the bedding on the terrace by

Mrs Charles Brocklebank

157

the house, and the large walled gardens. He mowed until dark on summer evenings with no overtime pay. His wages were about 30/- a week.'

Lady Harrod

'Gerald Berners didn't like any flowers near the house at Faringdon; there was no need, and anyway a lovely sweep of grass led from the house to the church. He once saw a flower and rubbed it out with his heel.'

Loelia, Lady Lindsay of Dowhill (*formerly Duchess of Westminster*)

'My love of gardening really developed at Eaton. Of course I never actually did anything myself; I never dug a hole with a trowel or put a bulb in or anything like that, but the head gardener there – Barnes, a Scotsman – was marvellous and creative, and fulfilled my extravagant plans.

'The garden was beautifully laid out, partly by Gertrude Jekyll. There was a huge lake: to walk down to the lake, round it and up again took one half an hour. In the middle was quite a big island, with trees, in which we put some wild monkeys. They really were wild, the most wonderful acrobats I've ever seen, flinging themselves from one branch to another. Only one ever missed – and broke its arm. When the lake froze round the island and people skatèd, there was a great deal of trying to get the monkeys to come and hold hands and skate, without much success. I did plant a lot of rare rhododendrons; the soil was right for them.

'The remarkable thing about the kitchen garden were the glass houses which ran along its sides – they were Crystal Palace size. Camellia trees grew on one huge long brick wall and flowered so that you could scarcely put a pin between the blossoms. They were cut every year for one of the table decorations for the National party: the whole thing was done with these lovely, large, pink reticulata camellias. Then the camellias would be swept away, and the whole table done with orchids – something differerent all four nights. I said to somebody, "What happens to all these wonderful flowers?" "Oh, I don't know; they're thrown out, I suppose." So then I organised that they went to the hospital.

'When we weren't there, we opened the gardens. I used to decide what I'd open them for, to make a nice lot of money for the different charities, and the whole of Chester would pour out to see them.

'Years after I left Eaton, a rather charming and funny thing happened to me. I was staying at Saighton with Sally, Duchess of Westminster, and she said to me, "Would you like to come and walk over

Opposite, above:
At Eaton, 'the garden was beautifully laid out – partly by Gertrude Jekyll.'

Below:
'The remarkable thing about the kitchen garden were the glass houses . . . Camellia trees grew on one huge long brick wall and flowered so that you could scarcely put a pin between the blossoms.'

the garden?" I was very keen to do so, as I was interested to see what had happened to things I'd planted. We were walking in a leisurely fashion past the remains of the house, which had been pulled down, and there was an old man picking up leaves between two boards. Sally said to me, "Go and talk to him; he was there in your time." I went over rather self-consciously, and said, "Oh, Jones, how lovely to see you again, and how things have changed since I was here with you. It's rather painful to come back, because of course the gardens were so wonderful, weren't they, when I was here. I can't remember how many gardeners we had – thirty-five, wasn't it?" He looked very puzzled and then said, "Oh, I see what you mean, Your Grace; not counting the glass." So I said, "Oh, of course, not counting the glass. Yes, how many did we have there?" "Eighteen." So, thirty-five and eighteen.'

Lady Mander

'Knowing Wightwick was secure after the National Trust had agreed to take it on, we took a new interest in the gardens and grounds. the earlier part on the west side was designed by Alfred Parsons in the late 1880s, followed by Mawson's terrace and landscaping on the south side about 1910. These are now famous names for enthusiasts of garden history. During the war, the flowerbeds were dug up for vegetables (Lance Thirkell, son of the novelist, and grandson of Burne-Jones, who was stationed nearby, came over to help). For reasons of economy these were not all replaced later, but we collected plants from the gardens of famous people for the beds below the terrace: from Kelmscott, from Kempe's garden at Lindfield, and also from Dickens' home at Gads Hill and Tennyson's at Farringford. Francis Meynell, well known for his work as a private press printer, gave us an iris that Meredith had called "Alicia" after Mrs Meynell. There are also trees that were planted by well-known politicians, such as Herbert Samuel and Clement Attlee, and one in memory of Stanley Baldwin, the Prime Minister, by his son, the third Earl. There was a special local connection, for four daughters of a Wolverhampton minister called Macdonald made remarkable marriages: one to Sir Edward Burne-Jones, another to Alfred Baldwin, another to Edward Poynter, and the last one, Alice, to John Lockwood Kipling.'

Anne, Countess of Rosse

'At Birr Castle two rivers go past in the demesne, and so although the castle and the town are on lime, not peat, they bring in alluvial sand. That is how Michael and I, over the last fifty years, managed to raise all sorts of things that they thought would never grow on lime, like magnolias.'

'Goodwood had a kitchen garden, but it simply didn't work. I remember my father struggling with this huge garden and saying to me, "It's much better to go to a greengrocer, I'm afraid, and buy what you need." You can never grow a sufficient amount of one thing to make it viable: it's no good growing an acre of peas for a small household – you would never eat them – and if you do grow a whole acre of peas, you've got to find someone who's prepared to buy an indefinite amount off you.'

The Duke of Richmond and Gordon

Ben, gardener at Eaton, was known as 'the Immortal Cellini'.

Overleaf:
The chapel at Catholic Oxburgh. 'The history of Oxburgh is inextricably bound up with the Bedingfelds' Catholicism.'

X THE CHURCH

Flete – Melford Hall – Ickworth – Wightwick Manor – Greenlands – Bartlow House – Oxburgh Hall – Whittington

The Hon Mrs John Mildmay White

'We always went to church on Sunday, usually twice – at eight o'clock and again at eleven – and my father always read the lesson. No one else ever read it when he was there. He was never patron of the living, either at Flete or at Shoreham, thank goodness.

'Vicars were treated quite differently in those days. You never thought of calling your vicar by his first name, like you do now, although he was always coming to meals. If my father had been expected to call the vicar by his first name, he'd have thought it was the end of the world. I suppose the fact was that you hardly called anybody by their first names.'

Ulla, Lady Hyde Parker

'When my father-in-law came back from Barbados, where he had his first curacy, to take over the estate after the death of his elder brother, he used to preach at Melford. He could preach in broad Suffolk, and then the large church would be crowded, because he spoke their language.

'In those days people walked to church. Even when my father-in-law and mother-in-law were elderly and were driven everywhere, they would still walk to church. It was very much the thing to do – I think it was a mark of respect. My husband always wore a bowler, and on All Saints Day I remember both of us wearing black for church. In my mother-in-law's day, the whole staff had to come to church, and sit in two rows in front of our pews. They were not allowed to have decorations in their hats, and they were very carefully watched.

'The eleven o'clock service was very much for the gentry; the others went to evensong. Retired army officers would all turn up in the morning, since that was the thing to do. But my husband always made a great point of trying to be aware of both services. Willy and I would often go to evensong: "We'll sit at the back," he would say, "I like to worship with my men."

'Everybody was involved at Harvest Thanksgiving: Long Melford church holds 1100 and could well be almost full. They came with marvellous vegetables – enormous marrows and cabbages from the allotments and from their gardens, which had all been kept for our Thanksgiving. Everybody brought flowers and put them just how they liked, and the village children came with wild flowers and put them in jam jars. There was an endearing charm about it. It was spontaneous and it all rang so true. For Easter we grew special Easter lilies and a white lilac here in the greenhouses.'

Opposite:
Church fêtes at the big house – above, at Flete; below, at Melford Hall.

Lady Phyllis MacRae

'My father's brother was the parson – he had the parish of Horringer

and Ickworth – and he had to do what he was told. If my poor uncle, Lord Manners Hervey, tried to bring in any modern ideas, any new hymn or any new prayer, my father got up in church and protested. On one occasion, my uncle tried to say a prayer for the League of Nations when the League first started. My father jumped up and said, "Let's have no more of these mumbo-jumbo prayers, Manners. Go on, stick to the Book."'

Lady Mander

'All my husband's interests were in Pattingham, about five miles away from Wightwick, not the local church. His father had had a lot to do with Pattingham and had been great friends with the vicar there; and when my husband was High Sheriff, he made the Pattingham vicar his chaplain – at that time the High Sheriff and his chaplain had to be present at any hanging in Stafford. My husband is buried in the churchyard at Pattingham.

'I became involved with the Friends of Friendless Churches as Ivor Bulmer-Thomas was at Oxford with me and put me on the original committee, respresenting the agnostics. The idea had always been to have nonconformists and non-believers who were interested in the aesthetic side. I come from a long line of Cornish clergymen. Most churches in south Cornwall have a Grylls on the list of rectors, so I've always been interested intellectually, and Ivor thought I was the ideal person to represent that point of view. It's now become something that people are completely unselfconscious about: they love the buildings and they symbolise something which is important to them, but there's no suggestion that they've got to do good works in the parish, and pull their weight in such things as the Mother's Union. And it's the non-believers now who make the most fuss about the new prayer books and the liturgy, not the church-going people.'

Patricia, Viscountess Hambleden

'We were on friendly Christian name terms with the vicar at Greenlands. He used to come and have all sorts of meals. And of course my husband was patron of the living. There was a gentleman called Dr Brinton when we first married; when he retired it was my husband's job to choose the new vicar, and he became a friend of the family.'

Mary, Duchess of Buccleuch

'In Scotland, the landed families had – indeed still have – a great responsibility for all the Episcopalian churches, as the Anglican churches are called there. They had a great say in who was appointed, and they helped to induct the parson. We contributed towards the upkeep and maintenance of the church. By and large the Buccleuchs are Episcopalian, so that a great many of the churches in the south of Scotland, round the Borders, were built by my grandfather-in-law. It was an enormous responsibility, with something like twenty-one churches. We didn't have any say in the appointing of the minister in the Presbyterian (Church of Scotland) churches.'

'My father-in-law was a "squarson". He owned most of the village. Bartlow, where he lived, was formerly a small early nineteenth-century house, which had been greatly added to by him. Besides the church, the village consisted of a handful of cottages, the rectory, the agent's house, the laundry, the post office and the Three Hills Inn. The hills – in fact four in number – are Romano-British, the largest in western Europe except for Silbury. From the top of the largest hill you could look down on a microcosm: my father-in-law's greyhound kennels, the large walled garden with peach houses and greenhouses, and the little station beyond.

'He had ceased to have a parish when I knew him, but he took occasional services, and both married us and christened our children. He continued his sporting and agricultural interests, breeding dairy shorthorns (the Bartlow herd was well-known), white game-cocks and Jack Russell terriers. He also had a black, curly-coated retriever, Best. He often judged at the Royal Show and at Smithfield. His greyhounds were sold just before we married; his yacht had gone long before. For a time he rented a lodge in Scotland – Rowardennon on Loch Lomond – and after that he took other shoots.

'Among his other interests was collecting editions of Bewick and Surtees, and Herring prints of horses and farmyard scenes. He was also a connoisseur of wine. The cellars at Bartlow were remarkable, running the whole length of the old part of the house, with compartments like catacombs cut into the chalk. Port and champagne kept in them for years, but they were less good for claret. He made sloe gin from an old receipt, which involved boiling the gin on the large iron kitchen range.'

'The history of Oxburgh is inextricably bound up with the Bedingfelds' Catholicism. The whole village was Catholic. The parish church, which was Church of England, used to have congregations of only about ten, and sometimes only five.

Mrs Charles Brocklebank

'My father-in-law was a "squarson" . . . He continued his sporting and agricultural interests, breeding dairy shorthorns . . . white game-cocks and Jack Russell terriers.'

Mrs Violet Hartcup

167

'In the days when Mass wasn't allowed to be said, the priests stayed upstairs in the attics. When a priest was coming, the message carried – if he turned up here, they used to put linen to be dried on the shrubbery just near the house, and the village people knew that that meant there would be mass the next day.

'There was a great deal of animosity between the Church of England and the Church of Rome, because the Roman Catholics felt bitter about the way their churches had been taken over. And we weren't allowed to build churches. As a family we lost money, we lost every sort of thing, we were fined very heavily, and people risked their lives hiding those priests. The change came in the early nineteenth century, when the chapel was built.

'In my grandparents' day, no Roman Catholic was allowed in the army, or in any position at all, so what was a young man to do? If you wanted to get into the army you had to get out of England. My grandfather was for years in the Austrian Cavalry – he rather wanted to go to a Roman Catholic country, and as he was artistic, Austria appealed to him for that reason.

'In my day we always had priests, and there was a presbytery in the village. We had various priests, some nice, some not so nice. They always were get-at-able and looked after the village. They always came to lunch on Sunday. We had a priest right up to the last war.

'I was brought up by my grandmother, who was a very strict, but very fair, Catholic. I went to five convents, because my parents always thought I'd do better elsewhere. My mother's two sisters went to be nuns, so I went to one of their convents in Cavendish Square. I was always very much in favour of the Church of England, which astonished my family, because I said, "We are *bound* to go to Mass on Sunday, and most of my friends who are Church of England are not *bound* to do anything. They just go, and there's a great deal of difference."'

Margaret, Countess of Lichfield

'Reginald Farrer, a famous horticulturalist who lived at Ingleton Hall, Ingleborough, had been converted to Buddhism. He wanted to convert my mother, who was a deeply religious Christian, and he asked if he might have a meeting in the drawing room at Whittington, to talk to people about being a Buddhist. Poor Reginald had no roof to his mouth, and my mother, who had superb manners, never showed that she couldn't understand a word he was saying – although she sometimes used to laugh, and you can't laugh at something unless you know what it is about. Very few people would have understood a word he said.

THE CHURCH

'The other side of the river at Kirby Lonsdale lived Lady Bective, who was very fond of Reginald Farrer, so she consented to have the meeting in her drawing room. My mother went to it for the sake of Reginald. She was amazed at what a lot of other people went. They were all rather queer people, sort of artistic types, people my mother had never met before. They must have been local, because few people had motors: it was only horse distance that you could go.

'He made his speech and I don't suppose anyone understood him. He had, however, produced the most enormous number of Buddhist statues. They got one very heavy one in. Then they couldn't get it out! There was Lady Bective, stuck with the Buddha for years. She was very upset and said to my father, "Could we have Kit Hodgkin, your house carpenter, to come and move the Buddha? He's such a wonderful man, there's nothing he can't do." My father never let him do it, because he thought more fool her, for allowing it there in the first place.'

XI THE SERVANTS

Flete – Goodwood House – Bartlow House – Giffords Hall – Melford Hall – Wilton House – Greenlands – St Paul's Walden – Boughton House – Drumlanrig Castle – Dalkeith Palace – Bowhill House – Mellerstain – Wightwick Manor – Birr Castle – West Wycombe Park – Holker Hall – Eaton Hall – Wallington House – Badminton House

'Flete wasn't one of the really grand houses. The really grand houses had a butler and a groom of the chambers. I'm not quite sure what their various duties were. We had a butler and two footmen. Because our butler was six foot three and wouldn't have underlings taller than him, the footmen had to be over six foot but not more than six foot two.

'The footmen wore livery when there were parties. Otherwise, they wore their ordinary clothes until midday – they were given two suits a year, one darkish and one more tweedy, and were allowed to choose them themselves, so they were rather inclined to choose the sort of suits they would wear if they left. Then for luncheon they put on their livery coats, which had silver buttons and a nice striped waistcoat, rather like a wasp.

'They used to have to start at seven o'clock in the summer, though a bit later in the winter, in order to call visiting guests who hadn't brought valets, and to lay the breakfast. They did all the washing up of the dining room china in the pantry and polished all the silver there. There was a lift, operated by hand, so that the china and silver could be raised to the dining room immediately above. They did this all morning and had their lunch in the servants' hall at one o'clock, brought in from the kitchen. (A bell on the roof at Flete always rang at one o'clock for the servants' luncheon.) Their washing up was done by the hall boys. The footmen had alternate afternoons and evenings free, except when we had visitors. Whoever was on had to bring in tea, which was left ready in the kitchen so that the staff could relax until it was time to cook and serve dinner.

'My father and I would just have some tea on a tray in the library, but when we had visitors it was much more elaborate. According to numbers, one or more folding tables were brought in, put up and covered with the white damask linen tablecloths. Plates and knives were placed round, and at one end, where I sat, all the cups and saucers stood on a large silver tray. There was a silver tea caddy with a division down the middle; one side had India tea and the other China. There were two silver tea pots, and a huge silver tea kettle was brought in at the last moment full of boiling water, with a spirit lamp underneath it to keep the water hot. When we were all assembled, I made the tea and asked each guest which sort they preferred, and then poured it out. The cups were passed from hand to hand. The footmen withdrew after loading the table with scones, delicious croissants of Ma'am's (the cook's) making, several sorts of jam, real farm butter, Devonshire cream, a fruit cake and various other cakes and little chocolate buns.

'One of the oddest duties of the footmen was to take out the electric lamps on the tables every morning and bring them in again when

**The Hon Mrs John
Mildmay White**

Opposite:
The heir and the old retainer
– Lord Herbert with Ward,
the major-domo at Wilton.

171

it got dark. I can see them now, groping about under the big table in the library on their hands and knees, plugging in these lamps. It was curious; it must have been a relic of the old days when oil lamps were always taken out to be filled and trimmed. They were kept in the lamp room. The footmen also cleaned the men's clothes, in the tremendous brushing rooms downstairs – if visiting people didn't bring valets of their own. Then there were two hall boys, who stoked the boiler, cleaned the shoes, and brought in the meals for the staff and that sort of thing.

'The housekeeper, Mrs Carr, engaged all the housemaids – a head housemaid and four under-ones, two of whom were "travelling" ones. The head housemaid remained at Flete, and there was a head housemaid at Shoreham and one other, and a head housemaid in London and one other.

'Mrs Carr used to come and see my mother every morning, but by about 1929 my mother had fallen ill and was in a nursing home, so I really ran the house after that, and, because Mrs Carr had been there so long, I used to go and see her. My brother and I always called her "Carr Carr", as she had come to my mother as lady's maid, years before we were born. She was with us for about fifty years, and was the most wonderful peacemaker: everybody used to go to her with their troubles, and she used to calm them down.

'The butler, the housekeeper, my father's valet and my maid had their midday meal in the servants' hall. But breakfast, tea and supper they had in the housekeeper's room, which was extremely cosy. They were waited on: their food was brought up by one of the hall boys. As they'd all been with us for so long – they were really our greatest friends – my brother and I, when we were on our own, always used to have a glass of sherry in the housekeeper's room at half-past six. We got to know everything that was going on.

'My father was a money worrier, really, although we were averagely well off. He'd never been the faintest bit overdrawn; it would have killed him, I think. I can remember when I was first given a bank account: he told me that on no account must I ever, *ever* overdraw. I used to have to borrow from the butler before my next allowance came in, so as not to be overdrawn.

'My father had a tremendously devoted little valet called Brown – very funny and very nervous of my father. He kept all my father's clothes in the most wonderful order: my father was still wearing his going-away suit when he died sixty years later.

'The cook, Mrs Woodman, had four in the kitchen: first and second kitchenmaids, the scullerymaid and herself. The women didn't get their uniform – well, the kitchenmaids didn't. They had to get their own overalls and things. The cook and the first kitchenmaid wore white overalls. The second kitchenmaid and the scullerymaid wore blue with white collars.

'When we had visitors or a special party, there were various women who used to come in from outside. The kitchen was not very convenient, because there was never a sink in it; everything had to be carried out to the scullery to be washed up, and when vegetables were being cooked on the black range, the water had to be carried in. Mrs Woodman did all the shopping. She had a room off the kitchen, her little sanctuary, where she would see the local tradesmen. Some of them were favourites; they'd be given cups of tea and cake.

'Mrs Woodman was the most marvellous cook. She was the opposite of a peacemaker – she was very touchy, an absolute troublemaker. But she and Mr Brown were tremendous friends and used to go out a lot together. Their favourite sport was greyhound racing: Mrs Woodman owned racing greyhounds in London at the White City, and in Plymouth, where they ran at the City Stadium. My brother and I were invited along one evening, and were treated like princes, entirely because Mrs Woodman was such a successful owner. Her dog won the West of England cup – a sort of greyhound Derby.

'Afternoons were free for the kitchenmaids and housemaids. In the evening, the housemaids had to turn down the beds, close the curtains and put hot water in a brass jug, wrapped round with a towel to keep it warm – my father and I had our own bathrooms, so we didn't need this.

'My maid used to come with me when I went away – to Cliveden for Ascot or to stay with friends in other country houses. She and I always used to drive off together. At one house we went to, in Shropshire – friends of my father, where I'd never been before – my maid, who was very pretty, found herself in the drawing room, while I found myself in the back regions. She looked so much better than I did! It was great fun taking your maid: you found out what was going on. She told you everything she'd heard.

'Flete had about fifty bedrooms. All the housemaids and maidservants slept on the top floor; all the menservants in a separate wing; the stablemen in a bit which you could get into from the stable yard; the men guests in the bachelors' wing; the other visitors in the main house; and then we had our rooms.

'Local girls would very often come when they left school. They would usually stay about two years, then they would go to another big house, to what they would call "better themselves". The scullery maid would, for instance, go off as third kitchenmaid, the second kitchenmaid to be first kitchenmaid. That's how it worked. But the heads of staff stayed. The butler would have got paid about £100 a year, the cook £60, something like that – I wouldn't really know. I knew about cooking bills, but my father's secretary paid the other bills.

'My father always had a secretary, who was neither fish, nor flesh, nor fowl, nor good red herring. She had to have her meals brought to her by one of the hall boys in the "business room", where she worked. Though she was only seventeen when she came, she was always called Miss Pearce by my father; her successor, who remained for fifty years, was never anything but Miss Coyte to him.

'In a house the size of Flete there was always something which wanted mending, so attached to the house was a house carpenter, who had to do all the mending and wind all the clocks. He also ran the dynamo, which made electricity for the house and for the estate sawmill. He worked for us all his life – his father had been house carpenter before him. He was rather inventive, very musical and a great character. And there was always a plumber and various masons – every mason had a mate (you can't have a mason without a mate) – outside the house and quite a few other estate staff, such as woodmen.

'As well as a chauffeur, and numerous grooms and gardeners, there was also a laundry at Flete, about half a mile from the house, with laundrymaids. Between the wars, all the sheets from London used to come down to be laundered and sent back by train, with the vegetables and farm produce.

'In case anyone came to call, there would always be the butler or my father's valet and one footman about. I'm told that our servants were very lucky, because when we were by ourselves, with no one coming to dine, we only had one on duty – one footman and hall boy were off every other night. And the same really with the cook and the kitchen staff. They paired off – the cook and the second kitchenmaid, the first kitchenmaid and the scullerymaid – so they had quite a lot of time off. They were always going off to dances and things in the surrounding villages. If there was a special evening, most of them were always allowed to go. They would hire a taxi and off they would go. Some of the younger ones have told me that they used to refrain from coming back in a taxi, if it was in the village, because it was such fun walking back through the woods with the young footmen. Because there were so many of them, they all tell me now what fun they had: dances, and whist drives, and every kind of thing. Every year they had a big expedition – they went off to some local play or something like that. And there were always romances going on between them.

'Every Christmas, we used to have staff parties for about seventy people. We would have an enormous meal, and then sometimes an

Above:
Cheering the heir – Anthony Mildmay applauded at his coming-of-age by the children of Flete.

Left:
Anthony Mildmay receiving a hunting crop and cigarette box given by the estate at Flete.

entertainment. Then they all had a song which they used to sing. Each man had his own song, and you had to hear his song year after year. There was a time when all the estate men used to get a round of beef and I think a plum pudding, which we used to dole out at the school. Somehow that got a bit embarrassing, I don't know why, so later they got money. Sometimes we had a summer school treat: races and games in the garden. This was for the Holbeton children, but we also had Christmas treats every year at Ermington and Kingston, and two other villages where we had land and a lot of cottages. These were held in the schools, as it was too far to bring the children to Flete. We had a huge tea, a Christmas tree with real candles and a footman standing by with a wet sponge on a stick to dowse anyone who caught fire. There were games after tea and every child got an orange and a bag of sweets at the end. And then we used to visit the old people who were ill in the almshouses and take them soup on Sundays after church.'

The Duke of Richmond and Gordon

'My mother and father lived first at Molcomb on the Goodwood estate, and they had £3000 a year, which in those days enabled them to look after four children, have horses for all four, two grooms, a car and a chauffeur, two gardeners, a cook, a butler, a footman, two housemaids, a nanny and a go-between nurserymaid. Wasn't bad, was it?

'Some servants lived in the house – in the end that faces east, overlooking the bottom of the garden – and plenty of them out of the house. Nanny lived upstairs. There were two rooms on the ground floor, beyond the front door on the right. Through the swing door on the right of the front door, the first room was the butler's pantry. Next was the servants' hall – a long room – and beyond that the kitchen. And then all sorts of outhouses outside the kitchen: sculleries and that sort of thing. And there were four cottages. The first was inhabited by Mr Wackford, the gardener, and I think one of his sons was the assistant gardener.

'Mr Johnson the groom lived in another of the cottages with his wife, his son Charles and twin daughters. He spoiled horse-riding for the whole lot of us, each one in turn. His idea of teaching us to ride was to take us up to the top of Halnaker Gallop, where he would line us up, pointing down the hill, and then crack his whip. Of course all our horses bolted. Invariably one of them swerved and bolted into the enormous beech wood. After that, one after another, we said we didn't want to ride any more. My mother, who was a really brilliant horsewoman and had absolutely no fear, couldn't understand it, to her dying day. I always said, when I went up to Oxford, that the reason my brother and I took to riding fast motor-bicycles was that we found that at least we could stop them.

'In the furthest cottage of all lived Mr and Mrs Kennet. Kennet was an enormous man – about six foot tall – who worked at the saw mill on the farm. He never worked in the house. His wife was about three foot high. Kennet is famous – there should really be a monument to him – because up the side of Hat Hill there are footprints called Kennet's Steps. Old man Kennet trod the same steps every day, so that he had worn stepping stones, a staircase, into the side of the hill.

'Marshall, the butler, a white-haired, splendid butler, a lovely man, never went to bed until we had. I said to him once, "I'm a bit worried about you. I want to see how far you walk." So I got one of those pedometers and put it in his pocket, and found he'd walked nineteen and a half miles in one day, all over the house. Amazing people, and they never complained. He died with us: overwork, I should think.

'My grandfather died in January 1928 – about a month after we married. Then, of course, my father and mother moved bodily to Goodwood. They disposed of the whole of the immense staff and ran the house with a staff of twenty-five. When we lived at Goodwood, we cut down to fifteen.

'One of the saddest things that's happened at Goodwood in recent times is that what was called "the gang" was dispensed with. The gang were pensioners. Instead of saying, "Well, thanks for all you've done, here's a bob, be off," and being suddenly whisked off into the Land of Nod and being really miserable, they would join the gang. This would mean that they would be seen round the house or the park, sweeping up the odd leaf or weeding when they felt like it. They all had their bicycles, and they were blissfully happy. Old McCarthy, who had been a very indifferent keeper and had lived in the Hatfield cottages, was always to be seen sweeping round the stable yard. About that time of year one time, I said, "Old Tom, you've got a busy job on there: the leaves are coming down smartish." "Oh," he said, "I was only saying to Leonard (another of the gang) this morning, 'We keep scratching around like a couple of old fowls' – but I don't know if he does much." I think practically all estates had their gang. There wasn't this thing of them all being pensioned off: they went on till they were jolly ill or died. I suppose what really happened was that when state old-age pensions came in, although they were practically nothing, the regulation was that you mustn't earn any extra money at all. So that's when it all stopped. Great mistake.

'My mother used to have a ghastly Christmas party for the servants, in the Stubbs Room – the long hall. One year, in about 1932, I should think, there was an enormous Christmas tree made of white cotton wool, and my cousin, the admiral, Sandy, had to get up on the ladder behind it, dressed as Father Christmas, and say, "I've got presents for all of you." He did this, and his beard caught on fire. He ran out of the room, through the hall, and all the way to the front door, followed by me and dear Charles Tilbury, the chauffeur. I managed to tackle him rugger-fashion just before he got to the front door, whereupon Charles Tilbury, who was just behind me, fully fifteen stone, fell on top of me! But I reckon we saved poor Sandy.

'Gordon North, the house carpenter, married one of the housemaids, Betty. She was gorgeous – so pretty. Gordon made every single thing in the house. If one wanted anything, one said, "Where's Gordon?" Gordon *was* Goodwood. He's just retired, which is ghastly, because he's been here since he was born. We gave a private party for him, which everybody on the estate came to. He enjoyed that very much.

'My brother, taken prisoner by the Germans in 1918 at the age of nineteen, was later killed fighting in Russia in 1919. He had returned from Germany in time for Christmas 1918, to the delight of all. My mother, proud of her gallant son, was keen to show him off to the neighbours after the early communion on Christmas Day.

The family went to bed on Christmas Eve with instructions that the car would depart at some early hour. The brother, of course, overslept. Car gone, he pondered on how to proceed, walked down the passage where the housemaids slept and found a bicycle. Walking the bike along a short cut, he was confronted by a high gate leading through a wood. "If I can get through here instead of going all round the road, I might just make it in time," he thought. The gate was locked, so he hurled the bike over it and climbed over. Landing the other side, he found he had buckled the front wheel, which spelt disaster for his plan. He then threw the bike back, put it over his shoulder and walked home defeated.*

'Too young then to attend the early communion service, I only

---

*The famous gate, in the flint wall to the Sealy wood by the stud farm (formerly the dairy), has been removed. It had great iron spikes on the top; whenever I passed by during the ensuing sixty-six years, I always saluted it.'

caught up with this drama at breakfast, where a dreadful rumpus took place. My mother, wildly frustrated at his non-attendance, had become near hysterical and was saying, "All I can say, darling, is you've broken my heart!" The brother, completely uncrushable, replied, "I don't know about that, but I do know one thing – that I have certainly broken the housemaid's bike!" Family dramas of that sort are not easily forgotten.

'In those times and at Goodwood, all the curtains, even the very big ones, were made by the housekeeper, as well as most of the chair covers. My wife's old lady's maid produced nightdresses, dressing gowns, underclothes and everything like that. Then, in the month of August when the family were always away, all the Goodwood carpets were taken up, hung over the great boughs of the huge cedar trees outside and beaten by hand. All the curtains were removed for cleaning and all the blankets went to the house laundry. Nothing ever went to an outside laundry. The laundry lady did all the net curtains and sheets. She was furious when we installed electric irons, much preferring the old irons heated on the tops of stoves and weighing tons.'

'The extraordinary thing was the value of money then: now, one could not afford to have twelve servants, plus chauffeur and nanny, and feed them all. My meat bill, today, for about two people is about the same as when one had the Giffords' household to feed.

Mrs Charles Brocklebank

'The servants got up so early. Everything had to be done before one appeared, and they were not to be seen after that, except when the butler came to announce a meal or the footman to make up a fire. One did not have to ring a bell – they just had to walk round and see the fires didn't go out.

'Willy Albon at Bartlow was a dedicated gardener, who kept the whole, quite extensive area in order, single-handed. He was often to be seen mowing the lawn until darkness fell. A hamper of vegetables was sent to us in London every week, listed in a beautiful hand by his wife, Jean.

'The gardeners got no overtime. Walter Ellum, at Giffords, even in the snow, would walk down, quite a long way, from his cottage, up to ten o'clock at night, to make up the boiler.

'One had very responsible head servants. The upper servants were harder on the young ones than the mistress of the house. I don't remember keeping eye on the morals of the household. The butler had to look after the menservants; the cook and head housemaid looked after the young servants. Some were very young – they went down to about sixteen or so – and they got small wages. They had to be in by ten o'clock.

'If they gave "notice", you knew that in a month's time you would have to get somebody else. It was sometimes done by getting a recommendation from a chef in another country house, but more usually from registry offices.

'At Bartlow the servants' hall did themselves very well. After the meat course, the head servants withdrew to another room to have their pudding. And in the days when servants had beer, off they went, carrying their beer with them to a different part of the house. English country house cooking before the war was about as good as you could have. At one time, one used to be able to send one's cook to somewhere like the Ritz or the Berkeley, where they could watch a particular dish being made. You gave the man ten bob for the privilege. But cooks generally learned by working under somebody else in the kitchen.

'For a short while – when we moved to Giffords – I had a secretary. She was good, and kept accounts and could engage staff. At Bartlow the staff were local, and there were no changes. At Giffords the staff came mostly from outside. They were nearly all resident.'

Ulla, Lady Hyde Parker

'The butler at Melford wore a morning coat, of course, and changed later into evening dress with a black tie. For the footmen, the livery was green and yellow, and they had long tail coats and crested silver buttons – buttons on the back on the long coat tails and more buttons on the front – and yellow and green striped waistcoats. The hall boy wore the same livery, but he had a little short jacket, a monkey jacket.

'When we had a ball here a firm in London, Searcy's, used to send down everything, and they had servants in red livery, with knee breeches and stockings. I said to my husband, "How lovely these men look," and he said, "That's how they used to be at Melford, but the war put a stop to that."

'The butler and the footmen wore white gloves only when they were serving dinner. On television I see that sometimes they wear gloves all the time, but I'm sure the menservants never wore gloves except at dinner. Outside the dining room anything handed to one of us was always on a salver.

'The housemaids wore striped cotton dresses and white caps, like little bonnets, in the mornings. In the afternoons they wore green alpaca dresses with frilly aprons, and frilly caps with green velvet ribbons through them.

'The upper servants were very strict with the under servants –

much stricter than we were. The butler told me that one of the footmen had had the cheek to ask if he could go to the pictures: "I said to him, 'You go round the house and look at the pictures here; that will do you more good.'"

'The upper servants trained the younger ones; for instance, the youngest housemaid would have to take the head housemaid a cup of tea in the morning, and the tray had to be just so, so that she learned how to do it that way. And the butler would train the footmen in their duties in the same way. So it was passed on from one generation of servants to another. I conferred with the cook, the head housemaid and the butler. If there were any complaints about any of the servants, the complaints went through the heads of department.

'The servants mostly came from the farms on the estate. The tenants' wives would come in with a timid young girl, who had just left school, asking if we would take her. We would find her somewhere to work and arrange how much money she should get: in those days a kitchenmaid was paid about £14 a year. We gave her the uniform, like the rest of the staff.

'The cook and the kitchenmaid were, of course, in the kitchen. You went down to the kitchen at ten o'clock, and by then the kitchen floor was spotlessly clean and the stove had been black-leaded, and all the brass knobs on the stove were shining. There was a long table where my mother-in-law would sit, and the cook would stand. They arranged the menus for the dining room and for the servants' meals. When the children came along, there was another menu for the nursery as well.

'I had to engage a cook for the first time two weeks after my marriage – I gave the old cook notice because she stole the game. I was very nervous, and I asked my husband what I should say. "Ask her if she can make a soufflé and pluck game and skin a hare – things like that." Long afterwards, she told me that I had asked her if she knew how to pluck a hare and skin the game. She came for a week's trial, and she and her husband worked here for forty-four years.

'When the cook and I had done the ordering, we'd go into the game cellar, where all the game hung – I loved it. Beyond that was the ham cellar. The hams were cured with a special receipt there was an old man who rubbed them with salt. I can see him standing at the big, wide stone sink rubbing the ham with salt. The hams were smoked with oak logs in a special cottage on the estate; it had a thatched roof with a huge chimney in the middle. In all the smoke people lived there! In the other cellar were all the bottled fruit and jams. It was all made here, in huge quantities: we thought nothing of making 150 pounds of marmalade at a time.

'Every week I had to give out the stores. I had the keys of the store room, and the butler would come for best candles for the drawing and dining rooms, and leathers for his silver and silver polish; and the cook would want next-best candles for the kitchen, and cleaning things, and soap; and the head housemaid would come to get candles for the maids' bedrooms, and brooms, and dusters, and polish. Most of the stores were ordered more or less wholesale from London about four times a year. They came by train and were fetched from the station in the pony trap.

'There were so many departments. I loved the laundry. In a Danish country house women were shown the laundry by the mistress of the house. She knew about it; it was part of her work, like Willy showing people the tractor. I don't think I ever took my guests out to the laundry, but I definitely went out to see how things were going, and I was interested. The stable yard has been pulled down, but it was an early Victorian building, and behind it was the laundry yard.

'In one room, which had sinks for rinsing and washboards, everything was washed by hand, boiled in an enormous copper. We washed about once a week. All the clothes were divided up, and put to soak the night before the washing day in various great tubs: all bed linen together, and all towels together, and all whites together, and all coloureds together. We started at the beginning of the week, on Monday; and had various soaps – brown salt soap and green salt soap, and soda (masses of soda they used), and then the fine white soap.

'Then everything was hung up to dry, either in the laundry yard, or inside the great long laundry. Wooden bars would be hoisted up and down and the clothes hung over them. Then there was an enormous mangle, about the size of a bed, or more, which stood in the airing room, where there were also wooden pulleys that went up and down. Certain things, like table linen, sheets and napkins, went into the mangle, so they hardly needed any ironing – they were just smoothed over lightly with an iron. The ironing was done in that room too; there were stoves with all the many irons. The early flat irons opened at the back, and you heated a piece of metal and put it in; but by then we already had the later ones, and you just had to heat the iron itself, take it with a cloth, and iron. The menservants had starched shirts and stiff collars, as well as Willy. I remember one old laundry woman who used to have a candle she rubbed the shirt collars with; and then there was an iron which was slightly rounded at the bottom to give it a polish.

'After everything had been washed and ironed, it was brought into the house and put into the airing cupboards. A well-trained house-maid would neatly pleat one's linen towels before hanging them over the towel horse or rail in one's bedroom and bathroom. Two linen towels were required per person, besides two bath towels, one large and one small. You had one "huckaback", linen towel, slightly rough, for your hands; and one "diaper", very smoothly woven and very fine. For the ladies this was often edged at one end only with lace, and this towel was for one's face.

'I always kept my own linen. That is very Scandinavian – I don't know what most people do in England. But that was inbred in me. The linen cupboard is something you are very proud of, not only in Denmark, but I think also in France and in Spain: red ribbons round everything that's linen, and blue round everything that's cotton. And you have lace pinned on the edge of the shelves. I've still got it.

'The menservants lived on the ground floor and all the housemaids upstairs. The laundrymaids lived out, in the village, and came in daily. There was a chauffeur in one cottage, the gardener in a stable cottage, and the grooms in cottages close by. We had the head groom, Howard, living on the premises in a flat over the stables. Willy was very keen on breeding horses, and of course, when the foals were due, he and Howard were up all night. Howard worked here until he was seventy-odd; he was still looking after the horses. As he actually lay dying, he said, "Well, you know, my lady, we must get a pony for Master Richard; he must have a little pony." And I said, "That's right, Howard, and you'll go out with him." "That's it," he said, "we'll take him for a ride, my lady." And he died thinking of riding alongside Richard.

'When staff retired, they were given a cottage, but I don't think most of them wanted to retire. Wally Mills, who had worked here as a woodman, came to Melford when he was twelve and died at eighty-two. He couldn't read or write, but he was amazingly strong. As he got older, he was given less and less work – he just did what he could. When he got too old, he was grateful to go into the garden.

'At Christmas-time we entertained everybody that we employed. We had over a hundred for Christmas tea, which started at three o'clock. It was a thing that I introduced, because in Denmark we make a lot of our Christmas, and I said, "We must have big parties at Christmas." So we had all the men – all the ones who worked for us – and their wives and children. We were well over a hundred – 130 or 140 – and tea was laid out in the front hall. There was a big table for all the children, and an enormous Christmas tree, with a present for everybody. To begin with, everybody was very

THE COUNTRY HOUSE REMEMBERED

shy; then the party got going, and after they had had something
to eat and the children had had their presents, they loosened up and
got much gayer. And then the beer came, the barrels of beer, which
were out in the back, and the butler would start pouring it out. He
would then give everybody beer, the wives and the men, and they
became quite gay. There was a grand piano in the hall, and
somebody would play, and then they would start singing local Suffolk
songs and speechifying. There was a point at which Willy would say,
"Now, look, I think it's time for us to leave," and we used to go
up where we could look down the big staircase and see what was
going on. They got gayer and gayer until Willy felt it was time to
close. After they had made all the appropriate speeches to us and
thanked us, we all sang "God Save the King".'

Patricia, Viscountess Hambleden

'We had quite a big retinue of staff at Wilton – well, we had a butler,
and what was called a groom of the chambers. As far as I can make
out, all he did was to clean pens and put blotting paper and water
on all the writing tables; and he was also valet to my father. There
were various footmen and odd men.

'We had an absolutely marvellous butler, called Mr Smith. He
had been at Wilton ever since I could remember, and he was there
till he retired. He had two very successful sons. He was a remarkable
man – he had everything under control and nothing ever worried
him. Everything was done impeccably. If he felt somebody was really
unsatisfactory, he would come and say, "I'm afraid George is no
good. I think you'd better get rid of him," and he would then find
somebody else. And the same for the housekeeper and cook.

'The menservants all had their livery, and when my mother and
father gave a coming-out ball for me, to which the Prince of Wales
came, they had very smart powdered wigs.

'My mother had two maids the whole of her life. They always
stayed till they retired or died. They were very very fond of her. She
was very stern and very strict with them, but extremely fair, and
they knew exactly where they were. My mother was too capable to
make her maid wait up, but I think some of the guests did. I remember the late Lady Curzon coming to stay, and it was very unfortunate,
because her make-up box for her face had gone on to Taunton, and
so she couldn't come down to dinner that night; everybody was very
put out.

'In every bedroom you always had a bell, so that the bell was on
the same circuit as your maid. I can see the bells now: they were
numbered 1, 2, 3, 4, 5, 6, and the maid went to the room that

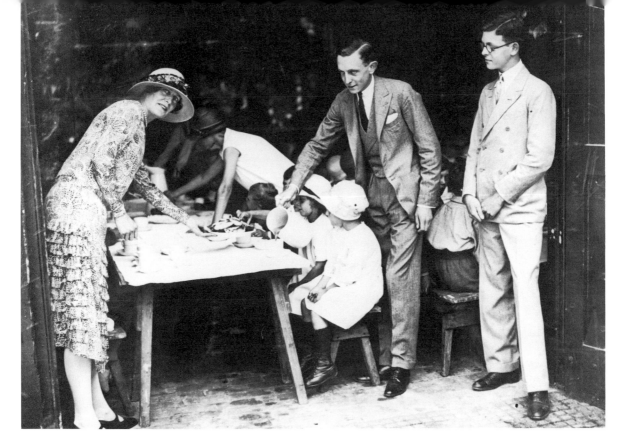

Above:
At a party for the tenants at Wilton, the Countess of Pembroke and her sons pour the squash.

Left:
Lord Pembroke with Deady, the Herberts' Nanny for generations.

belonged to the bell. The top floor was known as Maiden Lane, and the bottom as Bachelors' Row. The bell in my bedroom rang directly into my maid's room – No 2 Maiden Lane – and the maid would come padding along. There was another thing: nearly every bathroom had a bell, in case you fell down in the bath or something. And the bells were all connected up.

'There was a bell next to all the fireplaces, too: they were all very pretty, with beautiful brass coats of arms. You rang the bell to ask the footman to put more wood on the fire, or to bring more wood in, or to empty the ashtrays. You didn't empty them yourself – they were always removed and taken out of the room. The footmen would never knock on the door like they do in modern television productions; they just appeared, because you'd rung the bell.

'Housework at Wilton was a mammoth task – you just had brushes, brooms, dustpans. Unless you got huge great ladders on wheels, you couldn't clean the Double Cube Room, with all those swags and things. Now and then, every so many years, it has to be cleaned professionally; otherwise it's long feather dusters on canes, and you can't get to the top even then.

'There were two men whose entire job was to do the lamps. They used to carry them into the library, the drawing room, the sitting room, the Double Cube, the Single Cube, and take them out every morning to clean the wicks. We also had a man who rushed up and down the cloisters polishing the parquet floors. He was a gentleman called Sinka, who happened to be a Russian, captured in the Crimea and brought back as a little boy by our troops, because he had nobody to look after him (Sinka means "child" in Russian). He eventually lived at Wilton and became Mr Sinka; he married and had several children and his descendants live, I think, somewhere in Somerset. As a small child I remember Mr Sinka well.

'We had our laundry at Wilton, and very nice laundrymaids, who lived there and did all the laundry and the washing. Outside the house we had saw mills. A lot of men were employed in the mills, because there were extensive woods around. There was also a house carpenter – his entire job was mending anything that went wrong in the house; it was a full-time job. Then there was a plumber belonging to the estate. A gentleman used to come from Salisbury to wind the clocks. He came in every single week and wound all the clocks, which took him all day. We always wondered, as children, how he ever got it right, because by the time he got round it was three hours after he had arrived.

'If anybody on the estate was ill, it was immediately reported to the agent. There was a nice community feeling, even in those days.

We had very close connections with the town – my mother was mayor three times, and so was my father – and of course in many ways that was very useful, because a lot of people from the town would come in as dailies to help during busy times.

'The dance for the staff generally took place in the town hall in the town itself. I don't quite know why – well, it was a very big room, I suppose. We had the whole estate to it, and it was a very big estate in those days. We would hire a band and a caterer.

'When I married Billy in 1928, we moved into Greenlands straight away, because my father-in-law died just when we were engaged, and the wedding had to be put off. So we moved in, I suppose, in October 1928. Greenlands had quite a large farm in hand – a Jersey herd – and a vast amount of woods, great beech woods, which were nice for shooting. We did have quite a lot of staff. There was a butler – I think most people had butlers. I can only think of one person who had parlourmaids, and everybody rather noticed it. That was Lady Horner at Mells. She also had a most faithful parlourmaid in London. But on the whole I think it was butlers; it wasn't quite the thing to have parlourmaids. In fact, I remember my mother-in-law's brother, Lord Arran, being very upset after a financial crisis in 1932, saying, "Oh, Esther, the only thing left for us to do is to go abroad with parlourmaids," which was considered absolutely the end.

'My husband had a valet and there were footmen – they had a sort of uniform, with buckles and tails. When I appeared on the scene at Greenlands the housekeeper resented me to such an extent that she became extremely clever at making me look rather idiotic, like giving my grandest guests cotton sheets, unbeknownst to me, when we had linen ones. I'm glad to say she left after a bit and we didn't replace her. I got on very much better without her – with a charming old still-room maid and five housemaids.

'When I first married, I had as a maid a person who had been my brother's nanny, and she really looked after me. And then I had a splendid maid, who came to America when we went over there. I remember that we met her in New York; we were staying at a hotel, on about the fifteenth floor. It was a beautiful evening, and I said, "It's marvellous, New York. Isn't it a thrilling city?" and her reply was, "Much like any other city, milady".

'When the children were born, there was a nanny and a nursery-maid to start off with – two when there were four children – and a nursery boy. We didn't have laundrymaids in my day.

'In the kitchen there was a splendid, really very good cook – a charming lady called Mrs Robbins, the best type of English cook – with three under her. They used to come backwards and forwards to London every week. Mrs Robbins kept a beautiful book in which she used to write suggestions for the menu of the day. I used generally to go to her in the kitchen, because I detest breakfast in bed, so I always used to go down to see the menus; and the same in London.

'The bills were sorted out by a charming gentleman who was my husband's secretary, and he did the household accounts. The bills were sent to the estate office and they dealt with things like food.

'Some of the staff came quite young, but the housemaids very often moved from being third housemaid to go and be second housemaid somewhere else. Their duties started very early in the morning. There were no such things as hoovers – they used a dustpan and brush. The housemaids didn't wear uniforms – they just had nice print dresses and aprons.

'In my mother-in-law's time, all the staff had meals together in the servants' hall, but when the pudding came, the housekeeper and all the housemaids would process into the housekeeper's room. When we married, the housekeeper had her chums with her in her room.

'There was an odd man – two, one in London and one at Greenlands. Both, for some unknown reason, were called Percy. Those were actually their names – they were allowed to keep them. We also had a house carpenter and a clock man, who came in once a week. I think most houses did; it was an accepted fact that you couldn't ask somebody who didn't know about clocks to wind them.

'Of course we had a lot of gardeners – the head gardener had been there for ages. I can't remember how many. It wasn't a very big garden compared with many places. I used to do quite a lot of flowers myself, but they brought in all the beautiful pot plants – things like fuschias. They came into the house before breakfast to water them.

'We had a charming chauffeur, two in fact. One drove the enormous van, which looked rather like a hearse, to London each week with all the flowers and vegetables in it; originally he had been a groom, and then had learned to drive as well. Then there was our own chauffeur, who would drive the children to various things when we weren't driving ourselves. If it was a very long journey, then he would be given a tip.

'It always amazed me how many of the staff could write the most beautiful handwriting, with splendid spelling, having left school at twelve. They were also articulate conversationalists.

'Everybody had to have one day off a week, but as far as holidays were concerned, I think it was very meagre, about three weeks a year. They certainly never had weekends off, unless we happened to be away, in which case they could obviously do what they liked. Funnily enough, I think they had a rather jolly life downstairs – they always used to go out on expeditions to the river, for instance – because we were away in the middle of the week, so they were not overworked.

'They did have very nice rooms – it was only a two-storey house, so they weren't crowded up anywhere in particular. My husband was extremely far-seeing about things, and realised that you couldn't go on treating people the way they had been treated in the past.

'With the house staff and the garden and the woods and the farm and the stables, there really were a lot of people for our staff festivities. They all came with their wives or husbands. We always had a dance for the staff, and of course a Christmas party, at which all the children of the outside staff got presents as well, round the Christmas tree.

'As far as tipping was concerned, if you were a couple, the usual habit was for the gentleman to tip the butler, and the keeper something at the end of the day's shoot, while the lady, the wife, would leave some money on the dressing room table; probably a pound note – if you were very polite, with an envelope saying "many thanks", or just popped under an ashtray. Poor old cook never got anything: you see, she didn't appear, so they didn't bother about her. It was an awful shame. However, the cooks were paid quite well, I think. Once you became a very good cook, you were in rather a grand position, like the housekeeper.

'Some of the staff stayed with us for ever, until they retired – often they retired on the estate. Just before the last war, fortunately, my husband converted an old barn at Hambleden, on the estate, into five very nice cottages for the old people to retire to. Those who stayed were looked after for life; they tended to be very long-lived, so the houses used to get rather overcrowded occasionally.

'The estate was run at first by an agent, an old gentleman who had not only looked after my father-in-law, but had been with my grandfather-in-law before him. He was very old and very nice, and he ran the farm. It was rather difficult for my poor husband to get anything done the way he wanted: the agent considered he knew all about it, and did everything – if money didn't matter – quite efficiently. He was a great friend. He had a remarkable wife, who was an extremely capable lady and lived to just under a hundred. She was the most outspoken woman I've ever known: she used continually to come and tell me what I was doing right or wrong. A great character and great friends.'

'We didn't have a butler at St Paul's Walden – we had a parlourmaid, Nesbitt. She went through every department, and she was a formi-   **Lady Bowes Lyon** dable parlourmaid. Later (after the war) she became housekeeper and then cook. We had two in each department, and for a short time we had a sewing person for the children's clothes and clothes in general. Nanny had been our nurse, and she had a nurserymaid. Then there was a housemaid and a girl.

'There was one other member of staff, called Basket. He had been Lord Strathmore's valet for a great many years. He had one weakness – the bottle. So he was given notice about once a month, and the month would pass by . . . until unfortunately he upset a boiling kettle over Lord Strathmore, so it was decided that he should go and caretake at the family house in Hertfordshire, St Paul's Walden. When we came to live here, he did, I suppose odd jobs. I've got a photograph of him taken at the beginning of the war, hanging up the washing on the line, with a club in one hand and field glasses in the other, because German airmen were likely to parachute in.

'We paid the heads of department £10 a month, I think. Outdoor staff were paid 37/6 a week. I remember the cook had been here before the war – to get her back cost £5 a week, which I thought was an awful lot.'

Mary, Duchess of Buccleuch

'One was full of comforts in those days. The bedroom fires were lit early in the morning by a housemaid. They used to come bustling in. I can hear now the wonderful scraping on a dark morning, getting the ashes away, putting in the coal and lighting the fire. At Bowhill, when I first married, bathrooms were very, very scarce, and one very often had a bath brought in and put on a blanket in front of the fire. And I can remember the brass cans being brought up and put in the basin on the wash stand with a towel wrapped round them to keep the water hot.

'Breakfast was at nine o'clock. When I got to Boughton, I used rather reluctantly to offer my guests – the ladies, that is – nine o'clock breakfast in their beds, but that was considered fearfully over-pandering: the men always came down.

'I relied enormously on my staff. One had a housekeeper in each house, and a very good head butler, who travelled from house to house, and he nearly always had a second butler, who also travelled with us. Men staff always did, but the housekeeper remained in each house. And one usually had a travelling housemaid. In other words, there was always a staff left in each of the houses.

'I had an Austrian maid called Leonora, who was a genius at flower arranging, and did something like fifteen vases every single weekend, in all the houses, all matching the rooms: great big, what they call "arrangements" nowadays. I used to help her occasionally, but otherwise it was left to her.

'I left the menus and the ordering of the food entirely to the cook – I had rather a good cook, luckily, so I left a great deal to her, really. She had her own department – she never came out of the kitchen. She had her own sitting room and ate there, fed by her own minions. She was entirely separate and didn't join in with the household at all. She used to do everybody's food, the luncheons and dinners, but of course she had a great many servitors: two kitchenmaids and a scullerymaid. Don't forget that there was a still-room maid as well, who did the breakfasts, I suppose, and the baking – scones and cakes, endless scones – and the coffee. Certainly, until the war, we had a still-room maid at Drumlanrig and Bowhill, and an under-still-room maid. Goodness alone knows what they would have done – I can't conceive how they can have found work enough to do.

'There was a butler and an old odd man who had been there for ever. Another person carried the fuel, the logs, or whatever it was. It was a full-time job to keep all the fires going. Until quite recently one footman always came in every hour or so to make up the fires. One would never put a log on oneself. When one had fires upstairs, it meant a tremendous lot of carrying logs and firewood up and down. And it was a long carry, of course, round the various houses.

'The housekeeper and the steward used to eat together, then they used to move down to have pudding and cheese in the servants' hall, even in my day. Their meals were brought to them by some of the under-servants, by the under-footman and the under-housemaids. Visiting ladies' maids were always the same hierarchy as the housekeeper, and the valets as the butler and the steward. They were the upper strata, so to speak.

'When I first came to Boughton in 1936, everything was fairly primitive. And at Drumlanrig and Bowhill, the kitchens were miles and miles away; we brought them into the centre of the house, into the still-rooms, and made the still-rooms the kitchens.'

'Mellerstain has two big square wings and one long central house. The wings had a courtyard, and a separate part of one wing used to be for the housemaids. The footmen used to be in the other wing, which was where the grooms also lived. Naturally there was a separate staircase for each of the wings. The butler always had his special room downstairs in the basement of the main house, with his own bathroom. The chauffeur didn't live in the house – he had his own little house. The agent too had his own house, which was built by

The Countess of Haddington

191

my husband's father. It's on the way to Kelso, on the estate, some way from the house.

'The butler started as valet to my husband during the war, when he served in the Greys. Eventually he rose to the rank of butler, and another valet took his place. The butler was entirely responsible for the dining room and for all the wines. When we were first married, the butler had two footmen and an odd-job boy. The footmen wore the Haddington livery, which was deep red.

'One footman, who came to us very young and who was charming, excellent in every way, joined up when the war came. Unhappily for all of us, he was killed. We've always felt a sense of sorrow for him ever since. The staff were all part of the family, really. Our butler was with us for many, many years.

'We inherited the most wonderful housekeeper, who had already been at Mellerstain for about twenty years. She told me that she went to a "place" in England to be initiated. She had had to scrub a floor which was half a mile long every morning at six o'clock! At Mellerstain she had her own dining room; the butler ate with her, and my maid, my husband's valet and the cook. As housekeeper, she would go to the kitchen to tell the cook what to order – she would know the quantities. She was also in charge of the still-room, but the laundry always went out. Her heart was completely enveloped in the house and all that it contained. She loved it so much that she lived with us throughout the years and died at the age of ninety in her own room.

'The staff seemed to be very happy at Mellerstain, although the housekeeper was extremely strict with them all. Everything had to be perfect and very clean and polished. They all respected her, were devoted to her, and loved the house. They didn't wear a uniform. There was one moment, when we first started, that we put them in little pink dresses, with white frilly aprons, but that didn't last long. They preferred to wear their own little aprons and their own little dresses. They changed their dresses in the afternoon to a black dress with a white apron.

'Housemaids started, when we first moved to Mellerstain, at six in the morning and went on till six at night. The staff went up the back stairs and the family up the front stairs.

'The maids came at about fourteen. The scullerymaid was usually a young girl starting off – she came really to be trained. Then she'd go on to another house for something else, and gradually rise to be the cook. They worked their way up, and we always tried to help them as much as we could. When they contemplated going on, then we'd find them a place. Mostly they were Scottish – a few of them local – and others came from London.

'The wood was usually brought in by an under-gardener, and the second footman used to put the logs in place in the various different rooms. If the fire was running down, I would ring for the footman – unfortunately the bell system at Mellerstain wasn't very good; there was always something going wrong with the bells – to come and bring the logs in basket and put them on the fire. If the timber was damp, it burned longer, but if it was dry, it would burn much quicker, which meant that the wretched footman had to come more often.

'Spring cleaning was really a religious occupation for the staff. As soon as the time came – which was usually in April – we had to hasten to get ourselves ready to go down for the Season in London, so they could get on with the spring cleaning.

'The butler, cook and housemaids used to have quite long holidays: they'd go away for about three weeks at a time. But they always seemed to enjoy coming back, because they seemed quite devoted to the whole place. They were very happy with us, and I must say they were very comfortable. They had their own staff sitting room; they had everything they could want – music and all that sort of thing. They could enjoy themselves. We never had a complaint.

'We were very lucky with our head gardener: he was there for as long as he worked. That took him up to the age of seventy-two. We never had a great many staff in the garden; never more than six. I did all the deciding for the plants and the flowers – how we were going to organise the flowers on the terrace, for instance. We tried to grow grapes, but we didn't have sufficient staff, and it was too expensive, even at that time, to heat the two big glasshouses. So we decided to give up the grapes. The gardener always went to the kitchen to ask what vegetables were needed. The cook was in charge of that.

'When we went to London, we took down flowers and fruit and vegetables from here, and also our lady gardener. She did the flowers – here and in London – in the house, and she was absolutely excellent. It took her quite a long time to do them, so she didn't have much time to go outside at all! We actually sent her to be trained how to do them, to London, to Constance Spry or someone like that.'

'That the war changed the domestic staff situation (by finishing it off) I do not regret. When I came to Wightwick, the gardener's wife was housekeeper; her resentment at my arrival was not improved by my failure to impress her. Her standards may be shown by the fact that she asked my husband's permission to take me to the local

Lady Mander

Sir Geoffrey Mander's
chauffeur – 'a sure political
barometer'.

Woolworth – my prime shopping centre for three years in Oxford!
I was on the side of the maids against her. Apart from this and the
whole set up, it is a relief now not to have to try to keep up appearances or to guard one's speech at meals or to catch hostile glances
from the gardener for picking a flower instead of waiting for him
to bring plants in from the hothouse.

'The only member of staff I do miss is a driver. I learned to drive
during the war, so that the chauffeur could help in the garden, and
it was a sad day for us when he retired. He had enjoyed election
campaigns and was a sure political barometer, usually agreeing with
our Liberal principles. I remember, however, our disappointment
when we found that he did not share our indignation at the Nazi
occupation of the Ruhr – he had come out of the 1914–18 war much
preferring the Germans to the French.'

**Anne, Countess of
Rosse**

'There were still, when I went to Birr, for each day, six different lunches in six different rooms. The staff could on occasion meet and
talk together – Nanny could gossip with the housekeeper in the housekeeper's room, or Miss Martin the governess could gossip with Nanny
either in the schoolroom or the nursery. But eating together – NO.
Naturally the housekeeper was permanently at war with the cook
and her staff. The darling butler and his staff had a wing and a world
of their own.

'The lady of the house soon learnt her round. Down first to the
housekeeper's room. She would invariably ask me how many guests
and when and who. Then to the kitchen to give orders to the farm
that week. Then to the darling pantry boys, to tell them what sort
of guests and what silver and china to put out.'

**Helen, Lady
Dashwood**

'The butler really ruled everything at West Wycombe – he was very
very grand – and then the cook considered herself even grander, but
wasn't, I suppose, really. The butler, the cook and the housekeeper
were the king pins. Then I considered them middle-aged, but I think
they must have been in their late twenties. There were a great many
storms, and it was always very troublesome. Very often it was the
lady's maid who caused the problem. I had one maid, who I think
was German, because I was perfecting my German then and thought
that was the easiest way to do it; she fought with all the servants
and was very unpopular.

'I had several cooks, but the one I remember best was Mrs McKay,
who was an extremely good cook, trained at the Ritz. I thought it

Comber, the head gardener at Nymans, the Countess of Rosse's childhood home. In 100 years there have been just three head gardeners.

would be a good idea if I really learned to cook, so I said to her, "Are we doing anything on Wednesday, Mrs McKay? If I order a leg of lamb, will you teach me how to roast it?" At this Mrs McKay drew herself up and said, "Certainly not, my lady. While I'm here there's no possible reason for you to cook your lamb. I've been with you for twenty years, but I must regretfully hand in my notice if you're going to come in and interfere in my kitchen."

'Mrs McKay used to make the most wonderful fish cakes – the best I've ever had in my life. Morys Bruce, my son-in-law, loved them and always clamoured for some for breakfast. On one occasion he said to me, "What's gone wrong? No fish cakes for breakfast today?" I said, "Oh really? How extraordinary," and rushed out to the kitchen and said to Mrs McKay, "What's happened to the fish cakes?" "Oh, I'm sorry, I clean forgot, but there they are. Would you like to have them as a first course for lunch?" "Well, why not, what a good idea. Let's have them first, before the chicken." We had a very grand lady to lunch that day, the wife of the Chairman of the County Council. When the fish cakes were passed to her, with evident disgust and distaste she took one, a fearful expression on her face as if to say, "Fancy giving anyone *this*, in this sort of house. How disgraceful." I was a little put out, and then round they went to my son-in-law, who said, "Helen! Fish cakes! Thank God – may I have three?"

'I think the food in the servants' hall was as good as, if not better than, our own. I can remember one very funny occasion. We were going to a race meeting and I'd forgotten to order a cake for us to take, so I said to Mrs McKay, "Oh dear, how perfectly ghastly: I haven't got any cake, and Sir John and the boys will want some." She hesitated and then said, "I've just made a nice cake for the servants' hall and I'm sure we could let your ladyship have that if you'd like to." "Oh no, no, I'm afraid I meant really good cake." "I think you'll find it quite all right." When we got to the race meeting, at Hawthorn Hill, and I unpacked the cake, my guests exclaimed, "Goodness, what a cake! How rich, how wonderful! Where did it come from?" "Oh, it's the servants' cake." And they said to me, "It would be: you're the most extravagant, badly organised housekeeper I've ever heard of. Fancy letting the servants have a rich cake like this. *Poor* Johnnie!"

'Johnnie didn't have a valet; the butler valeted him. I had a maid, though, and always took her away with me for weekends – I hated places where they wouldn't have her. She did everything for me, although I remember my mother saying to me, "Why don't you let your maid put on your shoes for you, darling?" and I said, "Because

I'm quite sure this isn't going on for ever, and I don't want to have to learn to put on my shoes when I'm old."

'The chauffeur wouldn't teach me to drive, because he said he didn't wish to be with anyone who could drive themselves.

'I always wanted to be friends with various staff – some were nicer than others – but I noticed that whenever I got to like anyone very much and we had a sort of cosy relationship, it always seemed to go bad in the end, so it wasn't any good having a pet one.

'Once, when Sarah was in the Wrens in the last war, she came home and said, "Oh Mummy, all the girls want to know about West Wycombe. They're not a bit interested in the frescoes or the architecture or anything like that – they don't give two hoots. What they really want to know is, did we have footmen and what did they *do*." So I said, "Well, darling, what did you say?" "Well, I said, yes of course we had footmen, three of them, but I didn't know what they *did*, only that Stanley was a whizz-bang at Sardines." Just what a mother doesn't want to hear!'

'If you were a nine-servant house like Balcombe Place, you didn't have a lady's maid, nor a second footman, so you were rather looked down on. You either had three in every department, or three plus a lady's maid, plus an odd man or a second footman.

'Mama had a wonderful cook, a farmer's daughter who had run away from home on her father's second marriage. She had found herself a job as scullery maid at Carlton House Terrace, which was my grandfather's house. The servants there had to get up at five o'clock in the morning. When my mother was due home from Australia, my grandmother picked her out and said to her, "My daughter is coming back from Australia and has got to start keeping house all over again. You will go and cook for her." And so she did, and stayed for fifty years.

'When my mother was made Grand Dame of the British Empire, she said that she could never have achieved what she had done had it not been for the excellence of her staff, who took all worries off her shoulders and organised everything. All she had to do was to say how many people were coming for the weekend. It really worked like that. I remember the secretary putting her head round the door and saying, "Sorry to trouble you, but I can't remember whether Mr Hill-Wood is 'My dear Willy' or 'Dear Mr Hill-Wood'." They could do each other's writing: nobody knew whether it was her writing or her secretary's.

'I was married in 1931, and we came back from our two months'

Lady Burrell

honeymoon to find Knepp Castle opened up for us, with eleven servants in it, all engaged by my mother's secretary. The cook was paid £100, and later, when I had Nanny, who was a divine woman, she was paid £60. I quickly put her up to £100 and the cook to £120. The smart way to get servants was through two agencies in the West End of London; then there were local agencies and advertisements. In the great slump of the 1930s, with three million unemployed, I advertised in *The Welsh Daily Paper*. I only got one reply, though: they were too homesick. The one who came cried for a week, although I think she did settle after that. It was really pathetic.

'Although there were some terrible fights, especially between the lady's maid and the cook (the men didn't seem to fight as much: I don't think they took it quite so much to heart), the servants all felt part of the family, enormously so. It was their family and it was their house. They usually stayed for years – if they left it was because the head of department was a tough guy who was making life impossible for them, who really hated them, thought they were useless and never going to learn. They had at least one afternoon off a week, and if it was a special occasion – if a sister was getting married or something – they had it. You had long notice of the event and you couldn't have a lot of people to stay that weekend.'

Diana, Viscountess Gage

'The servants had a lovely time when people came to stay at Holker, because it was like a house party for them too. Rainald, my late husband, used to come and stay at Holker, and always brought a manservant with him. He said that the manservant liked staying with Philip Sassoon because the staff had their own lawn tennis court, but he liked to come to Holker because it was the best food. Many, many servants who worked together got married. My youngest sister was learning to ride – she was only four – and Libby, the nursery-maid, walked on one side of her dressed in white piqué, and the groom walked on the other side. Time went by, and they married. The Christie-Millers used to stay at Michael Duff's house a lot, and Veronica's maid was being courted by Michael's valet, and Michael was supposed to like Veronica or Lavender, but it was only the valet and the maid that married! It must have been terrible when they weren't asked together any more.

'At Christmas there was always a dance in the big front hall for all the household and the immediate people like the gardeners. Sometimes it was a fancy dress dance. One danced in the hierarchy: I was usually with the pantry boy, but my mother would dance with the butler and my father with the housekeeper. We all danced for a bit, and then they would carry on on their own. A local band came from somewhere. And then Molly Buccleuch would put on a play in the upstairs gallery, in which we all acted, and the audience was the staff.

'The housekeeper, the butler, my father's valet and my mother's maid and visiting maids ate in a room called The Room. The knives were marked with an R. The rest of the staff ate in the servants' hall; their cutlery was marked with an S. The cook didn't like eating with other people, so she ate in a little alcove off the kitchen. She had a perfect name for a cook, Mrs Hubbard. She was very good-looking – looked like Lady Hamilton – and frightfully grand.'

'One housemaid was dismissed from Eaton for being rude to Mrs Crockett, the housekeeper. She came to cry on my shoulder – it was awful. I really longed for her to stay, but Mrs Crockett said, "No, absolutely no way." She'd been cheeky and out she had to go.

'In London at Bourdon House we had five housemaids, although we never spent more than two nights there at a time. When one of the housemaids got married and left, the head housemaid came to me and said, "How shall I set about replacing the fifth housemaid?" I replied, "Well, I think that really, as we never spend more than two nights here a month, we ought to be able to manage on four housemaids." "Well, if that's the case, then I'm leaving." "Right," I said. How had I the guts to do that! But we only had four.

'I had to have two maids, because of this everlasting moving – packing and repacking, unpacking. The head maid had to do the packing and unpacking, because she was the only person who knew how to do that, and the other one used to stay behind to iron and put to rights things that were left behind. In those days, of course, dresses were infinitely more elaborate and none were creaseproof, so they never stopped having to be ironed. I think I took lots of unnecessary clothes with me, because I was so thrilled at having marvellous things to wear.'

Loelia, Lady Lindsay of Dowhill (*formerly Duchess of Westminster*)

'In my grandparents' day Wallington was, I suppose, a typical Edwardian house: a very much bigger staff of servants (twelve or fourteen in the house) and very much more formal. The servants in those days were not supposed to meet you in the gallery or on the stairs, and my father found, when he inherited the place in 1928, that the younger servants had never seen the front door or any of

Mrs John Dower

Above:
Estate workers at Wallington in the 1890s. Many stayed on after Pauline Dower's grandfather died and her father inherited.

Right:
Booa, for years nurse at Wallington, with the three Trevelyan brothers. Pauline Dower's father is on the left.

Opposite:
'In my grandparents' day Wallington was . . . a typical Edwardian house: a very much bigger staff of servants . . . and very much more formal.'

200

the big rooms. They had seen the Central Hall, of course, as they walked round the gallery, but they didn't know any of the beautifully decorated Italian stucco rooms at all.

'My father would never have any male servants indoors – he didn't like the idea a bit. His father's footman, whose forebears had always been gamekeepers, had been prevented from being a gamekeeper because he hadn't got very good sight. He begged my father to allow him to become his gamekeeper – which he did and was first-class, as it turned out.

'The housekeeper had been my father's and uncle's nanny, and she became housekeeper later, and then lived on at Wallington until she died in the 1920s. The cook we had, Mary Smith, had been my younger brother Geoffrey's nanny. After breakfast, my mother would go along to the kitchen to discuss with her about meals. But later on in our time at Wallington, the cook came along to her room, which was the parlour, now called Lady Trevelyan's Parlour, to take orders.

'The cook had two kitchenmaids under her until my mother got an Aga. Before that there had been a big range, into which a kitchenmaid had to shovel two large shovelfuls of coal every ten minutes during the whole of the day. I should think she started between five and six in the morning. The laundrymaid started at two in the morning in my grandparents' day. The kitchenmaids were local. When I became engaged and it was known that I was going to live in London, I had a lot of mothers coming to me and asking if I would take their girls. The wages for a girl, who was my only maid, were £26 a year.

'All the maids lived up in the attics on the second floor, and the housekeeper had a very lovely eighteenth-century room on the first floor, one of the north rooms. The butler lived in a house in the courtyard, and the footman's bedroom was a cupboard – with no window or anything – over the door in the pantry, entered by a ladder.'

The late Duke of Beaufort

'When I was very young, the old butler, Mr Head, had been at Badminton for many years. He was a very good man and a great character. The head gardener, the chauffeur, the keeper, everyone – they were all people who'd been at Badminton, or worked for my family, for generations past.

'The butler had five or six footmen under him; my mother had a special under-footman called Toby who looked after her in her end of the house. My father had his valet, and my two half-brothers, who lived here a great deal, had their own joint footman, who looked after them. Most of the servants were local. In my father's day we had a very large staff of housemaids, who were again practically all local girls. Gradually they got fewer and fewer, and more and more married women came and worked in the house as dailies. There was also a housekeeper, and a French chef, whom we replaced later by a lady cook.

'There was a housekeeper's room, a steward's room, where the senior male servants lived – and a servants' hall. The chauffeur had his own house. The butler and footmen slept in the men's passage, the housemaids in the girls' passage. The two were very far apart: the men's in the west end of the house, and the girls' up in the north.

'Before we had electric light in the house, the lamp man naturally played a very important part. He looked after the lamps and candles. In the big drawing room, for instance, I should think each chandelier contained thirty to forty candles. They were lovely in a way, but they took an awful lot of looking after, because when they got really hot and burnt down, they were inclined to drip.'

The cook and her kitchenmaids in the kitchen at Ickworth.

XII NURSERY & SCHOOLROOM

Compton Beauchamp – Bowood House –
Sheen Falls – Holker Hall – Whittington –
Ickworth – Giffords Hall – Goodwood House
– Wallington House – Melletstain –
Greenlands – West Wycombe Park

'My mother and father were never at Compton Beauchamp in the week. When we were tiny children it was absolutely straightforward: Nanny Abbott took charge of us and during the week we did exactly what Nanny said. We had walks, and then we rode our ponies – we never had a day without riding – we messed about and had a few lessons. We wore little summer frocks or winter leggings or whatever, but at weekends there were grand visitors and we were shoved into smart clothes. We were much too young to see what was going on in the dining room, but we used to hang about on the back stairs and get food and delicious things when they came out of the dining room.

'The butler, Frederick, was the nicest fellow that ever walked. When my parents were away, we were allowed to fish from his pantry window into the moat. There were enormous, beautiful golden carp in the moat, which we were absolutely forbidden to catch. But we did, out of the pantry window, with little sticks and string, and bread pellets on the end. We'd catch them and pull them out of the water for about five seconds, have a look at them and throw them back – we'd never hurt them.

'We went quite often as tiny children to our grandparents' house, Tredilian. We were normally there when our parents couldn't have us. We were incredibly spoilt while we were with our grandparents. We didn't go to meals, because we were tiny, but we came down to the morning room, where Grandmother played with us and read to us. Then there was misery time, when we were in the nursery. After tea Nanny dressed us up to the nines – put us into Irish crochet lace, sashes and white shoes and white silk socks, the whole bang shoot – and sent us downstairs. Then we were allowed to dig about in the plants in the conservatory and spill the dogs' water and get ourselves absolutely filthy. We did anything we liked, until finally Nanny came for us and was absolutely furious with us every night.

'We had the most beautiful clothes; we went to a shop called Wendy – I think it was in Bond Street. The little boys went to Rowe's. We also had a local dressmaker called Miss Newman. We used to walk to our fittings. She had been trained by some terrific London dressmaker, and we had lovely things made, absolutely beautiful clothes: Fairisle jumpers from top to toe.

'We didn't go to school; we had governesses always. They never stayed, because we were so nasty to them. The schoolroom was in the old billiard room across the courtyard. Neighbouring children came too – one used to ride there every morning from Shrivenham with a groom. She was then fetched and rode back, but always with a groom in attendance. We had hunting friends and pony club

Mrs Richard Cavendish

Opposite:
Elizabeth and Mary Paget, nieces of the Viscountess Hambleden, at the seaside.

Overleaf, above left:
Anne Lloyd Thomas in the moat at Compton Beauchamp. 'There were enormous, beautiful golden carp in the moat, which we were absolutely forbidden to catch. But we did, out of the pantry window . . .'

Below left:
Pamela Lloyd Thomas (later Mrs Richard Cavendish) with Simon Asquith at Frinton. 'As young children we used to go to the seaside for holidays . . . We adored it.'

Above right:
Pamela Lloyd Thomas with Sis. 'We never had a day without riding.'

Below right:
'One of my childhood memories is of the Prince of Wales coming down . . . and my sister and I being sent up onto the downs with a bundle of hay to light when the aeroplane arrived' – David Lloyd Thomas with Mouse Fielden, the Prince's pilot.

THE COUNTRY HOUSE REMEMBERED

Opposite, above:
Bowood in the Viscountess Mersey's grandparents' day: 'We were very very frightened of grandparents, and slightly of parents.'

Below:
And in her children's day. When both her brothers were killed in the Second World War, the house and title passed to her cousin, George Mercer-Nairne.

friends, and we went to a dancing class at Faringdon. When we got older, Sis and I went to Oxford, I should think twice a week, for French and dancing and skating. We had French governesses during the holidays – we were bilingual by the time we went to France.

'As young children, we used to go to the seaside for holidays, with Nanny and a nurserymaid, who used, I suppose, to muck out. We would go to places like Frinton. We adored it. We used to go shrimping and paddling – I don't know what we didn't do. And Nanny, who never let on when she was at Compton that she was able to cook, cooked like a dream. My parents would come down to see us once or twice during our seaside holidays – they loathed coming, absolutely hated it. Mummy used to get into the sea; I should think it was the nastiest thing that ever happened to her. They'd come down for about three minutes and go away again. They'd done their duty.

'At Compton, we never stopped playing tennis. In those days one used to have a pro to come and teach the children and exercise the host. Ours was called Mr Jacobs; he was terribly nice and taught us painstakingly through the holidays.

'My mother organised the stores – we were all made to do it. We gave out the stores once a week, things like Vim, loo paper, jam. She got it in bulk and it was put into a store cupboard. They gave in their lists: the pantry, the kitchen, the nursery or whatever. If they asked for too much, she used to say. "What have you been doing with it? I think that's too much; you must look after it a bit more."

'The first time anybody was allowed in the dining room was when they were public school age, which I suppose was twelve or something like it. I remember very well my brother David coming down for the first time. The butler and the footmen were handing round – he was so frightened that he took one green pea!

'One of my childhood memories is of the Prince of Wales coming down – my father was working for him as secretary – and my sister and I being sent up onto the downs with a bundle of hay to light when the aeroplane arrived, to show which way the wind was blowing, so that it could land safely. With the Prince, whom we adored and thought wonderful, was Mouse Fielden, the Prince's pilot. He was wonderful to us, and as he had hay fever and I had hay fever, that was a great bond.'

Katherine, Viscountess Mersey

'Nanny was always in the nursery with the children. She never let them out of her sight and never seemed to have any time off. Always, always there.

208

Pleasure Grounds.

views from Mummy's bedroom.
Sheamy

BOWOOD
January & April 1938
Charlie after stiching his heart at Derreen
Magnolia
in the spring.

January.

Richard

Elizabeth
& Richard

Orangery.
& Terraces

Above:
'The holidays were marvellous, because we used to go to a house called Sheen Falls in Ireland' – Lord Rayleigh bathing with the Fitzmaurice children.

Right:
'We bicycled and had a donkey cart and were allowed to go out for picnics in the donkey cart on our own.' A generation later, little had changed: Viscountess Mersey with her own children at Sheen Falls.

'The nursery had special food carried up by the odd man on a very heavy tray, up endless stairs. When I had a governess, I sometimes had my meals with her in the schoolroom, which was at the very top of the house. Some poor man had to carry the food from the kitchen, up some dreadful stone steps to the ground floor, along a very long passage, and then up to the first floor, and then up *again* to the second floor.

'I was quite fond of my governess; she was a very nice woman but very, very uninteresting. I did lessons alone with her. She was not at all clever, and the only lessons I enjoyed were when I went to an English Literature class once a week, run by a marvellous old woman called Mrs Woolf, who had taught my mother. She was very old by the time I went to her. It was the only proper education I had, because I got so bored with the governess that I never really listened to what she said.

'In those days boys went away to school and girls didn't, so when my brothers arrived home for the holidays it was just so exciting. Well, I suppose a few of my girl friends did go to school, but not many. I hadn't really got any friends then, so I don't know.

'We were very, very frightened of grandparents, and slightly of parents. Sometimes we used to go to Bowood to stay with our grandparents. We would be there with my cousins, George and Margaret Mercer-Nairne; my cousin George and I were great friends. It was during the First World War, so we pretended to be soldiers and had Union Jacks and trumpets and marched about. George and I did some naughty things – at least we were made to feel very naughty. Rushing about in the corridor, by mistake we broke an ornament, and we got into the most fearful trouble. We were both shut in our bedrooms, and I cried for about three hours. I was told that Grandmother would come to see me. She marched into my room in uniform (there was a hospital in Bowood in the war), which she loved wearing: a navy-blue skirt and coat and a sort of nurse's thing over her head. She made me feel that to break this vase was just about the wickedest thing anybody could do. My mother couldn't quite say so, but I think she thought we were much too severely treated by my grandparents.

'After my father inherited and we moved to Bowood ourselves, the house was often full. I remember Stanley Baldwin and Mrs Baldwin coming. Eddie Marsh was there a great deal and the Desboroughs, the Bentincks – they were almost my parents' best friends – and the Cavendishes. They were all very nice to us children, but I liked them much better as I got older. When I was small they always kissed one through the veil – the women always wore veils then. There was something rather horrible about kissing through the

veil, but as I got older the veil seemed to disappear. Nancy Astor came occasionally – oh, she was so funny. We laughed and laughed. She was wonderful: she was always imitating somebody or pretending to be someone else. She was brilliant at pretence.

'We five children used to get up onto the roof – through the housemaids' bedrooms – and smoke. The housemaids had some really rather ghastly attic rooms with no running water; they had to fetch the water for their washing, carrying it upstairs. They were not nice rooms. The servants slept in extraordinary corners.

'One didn't really make great friends with the servants, except for the nurserymaids (we had a good many of those) and the cook. We were always great friends with the cook, and used to go and collect scraps to eat, because we were always hungry – well, greedy. I was allowed to have, told to have, cooking lessons, and I adored that.

'The holidays were marvellous, because we used to go to a house called Sheen Falls in Ireland. My brothers and I had a most wonderful time there: we just adored it. We bicycled and had a donkey, and were allowed to go out for picnics in the donkey cart on our own. The parents and the family came – five of us. It was absolute heaven. There was always a delightful housemaid there, whom we adored, and one other. From Bowood we took the cook, Nanny, the kitchenmaid, the butler, a footman and the chauffeur. We went to Sheen Falls for our holidays from 1919 onwards, except for two or three years which had to be missed because of the troubles in Ireland.

'When I was seventeen and a half, I went abroad for a year with my governess and two other girls to learn French and Italian, and then the magic moment came when my education was supposed to be finished. I came out when I was seventeen and a half.

'I used to have awful clothes before I grew up, and I always used to feel that I was worse dressed than my friends. My mother used to give me some of her cast-off clothes; I don't know why, she just thought a child needn't be smartly dressed. My brothers were very nicely dressed, though – they had sailor suits. When I came out, everything had to come from a very good dressmaker or a very good tailor. One was always trying things on – I rather enjoyed having some nice clothes at last.'

'My sisters had originally had German governesses. When the 1914 war came along, they had to go back. I suppose it was difficult to keep German people in England; they were rather delighted. Then in about 1917 came the governess who had been with the Vanderbilts; she despised us very much. The governess would always travel

Diana, Viscountess Gage

between London and Holker with us. It really was a dreadful life for them, not part of the family nor the servants and not liked by the nanny either. We also behaved badly sometimes; for instance when my next sister, Mary Crawford, had a donkey cart and asked the governess to get out to relieve the donkey going up the hill, and the governess wouldn't, Mary unharnessed the donkey and rode off.

'We didn't have prayers. We had breakfast and did lessons and then went out riding. We all had lunch together, the whole family and whoever was staying, in the dining room. After that we all rather liked doing things on our own. We could play lawn tennis, or croquet, or anything. And then there was schoolroom tea. I didn't have dinner in the dining room till I was sixteen – I was virtually coming out – but we'd always seen so many people staying. Young men were rather alarming. The older ones were perfectly delightful, because one knew them.

'When I was in London my life was rather circumscribed. I did lessons with the governess, and went to the Zoo, and to a dancing class, and went sightseeing, to Lancaster House or the Wallace Collection or something. Sometimes I stayed away with my parents, but by no means always. There were a whole lot of other girls like me living in the same way, and one used to go and have lunch or tea with them, and they used to come to one. And they came to Holker all the time, too.

'We all used to go out riding together. We rode in order of age, and as I was at that time the youngest, my pony was friskier than the others. I had to keep to protocol and not ride in front of my next sister, but she was very good-tempered with a good-tempered horse, so I sometimes used to steer my pony into the back of hers, to stop it. We didn't look after our ponies at all. We used to go up to get onto them at the stables, and when we'd finished riding the grooms took them.

'My mother bought our clothes, from a shop in London called Wendy; it belonged to Lady Willoughby, who designed for her daughter Rosalie, who was just my age.'

Margaret, Countess of Lichfield

'Our neighbours at Whittington, the Paget-Tomlinsons, lived at Biggins, a mile up what was called Hostaker Lane. The house – built before I can remember by Dr Paget-Tomlinson, who had come into an enormous amount of money from a Miss Tomlinson – was a copy of Haddon Hall, with a great deal of the garden very like it.

'They hadn't been there very long when, alas, his wife went raving mad. She was shut up in a bedroom upstairs. Nobody ever saw her, but she had a nurse to look after her. The old doctor was very fond of us children and we went there a great deal. We were there one day for tea to meet a clergyman's children, and we played hide and seek. We were told never to go through a green baize door upstairs, but I was being chased, and when you are a child you forget what you have been told. I shot through the green baize door and found myself in Mrs Paget-Tomlinson's room. I've never forgotten it. She was the most extraordinary colour, a sort of grey, putty-coloured face: a dreadful-looking woman. She had a glass of water by her side. She said, "Come here, child, come here." She grasped me by the wrist and then, thank goodness, a nurse came in. I was terrified. The nurse was very good with her; at last she persuaded Mrs Paget-Tomlinson to let go of my wrist. The nurse said, "You ought not to have come in here. You know perfectly well you are not allowed in here." I said, "I was being chased. We were playing hide and seek. I'm so sorry." I was very breathless and absolutely petrified. I went downstairs, but I daren't tell anybody. Everybody said how quiet I was at tea!

'The Paget-Tomlinsons had a companion called Miss Evett, who looked after the old doctor and acted as hostess and altogether ran the place. She was terribly kind, very small and very capable, and she lived for making everybody happy and comfortable; she was a remarkable woman – the type of woman you often met then, but has now completely disappeared. Her hair was parted in the middle and she wore spectacles. She was very prim and proper and had to laugh to make herself seem cheerful, but you felt that she wasn't really laughing at anything that was funny: it was just put on to keep people going.

'My first husband, Humphrey Philips, his nurse was called Da – they never called her Nanny. She was a marvellous person. Humphrey was the youngest; when he went to school she was turned into a sort of housekeeper and ran Haybridge and looked after everyone in the same way that Miss Evett had done. All the servants respected her and she bossed them about a great deal but with great tact and discipline. Also with great justice: she was very fair to them all.

'Those days with Da, and the other people who brought me up, taught me that familiarity breeds contempt. You could be very intimate, but never familiar, and I think that is one of the lost arts of today. People are so familiar, everybody calls everybody by their Christian name at once, on sight. In those days Christian names were only used by your nearest and dearest, but very intimate friends didn't for a very long time call each other by their Christian names.

I was brought up very much to call people Mrs So-and-So, Miss So-and-So, Lady So-and-So, and never by their Christian name.

'The difference between Da and Miss Evett was that Da didn't have her meals in the dining room with us. She always had her own sitting-room and bedroom upstairs, which we all adored going to, as it was so cosy. You could go and tell her your troubles and you knew it was quite safe. But she didn't have her meals with us and wouldn't want to.

'Exceptionally, when my mother-in-law was giving a party and we were going to sit down thirteen, she would send for Da to come down to make it fourteen and safe. But she never took umbrage and was only too pleased to oblige. There was no feeling of class: it was all so natural and happy, full of affection and love, with no awful affectation.

'I think that if there were more people in the world now like Da and Miss Evett, there would not have to be any psychologists, because they were so wise and their advice was so sound. They always reminded me of a lovely china bowl with no cracks and when you flick it with your finger it rings with a wonderful true ring. Well, they had no cracks and rang like an uncracked bowl. The world is so cracked now, with the psychologists as cracked as the patients. They have extraordinary unwholesome theories and everything is based on sex. Well, sex never really crossed these wonderful women's minds. They really were pure goodness. Nowadays the world has become so polluted and impure and sex so out of context with truth – everything has gone all upside down. With these people sex was not mentioned, but I think they knew a lot more. I always remember when I was very young, hearing two nannies talking; I was in one room playing with the other children and I heard one of them say, "Oh well, poor soul, these men, it's either drink or women." That really made me think, and I wondered what kind of men they were talking about.

'One learnt a great deal from this wonderful friendship with Da, particularly that friendship is built on trust, and my goodness they could be trusted. When you told them something you knew it would never go an inch further. It went into their ears and there it stayed.

'There was also Mrs Thompson, my mother's governess, who brought her up – and all my aunts – at Trehill. In those days girls did not go to school, they had a governess. These poor governesses had to know everything. They taught the piano, history, French, German, arithmetic – everything that had to be learnt they taught. I think that they must have been extremely well-educated themselves to be able to pass it all on. She gave her charges a great love of history:

'Mrs Thompson came to us in the holidays when she became a widow and was very hard up' – seen here wearing a cardigan knitted at the age of 14 by Margaret Dawson Greene, later the Countess of Lichfield.

Left:
Da's mother, Mrs Rowe, was a great character who lived to be 100. She knew Dickens well, and was the model for one of his characters.

Below:
The Philips children with their nanny, Da (centre), nursery maid (left) and under-nurse (right). Humphrey Philips, the Countess of Lichfield's first husband, is flanked by his three sisters: Rose, Joan and Kitty.

my mother was very well read. They read extremely good books and were taught to love reading. Mrs Thompson came to us in the holidays when she became a widow and was very hard up. Again one of these wonderful women who are completely selfless and do all they can to make everybody else happy and comfortable.

'My mother wouldn't have had time to look after us in the holidays as she had so much writing to do. In those days there was the most enormous amount of post. There were no telephones, so to keep in touch with all the vast number of family and friends, it did mean endless letters full of news. So Mrs Thompson was invaluable.'

Lady Phyllis MacRae

'My mother did not like nannies. She had had a very middle-class upbringing, and therefore she did not believe in them. She believed in mothers looking after their own children, and it was only perforce that she was not looking after us. We were a long way before our time in that respect. She was regarded as revolutionary by the family in which she found herself. She had, as mother's helps, Swiss girls, so I cannot remember a time when I *learnt* French; I never had to learn "*la chaise*" and so on. I can never ever remember not knowing it; sometimes now a French word comes to me when I am looking for the English one.

'When my children came along, although I could not ever remember having a nanny myself, I did have one for them. I did not, as other people did – trust the children to her completely, because I had been brought up not to. My children were my children. No nanny would ever have stayed with my mother – no nanny would have been able to make rules for my mother – and they could not do that with me either. I always had Swiss girls, and so of course we all have terrible accents. My children also say that they can't remember a time when they ever *learnt* French, because, like me, they grew up talking it. The little one, she had no nanny, but a nice Swiss peasant girl, when she was only three. Of course, people used to say, "I wish I could hear her speak French," but how do you make a child say anything at three years old, if it has no inclination to show off? Once she was sitting, playing, and eventually she said, "*Tais-toi, je ne veux pas,*" without realising that she was speaking French – it came out just like that. You couldn't have made her do it; she hadn't any idea, she had meant to answer in English, but she didn't. And that is what my sister and I were like.

'The kitchen and the nursery were nearly always at loggerheads. When we were at home they fed the nursery quite well. When we went away, they could not see why they should go to any trouble

Opposite:
Lady Phyllis MacRae's children at Ickworth. 'No nanny would ever have been able to make rules for my mother – and they could not do that with me either.'

Below, left:
'The little one, she had no nanny, but a nice Swiss peasant girl, when she was only three.'

for the nursery. So Nanny was up in arms, in particular over her supper, which was not a meal the children had. She was furious if they only sent up a sandwich or something. One row, I remember, was when she was sent up scrambled eggs and bacon for supper – there was a terrible scene.

'I was eleven when my parents got a car, so when I was aged eight, nine and ten, which is, after all, the age when quite a lot of children go to children's parties, we always went in a horsedrawn carriage. We used to go twelve, thirteen and fourteen miles, horsedrawn. I remember going to a fancy dress party when I was six or seven. My father at that time was an MP (it was shortly before he moved to the House of Lords); the other children were dressed up as fairies and flowers and things like that, and I had to go as Protection. It was rather hard. (My sister was luckier – she was The Colonies.)'

Mrs Charles Brocklebank

'Starting as nurserymaids in a big house, nannies then either had the gift for it or they hadn't. Like teaching – you either have the gift or not. We certainly had an absolute gem of a nanny. She was with us for fifteen years, and went with us to North America in the war. She devoted her life to the children, with very little time off, as we divided our time between country and town, and were often away. So I gave her a month's holiday a year. She was never ill, and I never saw her fussed or put out. She used to make the children's clothes: she was very good at making frocks and party clothes, and at letting things out. People had things mended far more then, because they were made of much better and nicer stuff. She wrote excellent letters, many of which I still have.'

The Duke of Richmond and Gordon

'From about 1933 I used to fly all the people around Goodwood I could, because I thought it was something they would enjoy. The gardener, for instance, wanted to go round looking at his garden. I took Nanny up, too. I was flying from the field down in Chichester Lane, with its lovely hangar, which got burnt down. The boys were in the front seat, and they bounced up and down and said, "Nanny faster, Nanny faster." Nanny had a very heavy moustache, and she was dressed up in a leather flying jacket. Nicky, being rather naughty, said, "Oh, Nanny, you look just like a frog; you look just like a monkey." Charles, rather more tactful, said, "No, you don't, Nanny, you look just like Amy Johnson."

'Then we put Nanny in the front seat. The wind was south-westerly and I taxied up to the far end of the field. When we got up to about fifty feet, I thought this would be about the time to take Nanny's mind off things, so I said, "Nanny, if you look just over the left side of you now, you'll get the most wonderful view of Chichester Cathedral." Now, do you know what she replied? "Very good, Your Grace."

After the sale of Gordon Castle and the Scottish estate, 'we always spent August in Cornwall. After races week you felt you had to get away – to be completely free to wear old clothes. We'd had the house in the family for generations. The boys adored it – all the swimming and surfing. It was always absolutely gorgeous, a lovely wild place. Even so, one took a cook, a nanny and nurserymaid and a lady's maid. They enjoyed it enormously too, although whenever Nanny saw me approaching, she used to put on her mackintosh, because she was in her bathing dress.'

'On Sundays, as soon as we knew how to behave at table, one or other of us (I'm the eldest of six) went down for lunch with my grandparents. The grave difficulty in the summer was that my parents invented British summer time five years before the rest of the country, so every week during the summer there was a discussion as to whether we had to go down at 12.30 for their 1.30 lunch, or 2.30 for their 1.30 lunch! I still remember the anxiety about those lunches.

Mrs John Dower

'We had a nanny and a governess before we moved to Wallington. The governess left, but the nanny became cook/housekeeper at Wallington. She was from Redcar, where my mother was born and brought up, and she was the third generation of her family in service with my family, so that she wasn't necessarily a trained nanny – she just looked after the smaller children. She apparently *did* cook, and loved cooking. Certainly she cooked very well for us.

'Lunch was an important meal, the chief meal of the day. After lunch we all had to go out. On a wet day we would dam a stream; that was the etiquette. I remember once, when Clem Attlee was staying, as a young man, before he became a well-known politician (long before he became Premier, of course), we were going down to the Wansbeck to dam a stream to make a good bathing pool, and I said to him in the rather superior way that a young person will to a stranger, did he know anything about damming, and he said, rather shyly, "Well, I have dammed the Euphrates for three miles" – he was a water engineer and had built a super dam, which lasted for years! (The last time I saw him was as an old man in a white topper and a beautiful grey suit at a Buckingham Palace garden party. We sat together and reminisced about the days at Wallington.)

THE COUNTRY HOUSE REMEMBERED

'Tea was a great meal; we always ate a good tea. It was in the Central Hall at a huge refectory table. The Central Hall was very much the children's room, so it would be strewn with toys, and the big rocking horse and the bricks and all sorts of things were there.

'Only the older children stayed up for supper, which was therefore a much smaller party. The younger children would probably have supper after their baths – my father had put in three bathrooms – and it would be taken upstairs. I remember as children we always used to have brown bread, spread with butter and brown sugar. We ate it in the bathroom as soon as we had got on our nightdresses or pyjamas. It was a very good supper. After dinner we played all sorts of games in the Library. The Library was always our room. Card games, like rummy, racing demon, snap - but we were never allowed to bet. We were allowed to bet "time", though, which cures you of ever wanting to bet at all, when one's brother, just as one is putting on one's nice dance dress to go out with a friend, would say, "Now, look here, you owe me five minutes – you go and clean my bicycle!"

'We used to be very keen tennis players, but we only had a very soft grass court on the west lawn, and very much wanted a hard court. We knew that if we asked my father about it and he said "No", no it would be for ever. So we devised a way of getting round it, by making a charade at Christmas, "Ten is Court"; he took the point and gave us a beautiful court down in the field. The village were allowed to come and play too. We enjoyed shooting and fishing as well, but I don't think we ever went racing.

'Wallington had (and still has, but doesn't use) a very good fire engine, which lives in a little hut against the China Pond. Every year there were fire practices with great hoses, which came up with the fire engine to the courtyard. One summer my eldest brother – when he was at Cambridge, I think – devised a wonderful game: he and another Cambridge friend, dressed only in bathing suits and with tea trays as shields, had the whole of the great courtyard to maneouvre in, each armed with these terrific hoses. The object was to knock your adversary down. An excellent spectator sport!

'As children, we used to play with lead soldiers which lived up in a little cupboard with little drawers, each one housing a regiment. They had been collected by my father and his brothers with their pocket money ever since my father was ten, in the 1880s. They were German-made and bought in the Burlington Arcade. The boys got very little pocket money – sixpence a week – and the soldiers cost a few pence each. They took a long time to collect. There are 6000. Before his death, my father arranged the whole lot in one of the big cupboards in the museum.'

'The older five of us went to a Quaker school. My father was at Harrow, but he very much believed in co-education: he'd travelled as a young man in America and had decided, long before he married, that he would co-educate any children he might have. He sent us to Sidcot in Somerset, partly because he wanted to co-educate us, and partly because he had been a pacifist in the first war – he felt that no public school would accept his children because of his pacifist views. He also very much wanted us to be brought up in the Quaker tradition because of the Quakers' social point of view and attitude towards other people. The Quakers have no sort of snobbism about them: you are not any better because you have been born of a good family and because you own a big house. I think it brought us all up feeling that other people may be different from us because they haven't had as much chance as we have had, but in essence they are just as valuable as we are.'

'Both the children were born at Mellerstain, in the house, and so the nannies were there waiting. The nannies became our most intimate friends and we were really deeply fond of them all. One little nanny, who had been nurserymaid first and then rose to be nanny, went out to California, where she married and lived happily; we always keep contact with her. It was an isolated position, being a nanny, especially when we were in the big house. But then when the war came we moved into the wing, because the house was a hospital, so it was much cosier, really, for us all then. That's when life changed entirely. Before then the nursery was a separate existence. Nanny was absolutely all-powerful. Everybody had to kow-tow to Nanny.'

The Countess of Haddington

'When I was a child at Wilton, we had horses – my mother, who was a very good rider, used to ride, and my father did too – and we really had a very enjoyable life. We spent a lot of time on the river. Even though it was a small river, we had canoes on it, and every year we used to drag it. That was a great excitement; we loved that. And there were lots of dogs. My mother and father were both very fond of dogs, and we had dogs as children. I had a lurcher, and in fact took him to Greenlands with me when Billy and I married.

'My brothers had their friends to stay and there were lots of long leaves from Eton. In those days the Eton Corps used to go to camp

Patricia, Viscountess Hambleden

at Tidworth, and when they were there, my brothers used to bring masses of friends over.

'Before I married, as a girl, I had to join the Girl Guides. One was made to do certain things in those days – it wasn't just pure idleness.

'The nursery set-up at Greenlands wasn't really remote, because by the time I married, most of my generation saw much more of their children than we saw of our parents. It was always Nanny's day off on the Thursday – the whole day off. You looked after your children, put them to bed and everything. There was none of that total segregation in the way which there was when I was a child: although my parents were very very nice to me, I didn't see them in the same way that we saw our children. They never had to bother with that awful thing I remember as a child, having to go downstairs and sitting twiddling their thumbs and then going up again. Of course, if it was a large party, they perhaps were taken out of their rather muddy clothes, and came in for a bit, but they didn't have to sit like mice in the room. And when we took a house by the seaside, it was all hugger-mugger together; there was no question of protocol.'

Opposite:
The Viscountess Hambleden's children. 'There was none of that total segregation in the way which there was when I was a child . . . And when we took a house by the seaside, it was all hugger-mugger together; there was no question of protocol.'

'Queen Mary came to West Wycombe several times, by herself, or with the Duke and Duchess of York. She brought the two princesses – Princess Elizabeth and Princess Margaret – to a children's party we had once, and it was the best children's party I think I've ever been to, because we had turned the ball room into a circus ring, and tiny little ponies galloped up the steps outside and into the room, where they galloped round and round in the ring.'

Helen, Lady Dashwood

Francis and John Dashwood playing trains in the attic at West Wycombe.

XIII ESCAPE

'Ninety-nine per cent of our time was spent in the country, one per cent in London. We were never in London for more than a few days at a time, because Bendor hated it. We just managed to invite a few friends for lunch; and we occasionally went to the theatre or the opera; and he liked dining at the Savoy. When we were in Paris we certainly went out to good restaurants, but again we would probably only stay two nights. It was this restlessness, on a scale one can't imagine. We were never in the right place at the right moment. I was doing a lot to all the gardens, planting away like crazy, so I was dying to see what had come out in one place, and that was the one place one couldn't go to. By the time you got to that garden, there was no sign of whatever one was especially interested in.

'The Grosvenor estate at that time was being rooked by this arch-criminal, who knew that the only thing Bendor wanted in the whole world was to get out of London as quickly as possible. Bendor enjoyed going to a few shops – buying me a present at a jeweller, perhaps. My jewellery was contemporary; it came from a shop called Lacloche. And Van Kleef – that was another great one. Bendor never would go to Cartier under any circumstances: before my time he had had some row with them. He bought me some lovely old things as well; lovely old Russian jewellery. He collected Breguet watches, which are now practically unfindable, and very beautiful. He loved old things; he couldn't bear anything faintly modern. I insisted once on going to see an Epstein sculpture, and he very nearly killed me for even wanting to look at it. I said, "Well, I expect you're quite right, but one must go and look at it and make up one's own mind."

'I never knew beforehand that there'd be any question of getting anybody to dinner in London, because Bendor would make up his mind at the last minute to go somewhere, which would mean spending a night in London. So I'd say, "Let's try and have some people to dinner for this one night," and the secretary would telephone them. All the telephoning was always done by someone else. Bendor had his own telegram forms printed – quite large sheets of paper with Eaton Hall written at the top. He used to send sheafs of telegrams on these personalised forms, because he very, very rarely wrote a letter.

'The top-notch ball of the summer, which one saved one's very best dress to go to, was the one Lord Derby used to give at Derby House on Derby night every year. George V always had the whole of the Jockey Club to dinner before it. There was always tremendous fun on Derby night – people looked forward to it the whole way through the Season. Then Lord Derby's daughter, Lady Victoria Primrose, died, and he was so shattered by her death that he never gave another ball.

Loelia, Lady Lindsay of Dowhill *(formerly Duchess of Westminster)*

Opposite:
Georgia Sitwell, Sacheverell's wife, riding a camel when on holiday with the Westminsters in Egypt. 'The trips were whim – the whole of life was one long whim.'

227

Right:
Flying Cloud, 'a converted barge, like the pirate ship in *Peter Pan*,' was used by the Duke and Duchess of Westminster for their honeymoon.

Below:
A new craze for winter sports enthusiasts – bicycles on skis. The Duchess of Westminster is towed behind Sally Monkland and Eustace Long.

Left:
'The Cutty Sark was a converted destroyer . . . I hated her like poison.' Sacheverell Sitwell (left) with the Duke and Duchess.

Below:
Cecil Beaton, the Duchess of Westminster, Myrtle and Flash Kellett posing at the Hampshire House Hotel in New York below cut-outs of London society figures.

'There were dinner parties galore before any great dance. But of course you did not ask to bring a partner – you never tried to entertain your friends at other people's expense, which is what happens now, and which I deplore.

'I can never remember going to Ascot with Bendor – I don't think he enjoyed it – but it was a tremendous feature. A lot of people took houses all round, and had large parties, and gave cocktail parties in the evening, and balls. There was just non-stop fun and entertaining. Funnily enough, though Ascot was incredibly fashionable, Henley was exactly the opposite. Nobody in the *haute monde* saw themselves dead at Henley. It never got off the ground at all. It's very strange. Cowes was very different, because it was difficult to get there, unless you knew somebody with a yacht who asked you.

'I can remember very clearly being at Monte Carlo one Christmas. Bendor loved Monte Carlo, and we had the same suite in the annexe of the Hôtel de Paris each time (just as in Paris we always had a suite in the Loti). It was practically always on tap – I don't know what happened to it at other times. I suppose people were kicked out, or perhaps they never let it to anybody else. I don't remember that Christmas with any great pleasure. It was very lovely weather, that was the only thing.

'Friends had to do what they were told. You could ask them on the yacht, where you had them bottled up and then you saw something of them. We had two very large yachts. One was called the *Flying Cloud*, a converted barge, like the pirate ship in *Peter Pan*. She had a crew of 120, who were usually badly trained: very rarely was the wind in the right direction, nor did they seem to know how to put up the sails. That was just a joke: they'd get the sails caught up, and part of them would come crashing down onto the deck. That was the *Flying Cloud*.

'The *Cutty Sark* was a converted destroyer. During the First World War, the Keswicks, the enormously rich Hong Kong family, decided to build a destroyer of their own, as a present to the Navy. It wasn't finished by the time the war came to an end, and as the Navy didn't particularly need this destroyer then, they put her up for sale. Bendor bought her and converted her into a yacht. I hated her like poison – the only advantage was that she went like a bat out of hell. Poor old *Flying Cloud* could do about eight knots an hour, while the *Cutty Sark* went about thirty, so the martyrdom ended rather quicker. But she rolled and pitched like nothing on earth – I was always sick before we'd left the harbour, and never recovered till we got to our destination.

'The first time I went on the *Flying Cloud* was when we were engaged. She was too romantic and lovely for words, just like a tiny little Queen Anne house, on a barge. All the furniture was Queen Anne, just the right size for quite small cabins. Bendor was going to shoot snipe in Albania, and he said, "You must come with me to Venice" – where we were embarking. I tried to find out what sort of clothes to take, and whether I was supposed to pay for the ticket – my wretched parents didn't have any money, and I certainly didn't – and we didn't like to ask; it was torture. I did go and buy myself a tweed suit, because I didn't know what to wear down the Dalmatian coast; I'd hardly even *heard* of it. In Venice there was a pea-souper – you couldn't get round the Piazza without feeling your way from one pillar to the next.

'Both yachts were kept in this country, then it would be arranged for them to meet us in Venice or somewhere lovely. We entertained on board, probably the old guard, who were anything but jolly and who, I always felt, were secretly against me. We never stayed on board for very long though; we went to a place, got off, spent the day there, got on again. There was a cook on board, but we used to nip ashore if there was a restaurant with good fish, or lobsters. We travelled at any time of the year, and some of it I enjoyed enormously. In fact it was very difficult to come down to earth: if you were travelling by train, say, you had a maid, and you own *crêpe de chine* sheets and pillowcases put on your bed in the sleeper. You never had to worry about anything – and never saw a ticket. Bendor's valet (a horrible man called Albert, whom I didn't like at all) always had the tickets.

'The most popular trip was down the Dalmatian coast. I liked that: it was calm. Some land-locked places I enjoyed too. We went to Norway once on the *Cutty Sark* for the fishing; it was ghastly getting there, but marvellous in the fjords. The worst trip was when we left France to go to Alexandria. We got into an awful storm in the middle of the Mediterranean – it was so rough that even Bendor thought it was overdone, and he was a marvellous sailor. All the furniture got loose and crashed around us: it was terrifying. No joke. We crawled into Alexandria like wet sparrows; we could hardly totter. Even the others, who weren't nearly such bad sailors as me, were really frightened. We never went to different continents, alas. It was always talked about, and we were always planning to send the yacht out to South America and go to the Galapagos, but it was always talk and never do, because when the time came Bendor never really wanted to go anywhere except back to the old haunts.

'The trips were whim – the whole of life was one long whim.'

The Duke of Richmond and Gordon

'We went to Gordon Castle for several weeks in the summer – August and through September. I had to sell it two and a half years after my father died, though, in 1937, because we'd got no money, not a bob in the bank and no industrial shares. We had to make ourselves liquid and the only thing to do was to sell the Scottish property. There was a marvellous shoot up there – miles and miles of salmon fishing and a very nice, low-lying grouse moor, and then of course further inland the now-famous Glenfiddich, a divine and lovely place. We had another, lovely house, Kinrara, which was always let – I would love to have kept that.

'I used to fly all over the place – to Brooklands, to Cornwall, to Le Touquet. It was great fun: there was no air control in those days. We went to Le Touquet for the opening of the airport there; we arrived in the middle of a demonstration of old fighter pilots. Frightfully exciting – we became part of the display.

'We used to go on holiday to the South of France a great deal. Your car came with you on the aeroplane, a Bristol Freighter. We would go with friends, and stay in a hotel, but we didn't take the children when they were young. It was gorgeous, and so *cheap*.'

Lady Phyllis MacRae

'My mother was very keen to go abroad, so my father, reluctantly, was taken to Switzerland on short visits. He endured it, very much to please her – they were really very fond of each other. My husband would not go abroad either – it took me until I was forty to get to Paris. Except for going out to see my sister in Madras, and friends in the South of France, several winters, I didn't go abroad.

'When I realised that war clouds were coming, I told Mary, my eldest daughter, that she had to take school certificate early. At sixteen, I sent her out to Brillamont in Switzerland. She was able to be there for a year. I told her, "Don't come back for holidays," so she went to Italy for one and the South of France for another. I went out to see her, but I did not let her come home at all. In the July of 1939, I went to collect her, taking our youngest daughter to see the Prado pictures in Geneva. Then we went to Paris – I said they had better see it then, as they might not see it again. That was July 1939: I ran it as close as I could.'

Mrs Richard Cavendish

'I went to the most marvellous places on account of having hay fever. My mother and I both had it frightfully badly – I was so ill that I had to stay indoors with the shutters shut during the months of May and June. Then we discovered that if you got onto a ship it

A watercolour of the garden
pavilion at Melford by Beatrix
Potter – Cousin Beatie – who
often stayed in the house. 'The
number of flowers raised from
seed each year was quite
amazing. There were
larkspur, zinnias, helichrysum,
petunias, love-in-a-mist,
scabias, lobelias, alyssum,
foxgloves (at the back),
mignonettes, African
marigolds, antirrhinum . . .
They were planted out in
great clumps.' (*F Warne*)

Nymans garden, which the
Countess of Rosse inherited
from her father, Colonel
Leonard Messel, painted by
her brother, Oliver Messel.

Overleaf:
Before her marriage to the
Duke of Westminster, Loelia
Ponsonby had lived in St
James's Palace, where her
father was Keeper of the Privy
Purse. Victor Cazalet
commissioned this bookplate
especially for her from Rex
Whistler. St James's Palace is
depicted within the garlanded
and crested border. On their
visits to London during the
Season, the Westminsters
stayed at Bourdon House on
their London estate.

wasn't so bad. We went to the northern capitals, Denmark and all that; and to the Mediterranean. We didn't care where we went, as long as we were at sea. We travelled by ourselves, without a maid – roughing it.'

'We went to Russia on the way back from our honeymoon, across Siberia. We travelled on the Trans-Siberian Railway, and stayed in Moscow on the way back. It was in the days when Lord Chilston was ambassador – Lady Chilston was very knowledgeable on the history of Russia. The journey, which took nearly a fortnight, was very romantic indeed, because we went on another train that I love, the Shanghai Express. It was the most luxurious, Marlene Dietrich, train that you can imagine, all upholstered in lovely little buttoned velvet upholstery; the most romantic train in the world. Great big icicles the size of a man hung down the outside of the trains – it was mid-winter, Christmas in fact. I expected my darling husband to have my stocking put up and he didn't – he hadn't got used to me then. I had one put up for him, and he was very embarrassed.

'Train travelling was so thrilling, because people even dressed up for a train, and took a glow in looking rather exciting. You wondered who people were. (I wore my Tolly James clothes on the Trans-Siberian, but they didn't look eccentric; they were suitable to wear on the train. One didn't wear ball dresses, but his marvellous, thick clothes looked perfectly all right in Peking. He had the imagination, and the knowledge, of what you could wear, including extraordinary things for the tropics.) Then there was that wonderful business of going along to the dining coach. Of course, coming back from Siberia we had caviar practically every day. The service was perfect; it was perfectly comfortable. There was even a bath. I adored it all.

'On the way there, we went to Ceylon, by boat, then down to Bali, which in those days was marvellous: you went in a little boat from Java to Bali, where there was music tinkling all the time, and people dancing. Nothing like going by air. On another trip, we went to Egypt, and were some of the last people to see Abu Simnel before it was flooded. I adored America too. We've travelled in the States, and motored down to Mexico with American friends of ours, and we very often used to go and stay in the most wonderful garden, called Cypress Gardens, in South Carolina (we went back there after the gardens became public). My husband used to lecture in Charleston. That's a very magical city, beautifully preserved, with wonderful societies for preservation, great taste, and lovely magnolia gardens.'

Anne, Countess of Rosse

The Countess of Rosse in a Tolly James outfit (photographed by Cecil Beaton), and, below, in her peeress's robes.

The Hon Mrs John Mildmay White

'My father, to begin with, was a Member of Parliament. After that he was in the House of Lords, so he always went up to London from Flete in about the first week of February. Then sometimes, when he was on good form, we used to rent a house in Leicestershire and hunt up there during February and March. We took some of the staff up with us, but not the whole lot – the house we rented wasn't big enough.

'My brother and I used to go to Scotland in August, usually, to stay with friends. We would take the car and go off. Sometimes my father went up to Scotland, but abroad hardly ever came into it.

'The weekdays all summer we spent in Berkeley Square, where we had a very beautiful house, with Adam decoration in all the rooms (one of the original old houses in the square). It had been in our family about 100 years. The reception rooms were perfectly lovely, but the bedroom accommodation was not all that good – we were all rather cramped. My father used to give tremendous dinner parties there – that was one of the things he really loved doing. There were usually eighteen or twenty-two people (which works out so that the host and hostess sit at the top and bottom of the table). Mrs Woodman used to do the most delicious food, and an extra butler – a friend of our butler – was always got in to help, so that we had plenty of people waiting at table. I used to go off to Covent Garden with my father's secretary at the crack of dawn – about five o'clock in the morning – to buy the flowers, which we would do in all the rooms. The whole house looked simply fantastic, because it was the most beautiful place and was filled with lovely furniture and pictures.

'Those kinds of dinner parties were rather formal. People arrived in white ties, and the men were all given an envelope, in which there was a card saying "Will you please take Mrs So-and-So in to dinner?", and then you assembled in the library. You didn't have pre-dinner drinks – my father was not at all a pre-dinner drink person. I don't think a lot of people were. (I remember when the Prince of Wales came to stay at Flete, to ride in the local point-to-point, my father got into a terrible flap, because he knew he had to have cocktails for the Prince, and he hadn't a clue how to make them.) Then you solemnly assembled in twos, the man who had this ticket approached the lady whose name was on it, and you all walked in to the dining room, even though it was only next door. In the hall when you arrived there was one of those *placement* things, with little cards in it, so that you had already seen where you were sitting.

'Those London dinners were enormously long. You started off with soup, and then you had fish, and then you had an entrée, and then you had a chicken dish or something like that, and then a meat dish, and then a pudding, and then a savoury. When all that had been cleared away, there was the most delicious fruit – strawberries and things – piled into pyramids on the most beautiful Sèvres dishes. And there were lovely chocolates, which I used to go down to Harrods to buy, in silver baskets on the table.

'You waded your way through this enormous dinner, and of course it was very important that you should talk to the person on your right, because otherwise you threw the dinner party out. You had to keep an eye open to see that everybody was talking to the one on his right, and if not, try to switch it round, so that no-one was left out; halfway through everybody would turn and talk to the person on the other side. Then I caught everybody else's eye and the ladies all went to the drawing room upstairs, while the men were left downstairs. We had a gossip and a cup of coffee until they came up. My father often got in an entertainer of some sort – a conjurer, or we had a thought-reader once who did the most wonderful tricks. If we didn't have an entertainer, some people played bridge in another, very pretty, sitting room, or we just switched round a bit, because otherwise they got stuck with the same person the whole evening. The dinner parties took really rather a lot of organising, especially as my father always invited people when he was in one of his happy moods, and then quite often would forget who he'd asked: somebody would suddenly arrive just before dinner whom I wasn't expecting at all, or else somebody wouldn't turn up and I would have to do a quick rehash of the whole table just before we went in. They were always rather a source of anxiety, those dinners, but everybody seemed to enjoy them.

'When we weren't giving our own dinner parties, we often went to dances. In my day you went on going to dances until you were quite old, not just for the one year when you came out. We also sometimes had dinner parties for other people's dances. And then one went to the theatre an awful lot. That was great fun, because there were far more theatres in London then, and far more good plays – one could go to the theatre twice a week all summer. They were all so enjoyable, and it wasn't very expensive. You would wear evening dress – dinner jackets, not white tie, like it was before the first war – but you wouldn't be tremendously dressed up. There was nearly always something on, every evening.

'I used always to go to Ascot, and Wimbledon was a great thing. My father had got three debentures when Wimbledon was rebuilt, so we had three tickets for each day. And then we used to go down to Shoreham on Fridays, usually, so it was really Monday, Tuesday, Wednesday and Thursday in London, and we very often didn't come up again till the Monday morning.

'Moving from one house to another was a terrific business, because so much stuff had to go. First of all there was the staff and their luggage, and then there was the silver, which went into specially made boxes, great big wooden ones lined with baize, moulded into the shape of all the different bits of silver. Great buses would take everything up to the station at Ivybridge, where we practically had a special train to take us up to London. At Paddington Station there were buses you could hire to take you and your possessions to your house, and this was how we used to go, the roofs of the buses loaded up with trunks and every kind of thing. It was like a sort of exodus. This used to happen twice a year: when we moved up to London, and when we moved down again.'

Lady Burrell

'My mother always took time off from her work in London to go golfing in Thorpness. My grandfather was so horrified that we were all brought up in a soft house that he bought Dunecht so that we should all be braced up – at least, that was the intention. Mummy pretended that Thorpness was to brace up the grandchildren, but it also provided a nice golfing place for her. She used to play in the Ladies' Parliamentary quite often; adored her golf. Then she went sightseeing in Italy, and every January or February she'd be playing tennis in the South of France. She was very good at tennis: she played in Monte Carlo tournaments and on the centre court at St Cloud, where she played doubles with Neville Lytton.'

Patricia, Viscountess Hambleden

'We went to Ireland, once or twice, with the children, and to my brother-in-law's house on Islay. We used to go abroad occasionally: to Salzburg, for instance, and to Venice, and once to Canada, but our life was really divided between Greenlands and London. We were at Greenlands always during holiday times, especially later on, when the children arrived, but as my husband worked in London, we were at Belgrave Square during the week, and went down to Greenlands for weekends.'

Marcus Wickham-Boynton

'My grandmother had a house in London, 25 Eaton Square, and my father used to go to London during Ascot week and Derby week, and those sorts of things, and likewise my mother for a part of the Season.

'My mother liked travelling. She was a good linguist – she talked

German and French well. She travelled, I always thought, extremely uncomfortably: third class, with innumerable string bags and a bulging suitcase. She never took her maid – that was considered extravagance. She usually went with Lady Desborough or Mrs Hall from Settrington, to Italy and France and so on. She enjoyed that.'

Mrs John Dower

'My father and Walter Runciman, also of Northumberland, built two houses next door to each other in Great College Street, which is the street nearest to the Houses of Parliament. We still own 14 Great College Street. That was our London house. We went there at the beginning of each parliamentary session, and came up again when the House rose. A tremendous undertaking it was! A waggonette took the servants and the dogs and the cats and the smaller children to King's Cross. We had a whole carriage to ourselves on the train, and I remember one time there were fourteen pieces of luggage in the guard's van. The odd part was that there didn't seem to be any duplicates, because things like the nursery fire guards always went up and down, and the sewing machine, the children's high chairs and prams – all the things you would think a big household would have duplicates of. At Newcastle all this would have to be put on the Morpeth train, and at Morpeth on the Scots Gap train, and then the Wallington waggonette would take us and our things up here. In those days everything was much more leisurely.

'My parents used to have great parties in London, especially as theirs was the nearest house to the House of Commons. I grew up with constant dinner parties. We had a division bell in the house; if it rang once there was a pause in the conversation; if it rang twice the men got ready to run; and if it rang three times they all ran, because they could get to the House in less than six minutes. We women would be left sitting at alternate places at the table. Then they would come back. At one dinner party we were having some very nice rissoles, so my mother stood by the door and the men took a rissole each in their fingers and ran. That was in the days when my father was still a Liberal, so among the people who used to come was Winston Churchill. Winston was a tremendous talker, a tremendous conversationalist, and I remember my mother saying that she was determined to see whether she could keep the conversation general until after the main course. But she never succeeded: after a few minutes, the whole table would be listening to Winston.

'Entertaining was much more formal in London. I remember parties when my father was in Parliament, with a tremendous number of people: the drawing room and passages absolutely full. I remember Haldane coming to one party: he was rather large and simply couldn't get into the drawing room; he couldn't push his way in. They were very narrow houses, with a big drawing room on the first floor, and then down below a dining room and my father's study. At the back was a brick terrace. The neighbours' would let their cats out into the gardens at the back, where they yowled all night. My father sent a note round to all the neighbours, saying that he was going to bring his rook rifle south and shoot any cat in sight. They all let the cats out of the front doors after that. I remember the look of Father's bedroom with the rook rifle balanced against the bed – he was an absolutely first-class shot.'

'We had a house called Llangattock, near Crickhowell, in Breconshire, and a house in London (at one time it was 11 Portman Square), but we spent most of the year at Badminton. We were there certainly from the beginning of August right through to April, and then, when there was a water shortage, we used to go down to Wales for two or three months. Badminton was actually closed at one time from the first of May to the first of August, because of the shortage of water.

'I had to be in London a certain amount when I became Master of the Horse, but we didn't spend an awful lot of time there. We also went to Ireland a certain amount, to see friends there – I went to judge horses at the Dublin Horse Show and that sort of thing. I used to go up and stay with Hughie Northumberland, to judge his hounds, and shoot grouse; and then I went up to Scotland to fish.'

The late Duke of Beaufort

The Duke of Roxburgh, the Earl of Lascelles, the Duchess of York and the Duchess of Beaufort at Ascot.

Overleaf:
Melford after the fire started by troops occupying the house during the Second World War. 'The restoration of the house wasn't completed when Willy died . . . Willy wouldn't have let it down. I couldn't let it down either.'

239

XIV A RETREATING WORLD

Bowhill House – Boughton House –
Drumlanrig Castle – Langholme – Heath
House – Melford Hall – Wallington House –
Haigh – Balcarres

Mary, Duchess of Buccleuch

'War came, oddly enough, before one expected it. The army moved into Bowhill, with not a thing put away. The officers' sitting room was where all the Van Dycks were. It was terribly badly used; the army did terrible things to the house, all the proverbial things that troops are supposed to do – hacking down the banisters to make firewood, and throwing darts at the pictures. They couldn't have done more harm, and ended up by nearly burning it down twice. But it survived . . .

'Boughton was occupied by the British Museum, and so at least they kept the house warm, But we didn't really put things away – they just remained intact. Bowhill was a barracks; Drumlanrig was a school; and the other houses were also barracks. Langholm had to be pulled down after the war – it couldn't be shored up, because it had got such dry rot in it, through the troops being there for four and a half years.'

Margaret, Countess of Lichfield

Opposite, above:
During the war Heath House was turned into a hospital – staff and patients assembling for the blessing of the hospital by the Bishop of Lichfield.

Below:
A fleet of American Red Cross ambulances, which ferried blood supplies and patients to the hospital, drawn up in the drive.

'During the Second World War, Heath House—which belonged to my first husband, Humphrey Philips— and so many other country houses were turned into hospitals. The patients had the free run of Heath House, and loved and respected it and did all they possibly could to help. It seemed to bring the best out in all of them. They were always telling me that in the Army, Navy or Air Force, whichever they happened to be in, they all blasphemed in every sentence, everything "bloody this" and "bloody that", but there they found themselves never using any bad language in any shape or form – did not want to. They used to ask me why this was, they were so surprised. I pointed out to them that I had a collection of very young and pretty Red Cross nurses and they had too much respect for them to let themselves down in such a way, whether they knew it or not.

'The result was delightful and for six years we did have a very happy hospital. Their letters and poems used to pour in after they had left. So these country houses and their lovely gardens played a very large part in the healing of men in mind, body and soul, when they came out of hell and found themselves in heaven.'

Lady Hyde Parker

'A butler who'd been at other big houses like Stanhope had gone away to the war, and then come here to work at the Maltings. He saw us moving back into Melford, and he came one evening and said to me, "Can't I give you a hand, my lady?" I said, "Well, quite frankly, I can't afford a butler now." And he said, "Oh, but I don't want any money. Can't I just polish your windows and silver? I

The drawing room became a
ward, the stables a
gymnasium, and the library a
recreation room.

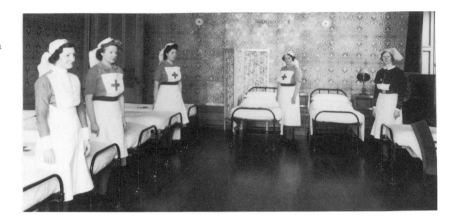

should so love to help." Later on, he did come every day, and he became our butler.

'After the war I'd moved out of a small, comfortable house to come back into Melford. It never struck me that I wasn't to carry on. I suppose I saw the difficulties, because I had had enough warning: "What are you going to do? You can't possibly live in that great big place," people would say. "But why not?" "You can't possibly move back. I know the family won't be sorry." My reply was "Well, Willy would have gone back to Melford."

'The restoration of the house wasn't completed when Willy died. But I knew how he loved this place; a house like this is not just bricks and mortar, it's more personal, something which has been going on for generations. Willy wouldn't have let it down. I couldn't let it down either.

'Nanny and I really lived here on our own. We took the furniture that had been stored in the stables, and I had a gardener and somebody else to carry the furniture out into the courtyard. We put scarves over our heads and brushed it all down, and then we furnished my sitting room downstairs completely as you see it today, with everything in it, photographs, flowers in the vases and all that; and my bedroom as you see it today. The kitchen we got going, and it looked a perfectly normal room, but behind it there were passages full of wood shavings. That's how we began. But it was amazing how people tended to step into the breach. They came, and I've never been short of any help since.'

'We were very involved in my father's decision to leave Wallington to the National Trust, which he made in about 1938, and which he finally signed in 1941 or 1942. We discussed it very thoroughly. It was a family decision: we agreed with my father that we had no absolute right to live in a place like Wallington, to live with all those beautiful things, unless we shared them. The mere fact that we were born to it was no special merit of ours. He searched round and decided that the National Trust was the body to which to leave it: more than anything else to guarantee that the public would have perennial rights to see the place, to be there and enjoy themselves. He and his brother, George Macaulay Trevelyan, together signed the deed of gift – it was a decision between them. He left the whole estate, not just the house, in order to keep the community together, because he felt very much that we were an entity. He was asked by the family whether he wouldn't like to leave it to the Trust then, in 1942, and take on the first tenancy, to build the thing up and show what he

Mrs John Dower

envisaged would be the relationship of the family with the Trust in future years. But he said, no, he'd like to keep it himself, during his lifetime. When pressed as to why he wouldn't hand it over earlier, he replied with what we thought was a perfect description of himself: "Because I'm an illogical Englishman!" My father was enormously interested in the furniture and pictures and things in the house, and knew a very great deal about them all. In his deed of gift he left every room completely furnished, although some other things he didn't leave to the Trust.'

Mary, Countess of Crawford and Balcarres

'Our London house, 7 Audley Square, had been bombed. All its contents came north, as also did quite a lot from various museums, to be housed in the capacious Haigh cellars. By now cars had replaced ponies and traps, but with wartime rationing and shortage of petrol I acquired a milk float and broke in a pony for driving and had a bicycle, so I was fairly mobile. An estate lorry fetched and carried essential supplies. The gardens produced vegetables and fruit, and I kept two cows for milk and butter, and at moments had two pigs, sadly to be fattened, slaughtered and eaten.

'My father-in-law died in 1940. For the next five years, after selling our London house, we lived at Haigh. Mrs Lickiss, who had been a rather grand housekeeper, who had kept Haigh in apple-pie order, now turned her hand to everything. Housemaids, footmen, kitchen-maids had vanished. An indoor and outside odd man remained, and sometimes we had a cook, at others not. Two young and inexperienced girls were gradually licked into shape, and I learned to cook after a basic fashion.

'Every year it became more apparent that we could not keep both Balcarres and Haigh. After much heart-searching, we decided to sell Haigh and move to Scotland, which was a very hard decision for my husband, as he loved Haigh and was deeply interested in its history and in the superb library. The decision having been made, books, pictures and furniture were selected for the move north, and the house and land were put up for sale. Mrs Lickiss retired to a cottage on the place, and Arthur Handley also retired and went to live in Haigh village. Eventually they decided to get married and lived happily together till Mrs Lickiss died. It is impossible to pay enough tribute to Mrs Lickiss for all the devoted care she gave to the family and Haigh; her wisdom and generosity and infinite patience in passing on her knowledge, and her gallant acceptance of ever more work when she might have looked forward to an easier life.

'Owing to the fact that we were moving a considerable amount of stuff from Staffordshire to Scotland, we had to make many changes at Balcarres to accommodate pictures and books and rather better furniture. We tried as much as possible to keep a feeling of what our forebears had contributed to the house, but it must often have been hard for my mother-in-law and the family not to feel resentful, though they never ever criticised. I think that nearly everyone has their own ideas of what they want their home to be like. When younger people take over, changes naturally follow. Sometimes the changes we made were in our eyes for the better, sometimes perhaps they were dictated by the circumstances of having to adapt to a different way of life. We converted the dining room into a library to house the residue of the Haigh library. We scrapped the old-fashioned kitchen with its enormous and ancient coal-burning stove, and made a new kitchen in what had been the butler's pantry, with an *Esse* cooker; and in 1947, when at last we were given a permit to put in electricity, we had an oil-fired boiler for heating the water. The house was then lit by electric light, and it was goodbye to oil lamps and candles, except for a few kept for emergencies. Later we moved the kitchen to the first floor, next to the small room we used as a dining room, to avoid carrying trays up and down the small staircase.

'Our household varied in numbers over the years – sometimes we had foreign couples, mad cooks and bad cooks, an ex-housemaid married to an ex-footman who remained with us as a couple till they retired. The head gardener's wife, who came as cook, was with us for eleven years and though a good cook was a woman of uncertain temper and very jealous. When she departed in a huff and took her reluctant husband with her, the relief was enormous. Two dailies then came to our rescue with the housework, and I took on the cooking, and, if the house was full, got outside help.

'With memories of Holker, I used to go through the linen once a year, checking and listing, but with wartime shortages and rising costs, it was no longer a question of regular replacements, but rather of making things last longer, or of repair and adaptation. Fashions were changing: blankets were giving way to downies, so that bed-making was quick and easy: washing was simpler and there was less ironing – white damask table cloths being replaced by patterned drip-dry materials on polished wood. Hoovers took the place of brooms and mops in the housemaids' cupboards on every floor and wash basins in bedrooms meant no more carrying of hot water cans. Milk and eggs and butter came from the farm, vegetables, fruit and potatoes from the gardens, and as in the old days the making of jam continued, but on a smaller scale. With the advent of cars and easy transport came greater dependency on shops, with their varied and ready-made manufactured products. The old self-sufficiency and independence were lost. So were many old skills, and specialities, and treasured secrets handed down from past generations, which gave so many country houses their individual flavour.

'There was always a lot to do, but I for one never regretted that I was not a "chatelaine" of a large household, and in fact I think that I would not have been any good as one. Life at Balcarres was very pleasant and happy, and if one couldn't have everything, one was happy with less and quite content to do more oneself.'

POSTSCRIPT

Despite the bomb that fell on Oxburgh, the bricks and mortar of most country houses came through the first war relatively unscathed. The way of life they represented was rapidly revived, at least to outward appearances. In all too many cases, this was no more than a brave show: although only hairline cracks may have been discovered on a still opulent glaze, the vessel itself was cracked and irretrievably weakened. Country houses had survived for the duration, but frequently only as vain citadels in a retreating world. It must have seemed that Simon Harcourt-Smith's *The Last of Uptake* (1942), with its illustrations by Rex Whistler, was to be an epitaph not just for one house, but for most. There, the collapsing masonry, the dripping, decayed marble and the dismembered statuary are given an almost welcome release when its estranged owners commit Uptake to flames rather than let it fall into unsympathetic hands.

The great estates faced mounting, often irresistible attrition. But not all. For those who have contributed to this book, the country house is still a potent symbol, still deserving to be cherished. There is an understandable reluctance to talk about the casualties, the houses which were abandoned. The traumas of the Second World War seem to have encouraged a far more open acknowledgement of irrevocable change. Some was unexpected, but to Beatrice Brocklebank not unwelcome:

> It was so quiet after one no longer had any staff: one now found hares sitting just outside the window. In earlier days there was so much noise going on, with all the people in the house; no wildlife at all.

There are other things to be grateful for: less of the silly, damaging cult of philistinism; a greater understanding of the evolution of so many country houses, so that the contribution of each period can be respected and preserved; and a revival of those aspects of the art of housekeeping which ensure the careful protection from sun, dust and damp of fragile paintings, veneers and textiles. Would these values have emerged without the more immediate threat of destruction?

There have also been the efforts to find new roles for country houses, without subjecting them to the indignities that all too often attend their conversion to school, business or hospital use. Their preservation has sometimes fallen to local authorities, as at Tatton Park, Heaton, Sudbury, Kenwood and Lyme. Like many other houses on the outskirts of industrial cities, Lyme came perilously close to being swallowed up by suburban housing. Lady Newton's premonition of the end of the Legh family's six-hundred-year tenure was proved right all too quickly. As her daughter, Phyllis Sandeman, has written:

> The advent of the 1914 war brought to an end all the social activities such as the Servants' Ball and the theatrics. It was the beginning of the end, not only for Lyme but for virtually all the big houses ... To his great credit, my brother continued to maintain Lyme, although on a less grand scale, for about twenty years. But the Second World War was the *coup de grâce*, again the chief difficulty being the impossibility of finding and keeping adequate staff. So much had depended on them and their devotion to the place.

When Lord Newton approached the National Trust in 1943, its adviser on historic buildings, James Lees-Milne, noted in his diary: 'The world is too much for him, and no wonder. He does not know what he can do, ought to do or wants to do. He just throws up his hands in despair.' Although Lyme eventually passed to the Trust, much of its furniture was dispersed in 1947, at a completely pointless sale which saw eighteenth-century gilt pier glasses knocked down for twenty-odd pounds apiece, and the relics of centuries of occupation scattered at little benefit to the family. Lord Newton made the long walk down the entrance drive alone, resolved never to look back or to return. There could scarcely be a sadder note of disappointment or failure than the printed message he sent out in May 1946 to his former staff:

> Before leaving Lyme we wanted to have a farewell party in the house for all our friends and neighbours so that we might say goodbye personally. Unfortunately the business of moving has caused so great a confusion that a party is impossible. But we are unwilling to depart and to

end without a word the associations of five and a half centuries and so we hope that you will accept this as an expression of our best wishes and as an indication in some measure of our sadness.

In a sense, Lord Newton and those who felt like him were correct. Lyme was a great building architecturally, but it was also a home; and to him the two were inseparable. The fact that others might assume the burden of maintenance, or might camp, like *banditi* in the ruins of the *campagna*, was little consolation. The way of life Lyme represented was gone for ever. Lord Newton and many country house owners of his generation saw themselves as victims of brutal eviction. But there were new opportunities for those young or vigorous enough to accept the challenge; and for them more to welcome than to regret.

In October 1950, *Illustrated* published a feature on the seventh Marquess of Anglesey, describing how he was planning to preserve Plas Newydd despite staggering death duties of £1,750,000: his father's yacht had been sold, the golf course ploughed, and much of the house let to *HMS Conway*, the naval training school, to cover the rates and heating bills. 'The idle rich, who were never very idle, are no longer rich. Old families, which have helped to build the greatness of Britain, struggle today to make two end meet. Young aristocrats, adapting themselves to a more democratic age, rack thoroughbred brains to discover how they can keep, if only for another generation, some fraction of their historic possessions.' That a popular magazine should write in such terms was itself symptomatic. 'Unless he is to abandon his heritage altogether, the aristocrat in the democratic age must have a head for mathematics and an eye for commerce. . . . a large house and estate, once run for pleasure, can only survive today as a business proposition.' The feeling that country house life and self-indulgence were no longer synonymous was, for the Countess of Haddington, a not unwelcome change:

> I look back on the 'twenties and 'thirties as a golden age, an absolute golden age. But I don't regret the present age, not at all. I think I approve of it much more than the old days. It was rather a selfish life, really, except in between one did good works and that sort of thing, with one's various charities. But on the whole it was a selfish life.

NOTES &
BIBLIOGRAPHY

Most of the quotations in the book are taken direct from recorded interviews. Some, however, are from books and magazines. Thanks, therefore, to those authors, copyright owners and publishers who have allowed quotations from these sources to be used.

Chapter 1

Wodehouse, P G, *Something Fresh*, 1915. See also: Usborne, Richard, 'My Blandings Castle' in *Blackwoods Magazine*, November 1972

Information given by the Marquess of Anglesey in 1982

Information given by the late Lanning Roper in 1983

Nicolson, Harold, *Diaries and Letters* 1930–1964, 1966, 1967, 1968

Correspondence in the possession of Lady Phyllis MacRae

Lawrence, D H, *Lady Chatterley's Lover*, 1928. See also: Gill, Richard, *The Happy Rural Seat: the English Country House and the Literary Imagination*, 1972

Bedford, Sybille, *Aldous Huxley: a Biography*, 1973

Huxley, Aldous, *Crome Yellow*, 1921

Waugh, Evelyn, *A Handful of Dust*, 1934

Donaldson, Frances, *P G Wodehouse*, 1982

Clemenson, Heather, *English Country Houses and Landed Estates*, 1982, especially Chapter 8; and Thompson, F M L, *English Landed Society in the Nineteenth Century*, 1963, especially Chapter 12

Unpublished typescript at Dudmaston

Brigden, Roy, 'Norfolk's Great Farm Strike', in the *Eastern Daily Press*, 26 March 1983

Newton, Lady, *Lyme Letters*, 1925

Information given by Margaret, Countess of Lichfield

Sandeman, Phyllis, *Treasure on Earth*, 1952

Amery, Colin (editor), *Lutyens*, Arts Council Exhibition Catalogue, 1982, page 142

Dean, David, *The Thirties: Recalling the English Architectural Scene*, 1983; and Aslett, Clive, *The Last Country Houses*, 1982

Jackson-Stops, Gervase, 'Rex Whister at Plas Newydd', *Country Life*, 4 August 1977

Mitford, Nancy, *The Pursuit of Love*, 1945

Information given by Anne, Countess of Rosse, 1984

Wodehouse, P G, *A Damsel in Distress*, 1919

Chapter XIV

Harcourt-Smith, Simon, *The Last of Uptake*, 1942

Sandeman, Phyllis, 'Lyme Park and the 2nd Lord Newton', *National Trust Studies*, 1981

Lees-Milne, James, *Ancestral Voices*, 1975

Lord Newton's letter to his tenants, reproduced in Laurie, Kedrun, *Cricketer Preferred : estate workers at Lyme Park, 1898 to 1946*, 1979

INDEX